"The HEAR Approach™ to negotiation has improved healthcare and will make you better. Its relational context anchored in emotional intelligence aligns beautifully with the principles that underlie optimal clinical practice. *Transforming Healthcare Through Negotiation* is a 'must read' for caregivers!"

James K. Stoller, MD, MS, *Chair of the Education Institute, Cleveland Clinic*

"As Director of the Division of Pulmonary, Critical Care & Sleep Medicine at NYU Langone Health in New York City, I have often seen firsthand how vital sophisticated negotiation skills are for advancing multidisciplinary care and clinical innovation. In my own role, I must navigate negotiations with various stakeholders across our health system, including those in the clinical, educational, and administrative realms. It is imperative, therefore, to acquire nimble and substantive skill sets to allow me as leader in healthcare to successfully traverse these domains and to advocate effectively for my faculty, staff, trainees, and, of course, our patients and their families. Stacey Lee's HEAR Framework offers a practical, evidence-based approach that resonates with the complex realities of modern academic medicine. Her book provides healthcare leaders such as myself with innovative, concrete tools for driving collaboration across clinical, research, and educational domains. I have had the privilege of witnessing Ms. Lee's negotiation seminars in person, and her book takes these crucial lessons to the next level for the reader, who will benefit immeasurably by the experience."

Daniel H. Sterman, MD, *Director, Division of Pulmonary, Critical Care & Sleep Medicine, NYU Langone Health*

"Dr. Lee understands that the complex environment of the healthcare environment requires a unique negotiating framework that is relationship centered versus traditional transactional exchanges. Having spent a career as a healthcare entrepreneur, I have been involved in countless negotiations with constituents including medical professionals, managers, bankers, and private equity sponsors. Looking back, I see so many instances where Dr. Lee's HEAR

Framework would have provided a more structured, thoughtful, and actionable approach to align stakeholder interests and shift negotiations from adversarial exchanges to strategic collaboration. Her book is an invaluable guide for all clinical, operational, and financial professionals working to achieve sustainable innovation."

John Heller, *Healthcare Entrepreneur and Executive; CEO of myOrthos; Founder and Former CEO of HealthPRO-Heritage*

"*Transforming Healthcare Through Negotiation* is an essential read for healthcare leaders navigating today's complex landscape. Stacey Lee's HEAR Framework masterfully aligns with the principles of market-driven healthcare innovation—a core focus of our work—by providing a structured, relational approach to negotiation that balances clinical, operational, and financial priorities. This book is a powerful tool for those looking to drive transformative change in patient care, organizational strategy, and health system leadership."

Regina Herzlinger, PhD, *Nancy R. McPherson Professor of Business Administration, Harvard Business School*
Brian Walker, DrPH, *Executive Fellow, Harvard Business School*
Ben Creo, MDiv, *Visiting Lecturer of Business Administration, Harvard Business School*

"In describing a negotiating approach uniquely tailored for use across the different 'pillars' of health care—the practice of medicine, care delivery, and the business of health care—Professor Lee advances an appropriately aspirational paradigm of 'empathetic cooperation that advances the profession's higher calling.' Its underlying principle—that the best outcomes are achieved when everyone's needs and perspectives are considered—is a welcome antidote to a cynical winner-take-all mindset that too often characterizes the business and its stark realities of costs."

Susan Dentzer, *Healthcare Policy Analyst; Former Editor*, **Health Affairs**

"Stacey Lee provides a thought-provoking and personal guide for navigating successfully through the challenges of work, bias, and self-confidence in turbulent healthcare settings."

Leonard J. Marcus, PhD, *Founding Director, Program for Health Care Negotiation and Conflict Resolution, Harvard T.H. Chan School of Public Health*

Transforming Healthcare Through Negotiation

Every day, healthcare professionals face high-stakes negotiations that directly impact patient outcomes, organizational success, and career advancement. *Transforming Healthcare Through Negotiation* introduces the HEAR Approach™—a proven system developed specifically for healthcare's unique challenges across clinical care, service delivery, and business operations.

This practical guide equips physicians, administrators, and healthcare leaders with immediately applicable strategies to transform potential conflicts into collaborative solutions that advance patient care while balancing competing priorities.

Inside, discover:

- A Relational Mindset that builds trust across professional boundaries
- Field-tested negotiation strategies tailored to healthcare's distinct environments
- Tactical approaches for maintaining momentum in time-sensitive situations
- Ready-to-use tools, including the Negotiation Planner and Trilingual Planner

Stacey B. Lee, JD, is a Professor at Johns Hopkins Carey Business School with a joint appointment at the Bloomberg School of Public Health. A Fulbright Specialist and healthcare negotiations expert, her work has been featured by CNN, *The Washington Post*, and NPR.

Transforming Healthcare Through Negotiation

A Guide to Success in Medicine, Care Delivery, and the Business of Health

Stacey B. Lee, JD

Routledge
Taylor & Francis Group
A PRODUCTIVITY PRESS BOOK

Designed cover image: Web Large Image (Public)

First published 2026
by Routledge
605 Third Avenue, New York, NY 10158

and by Routledge
4 Park Square, Milton Park, Abingdon, Oxon, OX14 4RN

Routledge is an imprint of the Taylor & Francis Group, an informa business

ISBN: 978-1-032-37244-0 (hbk)
ISBN: 978-1-032-37242-6 (pbk)
ISBN: 978-1-003-33601-3 (ebk)

DOI: 10.4324/9781003336013

Typeset in Garamond
by Deanta Global Publishing Services, Chennai, India

Contents

Preface

"Negotiate? I'd rather be on call for 48 hours straight."

The anesthesiologist's candid remark during my workshop at Johns Hopkins drew knowing laughs from around the room. As heads nodded in agreement, I couldn't help but smile – not because it was funny, but because it captured a truth I've heard countless times from brilliant healthcare professionals who masterfully navigate complex decisions daily, yet view negotiation with something between dread and outright hostility.

It's a paradox: These are professionals who coordinate intricate care plans, manage interdisciplinary teams, and make split-second decisions that impact lives. Yet traditional negotiation approaches seem to speak a different language entirely – one focused on "winning" rather than healing, on claiming value rather than creating better healthcare outcomes.

I discovered this disconnect firsthand when I transitioned from a litigator to a professor at Johns Hopkins. The negotiation tactics that had served me well in the courtroom felt jarringly out of place in an environment where patient care, not winning, was the primary goal. During one particularly memorable workshop, a surgeon pulled me aside: "Look," she said, "I know how to advocate for my patients in the OR. But when I'm trying to secure resources for my department or implement a new protocol, that's when I feel completely lost."

The Birth of the HEAR Framework

Through countless discussions with providers, administrators, and leaders across the country, a clear pattern emerged: The challenges they faced weren't just about negotiating better deals – they were about fostering collaboration, improving patient care, and driving meaningful change in a complex system. This realization inspired me to develop the HEAR Framework (Healthcare-Specific Empowerment, Acknowledgment, and Recasting), a comprehensive approach designed specifically for healthcare's unique landscape.

Rather than forcing healthcare professionals to adapt to traditional business tactics, the HEAR Framework builds on the skills they already possess: clinical judgment, empathy, and a dedication to improving patient outcomes. Rooted in daily experiences and the latest field research, it moves beyond the traditional "win-lose" paradigm to offer a practical, collaborative approach that enhances professional life, smooths daily interactions, and fosters a positive environment for both healthcare professionals and patients.

The HEAR Framework is built around four core principles:

- **Healthcare-Specific Strategies**: Tactics tailored to navigate healthcare's interconnected pillars effectively
- **Empowerment**: Enhanced self-awareness within the larger patient care and team context
- **Acknowledgment**: Understanding and valuing diverse viewpoints for more empathetic negotiations
- **Recasting**: Transforming challenges into opportunities for collaborative, creative solutions

I've watched this approach transform how healthcare professionals view negotiation. Recently, a nurse manager who had struggled with interdepartmental conflicts told me, "For the first time, I feel like I have tools that actually fit our environment. I'm not just managing conflicts – I'm building partnerships that make our unit stronger." Dr. Eric Nguyen, a primary care physician, put it this way: "Learning the HEAR Approach™ transformed the way I handle negotiations in my work. Whether I'm discussing treatment plans with patients, collaborating with colleagues on quality improvement initiatives, or advocating for resources with hospital leadership, the strategies I learned have made me a more effective communicator and problem-solver."

By integrating the HEAR principles into your practice, you can expect improvements across the healthcare spectrum:

1. **Enhanced Operational Workflow**: Navigate complex patient care negotiations more efficiently.

2. **Improved Interprofessional Collaboration**: Move from siloed efforts to fostering open communication and cooperation.
3. **Alleviate for parallel structure**: Reduce tensions common in healthcare negotiations.
4. **Elevated Patient Care and Satisfaction**: Create more cohesive care practices that benefit outcomes.

By mastering these strategies and tactics, you'll be well-prepared to navigate the ever-changing landscape of healthcare negotiations.

The Three Pillars of Healthcare Negotiation

This book is designed for anyone who navigates the delicate balance of patient care, operational needs, and financial constraints in healthcare: providers, administrators, researchers, senior leaders, faculty, students, development specialists, and CEOs. Whether you're negotiating treatment plans with patients, managing team resources, discussing funding for research, or navigating reimbursement approvals, the HEAR Framework offers a tailored pathway to more effective, empathetic, and successful engagements.

At the heart of this framework lies the essential art of "trilingual" negotiation across healthcare's three core pillars:

- Delivery of Care (Exam Room)
- Practice of Medicine (Operating Room)
- Business of Health (Boardroom)

Consider what Dr. John Miller, the Chief of Oncology at a major cancer center, faces upon implementing an innovative immunotherapy program. In the Operating Room (Practice of Medicine), he worked with his clinical team to develop evidence-based protocols for this cutting-edge treatment while maintaining rigorous safety standards. In the Exam Room (Delivery of Care), he collaborated with nurses and care coordinators to create comprehensive patient education programs and streamline the complex treatment scheduling process. In the Boardroom (Business of Health), he negotiated with insurance providers for coverage, developed cost-sharing programs for patients, and secured institutional funding for essential equipment and staff training. Through this trilingual approach, Dr. Miller not only launched a successful program but created a sustainable model that balanced clinical excellence, operational efficiency, and financial viability.

The interdependence of the pillars shapes every significant healthcare initiative. A change in insurance reimbursement policies (Business of Health) ripples through clinical practice guidelines (Practice of Medicine) and impacts how care is delivered (Delivery of Care). Introducing new treatment protocols requires adjusting staffing models and workflows while considering budget implications.

The challenge – and opportunity – lies in developing fluency across these domains. It's not enough to excel in clinical decision-making or financial analysis alone. Modern healthcare leaders must become "trilingual," able to communicate effectively across all three pillars. This means understanding how a pediatrician's request for additional specialists (Practice of Medicine) affects departmental workflows (Delivery of Care) and budget allocations (Business of Health). It means appreciating how a new patient scheduling system impacts everything from clinical workflows to financial metrics.

I've seen this trilingual approach transform seemingly intractable challenges. Recently, a nurse manager struggling with chronic understaffing shifted her approach. Instead of focusing solely on care delivery concerns, she learned to articulate how adequate staffing affected patient satisfaction scores (Business of Health) and clinical outcomes (Practice of Medicine). By speaking the language of all three pillars, she successfully advocated for sustainable staffing solutions that benefited everyone – patients, staff, and the organization.

Throughout this book, you'll develop this trilingual fluency. You'll learn to anticipate how decisions in one pillar affect the others, to communicate effectively with diverse stakeholders, and to craft solutions that honor the interconnected nature of modern healthcare. In today's complex healthcare environment, the ability to negotiate across these pillars isn't just helpful – it's essential for driving meaningful change and improving patient care.

A Path Forward

I understand the skepticism some readers might feel. When you're already managing heavy patient loads, complex regulations, and endless administrative demands, the idea of learning new negotiation skills might seem overwhelming. But I've seen up close how the right approach can transform dreaded confrontations into opportunities for positive change.

Consider how Dr. Miller's immunotherapy program might have faltered without this comprehensive approach. Clinical excellence alone wouldn't have secured insurance coverage. Financial savvy without attention to care delivery could have created unsustainable workflows. Only by applying both the HEAR Approach's™ collaborative principles and a deep understanding of healthcare's three pillars could he navigate the complex challenges successfully.

What makes me most excited about sharing this work is knowing its ripple effect. Every time a healthcare professional becomes more effective at negotiating across all three pillars while applying the HEAR principles, it improves not just their work life but the entire healthcare ecosystem. Whether it's securing resources for better patient care, implementing innovative protocols, or building stronger interdisciplinary teams, these integrated skills create positive change that extends far beyond individual interactions.

Through this book, you'll discover how to transform daily challenges into opportunities for improvement. You'll learn to apply the HEAR Approach's™ empirically-grounded principles while developing fluency across Approach three pillars. My goal isn't just to make you more comfortable with negotiation – it's to help you become a more effective architect of healthcare transformation. Because ultimately, that's what this is about: equipping dedicated professionals with comprehensive tools to drive positive change in a system that impacts us all.

Healthcare transformation happens one conversation, one decision, one negotiation at a time. Let's begin this journey together. You're about to become a much more effective catalyst for that change.

Acknowledgments

Writing this book has been a journey filled with growth, reflection, and inspiration, and I am deeply grateful to those who have supported and guided me along the way.

Capturing My Voice: First, I must thank Olson Pook, whose tireless effort to truly capture my voice on the page has been remarkable. Olson, you listened to hours of my lectures and conversations, helping me refine and articulate ideas in a way that felt genuinely "me." Your thoughtful approach and dedication to preserving the essence of this work made all the difference.

Publishing and Editorial Support: I am especially grateful to Kristine Mednansky and the team at Routledge Taylor & Francis. Kristine, your expertise in publishing and exceptional patience guided me through the process step by step. Your support made this complex world feel manageable, and I genuinely appreciate your role in bringing this book to life.

Patrick Dempsey, thank you for making the initial introduction to Kristine. Your encouragement to pursue this project helped make it a reality.

Sarah Cole, thank you for your early editorial feedback, which helped shape the book's initial drafts. Your insights were valuable in guiding the early stages of development.

Conceptual Contribution: I am grateful to Jake Guzman for his significant contributions, particularly in developing the "boardroom, exam room, and operating room" framework. Jake, your strategic thinking and industry insights added clarity and impact, helping me translate complex ideas into tangible concepts.

Motivation and Content Inspiration: A special acknowledgment goes to Spriha Modi, a dear friend and the motivating force behind this book. Spriha, you encouraged me to put pen to paper and get this project off the ground, and for that, I am eternally grateful.

I am also deeply indebted to Krishna Patel, Julie Grant, Lisa Brown, and Brian Strauss. Your stories brought theory to life, illustrating the power of effective negotiations in real-world healthcare settings. Through you, I was able to highlight the tangible impact that thoughtful negotiation can have on patient care, collaboration, and overall outcomes.

Academic and Research Support: I am especially grateful to my students at Johns Hopkins Carey Business School and Bloomberg School of Public Health. Your engagement and thoughtful perspectives were integral to shaping this book.

To Alexandra Murata, my research teaching assistant – thank you for your tireless support in refining key concepts, offering constructive feedback, and assisting in the development of this book. Your insights and commitment have been invaluable throughout this process.

Publicity and Outreach: I'd also like to thank Smith Publicity for your efforts to amplify this book's message. Your work connecting this book with readers has been critical, and I appreciate your energy and dedication in spreading the word.

Personal Support: To my mother Joyce Boyd – thank you for instilling in me the belief that anything is possible. Your resilience continues to inspire me. In loving memory of my father, Reese Boyd – your talent as a communicator has been a guiding light in my approach to words and their impact.

To Brian, Devin, and Flannery – thank you for your love, patience, and understanding. Brian, your unwavering support, from cooking meals for the kids to offering a listening ear, has been the bedrock of this journey. I couldn't have done this without you. Devin, your creativity and compassion push me to think outside the box and approach challenges with empathy. Flannery, your determination, passion, and advocacy have provided countless opportunities for me to refine my negotiation skills. Thank you both for your love, patience, and inspiration – I am so proud to be your mother.

To the Readers: Finally, to you, the reader – thank you for investing your time in this book. I hope it serves as a valuable resource, inspiring more collaborative and effective healthcare negotiations.

This book would not have been possible without each of you. I am deeply grateful for your contributions and the roles you played in this journey.

About the Author

Stacey B. Lee, JD helps healthcare leaders revolutionize their approach to negotiations across medicine, care delivery, and business through the innovative HEAR Approach™. As a Professor at Johns Hopkins Carey Business School and the Bloomberg School of Public Health, she bridges the worlds of healthcare law, business strategy, and negotiations to transform how healthcare leaders approach complex challenges.

Drawing on over a decade of experience as a securities litigator and in-house counsel for major healthcare corporations, Stacey developed the HEAR Approach™ – a revolutionary framework for healthcare negotiations that span the Practice of Medicine, Delivery of Care, and Business of Health pillars. As CEO of Praxis Pacisci, she trains healthcare professionals to master these essential skills.

Her expertise in healthcare negotiation and law has earned her recognition as a Fulbright Specialist and numerous teaching excellence awards at Johns Hopkins. Stacey served as the Academic Program Director for the Full-time MBA program and the founding Faculty Director of the Teaching Excellence Initiative.

A featured TEDx speaker on "Patient Voice," Stacey brings passionate advocacy for patient-centered healthcare to her work. Her insights have been featured in *The Washington Post*, CNN, CBS, Bloomberg Radio, and *USA Today*, where she provides expert commentary on healthcare negotiations and policy. Her research on pharmaceutical access and healthcare negotiations appears in the *Yale Journal of Health Policy and Ethics*, *Journal of Business Ethics*, and other leading publications.

BUILDING THE HEAR FOUNDATION

I

If you want to go quickly, go alone. If you want to go far, go together.
– African Proverb

Healthcare negotiations demand more than transactional exchanges – they require a deep understanding of how clinical excellence, operational efficiency, and financial sustainability interweave to create optimal patient outcomes. Part I of this book introduces the foundational elements of the HEAR Approach™, a comprehensive framework designed specifically for healthcare's unique challenges across the Practice of Medicine (Operating Room), Delivery of Care (Exam Room), and Business of Health (Boardroom).

Navigating Part I: Your Roadmap to Understanding the Core Elements of Healthcare Negotiation

Each chapter in Part I systematically develops your understanding of essential HEAR concepts, moving from basic principles to practical implementation strategies. This foundation is crucial before advancing to the more complex applications presented in Part II.

The HEAR Framework

Chapter 1: The HEAR Approach™ Overview

Your journey begins with an introduction to Healthcare-Specific Strategies: Empowerment, Acknowledgment, and Recasting. Learn why traditional

DOI: 10.4324/9781003336013-1

negotiation approaches often fall short in healthcare settings and how the HEAR Framework addresses these unique challenges.

Chapter 2: The Relational Mindset

Discover how Emotional Intelligence and Theory of Mind create the psychological groundwork for effective healthcare negotiations. This mindset transforms potential conflicts into opportunities for collaboration and mutual understanding.

Chapter 3: Healthcare-Specific Strategies

Master navigation of healthcare's three pillars – Practice of Medicine, Delivery of Care, and Business of Health – through strategies tailored to each domain's unique challenges and opportunities.

Core Components of HEAR

Chapter 4: Empowerment

Learn how embracing vulnerability while developing self-awareness enhances your negotiation capabilities and enables more effective advocacy for patients and resources.

Chapter 5: Acknowledgment

Develop mastery in active listening and perspective-taking to build trust and foster collaboration across healthcare's diverse stakeholder landscape.

Chapter 6: Recasting

Transform healthcare challenges into opportunities for innovation and shared value creation while maintaining an unwavering focus on patient-centered outcomes.

Making Part I Work for You

Each chapter includes practical exercises, real-world examples, and reflection activities designed to help you internalize these foundational concepts. By thoroughly mastering these building blocks, you'll be equipped to navigate complex healthcare negotiations with confidence, build stronger relationships across disciplines, create sustainable, patient-centered solutions, and drive meaningful change in your healthcare organization. Whether you're negotiating patient care protocols, resource allocation, or organizational change, understanding these core principles will enhance your ability to drive positive outcomes across all three healthcare pillars.

Chapter 1

The HEAR Approach™

An Overview of Transformative Healthcare Negotiation

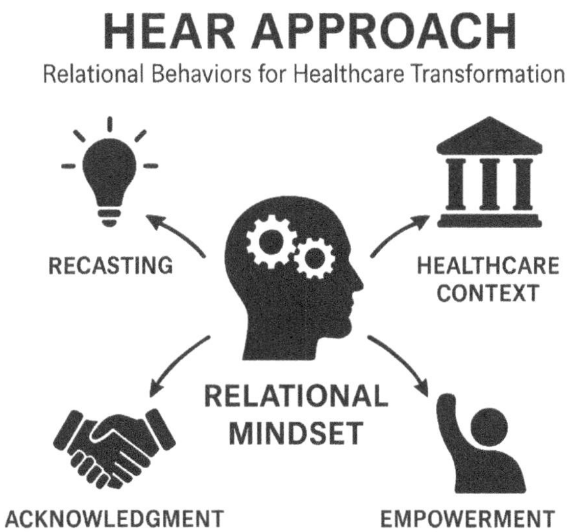

Healing is a matter of time, but it is sometimes also a matter of opportunity.

– Hippocrates

DOI: 10.4324/9781003336013-2

I can distinctly recall a conversation I had seven years ago with an oncologist at a major academic medical center. She walked me through a typical day, highlighting the constant negotiation challenges she faced:

> This morning was hectic, but honestly not unusual. I was in a multidisciplinary meeting going over surgical options for a patient with advanced pancreatic cancer. It's always a delicate balancing act – looking at the medical factors but also the patient's emotional state and quality of life concerns. I had to lay out the pros and cons of doing a major Whipple procedure versus something less invasive with the laparoscopic approach. And then there were the family members, understandably anxious, so I had to address all their worries, too. It's a tightrope walk, presenting the clinical realities while being sensitive to the human side.
>
> After that, I got pulled into a heated discussion with the surgeons and procurement about investing in this new da Vinci surgical robot system. The technology allows for more precise, minimally invasive procedures, which can lead to faster recovery times and less post-op pain for patients. But yeesh, the costs! We were debating whether the potential benefits justified the enormous price tag, especially considering the learning curve for the surgical team and the ongoing maintenance expenses.
>
> And I still had to prep for a panel later to review grant proposals, including one for an Alzheimer's study our researchers are leading. That room is filled with strong personalities and competing interests to navigate around when evaluating the scientific merits and strategic priorities. We've got basic scientists pushing for more fundamental research into the disease pathology, while the clinical researchers are advocating for trials of new diagnostic tools and therapies.

She smiled, a glimmer of determination in her eye. "So yeah, it's a constant push and pull. But it's also an incredible opportunity. Every negotiation, every tough conversation – that's a chance for us to make a real difference. To fight for our patients, to advocate for better resources, to champion research that could change lives. It's not easy, but it's worth it. Because at the end of the day, that's what we're here for – to do everything in our power to help the people who trust us with their care."

That conversation was just one of many I'd had, but it crystallized a crucial realization: healthcare professionals weren't just negotiators – they were orchestrators of complex, high-stakes discussions involving multiple stakeholders, each with their own concerns and priorities. Traditional negotiation tactics simply fell short in these scenarios. This epiphany sparked a years-long journey of research and development, culminating in a specialized methodology designed specifically for healthcare negotiations. This new HEAR Approach™ aims to empower medical professionals like this oncologist, equipping them with the tools to navigate the unique challenges of their field. By mastering these skills, healthcare providers can more effectively advocate for their patients, secure vital resources, and drive the kind of groundbreaking research that transforms lives. Ultimately, the HEAR Approach™ has the potential to revolutionize how the entire healthcare industry views negotiation, paving the way for better patient outcomes and accelerated medical progress.

The Shortcomings of Traditional Negotiation Approaches in Healthcare

All too often, healthcare professionals attempt to navigate complex situations using one-size-fits-all negotiation tactics carried over from other professional sectors. Whether learned in business school, legal debates, or sales environments, these traditional strategies falter when applied to healthcare's unique dynamics.[1]

At their core, many conventional negotiation models operate on fundamentally misaligned principles:

- A strict focus on claiming as much value as possible, with a winner-takes-all mindset.
- Adversarial positioning of parties against each other, with compromises viewed as failures.
- A transactional, dehumanized approach that overlooks the nuanced personal elements at play.
- Rigid strategic frameworks that are ill-equipped to adapt to the reality of fluid, high-stakes healthcare negotiations.[2]

In healthcare settings, these strategies simply cannot account for the complex interplay of patient well-being, ethical principles, resource constraints, power dynamics, and emotional undercurrents. Unfortunately, this approach often leads to institutions crippled by power dynamics, mistrust, and an inability to evolve, even when lives are at stake. Researchers like Jodi Halpern, a professor of bioethics and medical humanities at the University of California, Berkeley, who specializes in the emotional and interpersonal dimensions of healthcare, have observed that clinging to positional bargaining or distributive mindsets in healthcare negotiations leads to diminished rapport among healthcare providers and suboptimal outcomes.[3] Ultimately, enhancing human health and dignity should be the core driver of any healthcare negotiation – a principle fundamentally at odds with traditional negotiation's zero-sum, value-claiming approach.

The Critical Need for Healthcare-Specific Negotiation Skills

In the fast-paced world of healthcare, effective negotiation skills are not just valuable but essential. As Kathleen G. Sebelius, former U.S. Secretary of Health and Human Services, emphasized in a *New England Journal of Medicine* article, "Effective negotiation skills are essential for healthcare leaders seeking to navigate the rapidly changing landscape of healthcare delivery and financing."[4] Numerous studies underscore the importance of strong negotiation skills in healthcare, as the ability to negotiate adeptly can be the difference between positive patient outcomes and preventable harm. Research consistently shows that professionals who possess these skills are better equipped to advocate for patient needs, secure crucial resources, and drive positive change within their organizations.[5]

Yet the high-stakes nature of these negotiations demands an approach tailored specifically to the distinctive complexities of the healthcare sector. Physicians, advanced practice providers, clinical staff administrators, and researchers face a never-ending series of critical negotiations requiring a specialized skill set. By mastering Healthcare-Specific negotiation strategies, healthcare professionals can foster collaborative, patient-centric decision-making processes that lead to better outcomes and more efficient use of resources. From the exam room to the operating suite to the boardroom, skilled negotiators who emphasize collaboration over confrontation can transform healthcare's three pillars – the Practice of Medicine, Delivery of Care, and Business of Health.[6]

WHO NEEDS HEALTHCARE-SPECIFIC NEGOTIATIONS?

For physicians, advanced Healthcare-Specific negotiation skills enables:

- Engaging patients as partners in care decisions.
- Resolving interdisciplinary team conflicts.
- Securing resources for innovative treatments.

For advanced practice providers, strong Healthcare-Specific negotiation skills are key for:

- Advocating for adequate staffing levels to ensure quality care.
- Addressing operational challenges that impact patient well-being.
- Driving policy changes to advance clinical practice and improve patient outcomes.

For administrators, mastering Healthcare-Specific negotiation strategies is essential to:

- Facilitate buy-in on strategic initiatives across diverse stakeholders.
- Procure supplies and services that maximize healthcare value.
- Resolve inter-departmental resource conflicts that affect patient care delivery.

For those in the Business of Health, effective Healthcare-Specific negotiation skills are crucial for:

- Forging strategic partnerships with payers, suppliers, and other healthcare organizations.
- Advocating for sustainable policies and regulations while managing complex stakeholder relationships and competing interests.
- Driving financial performance and optimizing reimbursement rates while ensuring high-quality patient care.

For researchers, comprehensive Healthcare-Specific negotiation abilities are useful for:

- Securing funding and institutional support for critical studies.
- Building cooperative multi-site partnerships to advance medical knowledge.
- Navigating complex regulatory issues and data-sharing agreements.

Introducing the HEAR Approach™

Given the complexities and shortcomings of conventional negotiation tactics in healthcare, a new approach is needed – one that addresses the sector's unique demands while prioritizing patient outcomes and ethical considerations. The HEAR Approach™ offers a comprehensive toolkit that integrates insights from negotiation experts and the real-world experiences of healthcare professionals. This method empowers providers to navigate the multifaceted negotiations they face daily, fostering collaborative, patient-centric decision-making and efficient resource allocation. Comprised of several critical elements, the HEAR system ultimately drives better outcomes for patients, teams, and organizations.[7]

The Relational Mindset

The Relational Mindset is the foundation for the HEAR Approach™, promoting collaborative, empathetic negotiation focused beyond individual objectives. This mental framework is grounded in the understanding that all parties in a negotiation are interconnected and that the best outcomes are achieved when everyone's needs and perspectives are considered. At its core, the Relational Mindset is about adopting an "us" rather than "I" outlook in conversations. The two elements of the Relational Mindset – Emotional Intelligence and Theory of Mind – stress positive relationships, foster trust, and promote collaboration among stakeholders, underpinning and amplifying the effectiveness of each stage of the HEAR Approach™.[8]

By internalizing the Relational Mindset that forms the basis of HEAR's methodology, healthcare professionals can cultivate self-awareness and resilience to advocate with poise, develop Emotional Intelligence to grasp all stakeholders' perspectives, and foster creative flexibility to recast roadblocks into breakthrough solutions. This mindset positions practitioners at the forefront of championing a new era of healthcare negotiation – one rooted in empathetic cooperation that advances the profession's higher calling. Chapter 2 will go into greater detail about the Relational Mindset.

Healthcare-Specific Strategies

The first step of the HEAR Approach™ targets developing "trilingual" negotiation skills so professionals can navigate across the three pillars of healthcare: the Practice of Medicine, the Delivery of Care, and the Business of Health. By adapting negotiation strategies to align with the distinct challenges inherent in patient care, clinical decision-making, and the broad business of healthcare, the HEAR Approach™ utilizes proven methods for balancing competing priorities across healthcare's interconnected three pillars, ensuring that healthcare professionals can drive value across each. Equipped with the Healthcare Negotiation Mapping Tool, healthcare professionals can identify stakeholders, understand priorities, and tailor strategies that balance clinical excellence, operational efficiency, and financial sustainability while understanding how their decisions in one realm impact others.

The strategies of the HEAR Approach™ apply across various healthcare settings, from boardrooms to operating and exam rooms. In the Practice of Medicine, negotiations involve treatment discussions, interdisciplinary collaboration, and patient advocacy. The Delivery of Care focuses on operational aspects, including resource allocation, conflict resolution, and process improvements. The Business of Health encompasses financial and administrative negotiations, balancing cost considerations with care quality, and aligning stakeholder interests. By applying the HEAR Approach™, healthcare professionals can effectively navigate complex negotiations, drive positive change, and improve patient outcomes across all three pillars of healthcare. Chapter 3 will look at these negotiation strategies, setting the stage for Part II's exploration of effective trilingual communication and decision-making in real-life scenarios.

Empowerment

The second step of the HEAR Approach™ equips healthcare professionals with tools to effectively navigate high-stakes negotiations and advocate for their patients and their own professional needs.[9] By embracing vulnerability and enhancing self-awareness within a patient care and team context, healthcare professionals can explore practical Empowerment strategies that provide a roadmap for asserting the value of evidence-based practices, ultimately enhancing care quality and operational efficiency.[10] By mastering the RESET technique (Recognize, Evaluate, Step Back, Empathize, and Transform), healthcare professionals can practice real-time emotional management and offer constructive responses during challenging interactions.

Empowerment leads healthcare professionals to develop the emotional grounding to confidently advocate for patient needs and professional goals. For instance, an administrator involved in the Business of Health might conduct an internal scan to identify their own biases and emotions before negotiating with an outside supplier, ensuring a more objective approach that recognizes their unique position within the healthcare environment. Chapter

4 demonstrates how healthcare professionals can embrace an empowered mindset to navigate biases, stereotypes, and assumptions, fostering a more inclusive, equitable, and collaborative healthcare environment.

Acknowledgment

Acknowledgment serves as a powerful catalyst in healthcare negotiations, fostering more collaborative and impact-driven discussions by valuing different viewpoints and leading to more empathetic and effective negotiations.[11] By embracing active listening, validating concerns, and demonstrating empathy, healthcare professionals can break down barriers and shift negotiations from problem-centric to opportunity-driven. The concept of "Multiple Selves" provides a framework for recognizing diverse perspectives, leading to more inclusive solutions that address the complex realities of healthcare delivery.[12]

Actively listening to validate diverse perspectives and fostering mutual understanding and collaboration are key elements of Acknowledgment. For example, during a care coordination meeting, a social worker could practice Acknowledgment by summarizing each team member's concerns, such as a physical therapist's insights on mobility challenges or a pharmacist's input on medication management, before working together to create a comprehensive discharge plan. Chapter 5 illustrates how healthcare professionals can harness the power of Acknowledgment to foster a collaborative problem-solving environment and become more effective negotiators, compassionate leaders, and catalysts for positive change.

Recasting

Finally, Recasting offers techniques for shifting from traditional, positional negotiation tactics by externalized selves into an innovative and collaborative exploration of underlying shared goals by mutually vulnerable stakeholders.[13] Because parties are no longer as defensive (due to the Relational Mindset and Empowerment and Acknowledgment stages), during Recasting they are more willing to share information and adopt an "us" rather than "me" approach – leading to entirely new negotiations because the initial issues are now seen in an entirely different light.[14] By reframing challenges as opportunities for creative, breakthrough solutions, Recasting reflects a collaborative problem-solving that can lead to healthcare negotiations that foster trust, innovation, and mutual understanding – showcasing the potential of iterative adaptive strategies to foster continuous improvement and patient-centered care.

The key to Recasting is learning how to transform constraints like budgets or policies into opportunities for innovation that prioritize patient care. For example, when faced with overcrowding and long wait times, the emergency department (ED) team brainstormed creative solutions for improving patient care and operational efficiency. They proposed implementing a rapid triage system to prioritize patients more effectively while simultaneously collaborating with local primary care providers to develop a community education program on appropriate ED use. The team also suggested creating a "fast track" area for minor injuries and illnesses, complemented by a partnership with nearby urgent care centers to redirect non-emergency cases. Chapter 6 looks closely at how healthcare professionals can reframe

Figure 1.1 This illustration represents the HEAR Approach™ introduced in Chapter 1. At the center is a human profile surrounded by interconnected gears, symbolizing the Relational Mindset – the foundation of the HEAR framework – powered by emotional intelligence and theory of mind.

From this center, four core elements extend outward:

Top right – Strategy (Institution): Healthcare-specific negotiation strategies across the three pillars
Top left – Recasting: Turning challenges into opportunities for collaboration and problem-solving
Bottom left – Acknowledgment: Recognizing and validating diverse stakeholder perspectives
Bottom right – Empowerment: Cultivating self-awareness and advocating effectively
Curved arrows link each element, underscoring the integrated nature of the HEAR Approach™. Rather than isolated tactics, these components work in concert to transform traditional negotiations into patient-centered, collaborative solutions.

discussions to advocate for sustainable business practices aligned with the healthcare mission.

Throughout this book can be found explanations for how to develop enhanced negotiation skills and strategies tailored specifically for healthcare contexts. These skills build upon the foundational principles of the HEAR Approach™, providing a toolkit to navigate the complex negotiations encountered across the three core pillars of healthcare. Embracing this comprehensive methodology leads to negotiations that shift from being purely transactional to collaborative and patient-centric. By integrating the Relational Mindset, the HEAR steps, and optimized negotiation skills, healthcare professionals will be better equipped to drive positive change across patient care, clinical decision-making, and not just healthcare administration but the business of healthcare, leading to improved patient outcomes, strengthened interprofessional collaboration, optimized resource allocation, and a healthcare system more prepared to meet the evolving needs of the communities it serves.

What Healthcare-Specific Negotiations Look Like

The "Healthcare-Specific" component of the HEAR Approach™ is crucial as it equips healthcare professionals with the skills to navigate the industry's challenges across the three pillars of healthcare. Mastering this form of contextual negotiation means aligning strategies with the nuanced realities of patient care, regulatory frameworks, and healthcare policies to enhance their effectiveness and impact. Healthcare providers can achieve these goals by applying the different stages of the HEAR Approach™ in multiple contexts.

Example: The Operating Room (Practice of Medicine Pillar)

An ED nurse, Alex, recognizes dangerous understaffing during peak hours. Alex initially feels frustration and anger with the administration for not addressing this sooner, assuming they don't understand the realities of the ED.

Recognizing these feelings as counterproductive to achieving the outcome he seeks, Alex takes time to prepare a data-driven presentation for a meeting with the ED director and hospital administrator. Instead of complaining about understaffing, Alex reframes the issue: "I've analyzed our patient flow data, and I believe we have an opportunity to enhance patient safety and satisfaction while potentially reducing overall costs."

Alex presents data showing how proper staffing during peak hours could reduce wait times, prevent adverse events, and potentially decrease costly readmissions. Initially defensive because they were anticipating an emotionally charged meeting, the administrator becomes engaged when Alex acknowledges budget constraints and suggests testing the proposed staffing model. The participants agree to implement a three-month pilot program with flexible employee scheduling during crunch times, with clear metrics to evaluate its impact on patient outcomes and overall costs.

Coordinating operational aspects like staffing, process improvements, and quality initiatives across departments require constant negotiation. By using the HEAR Approach™, negotiations that could easily become confrontational instead turn into collaborative problem-solving sessions.

Example: The Exam Room (Delivery of Care Pillar)

Dr. Rossi, a pediatrician, is discussing a child's developmental delays with concerned parents. During the discussion, the parents expressed reluctance to pursue an Individualized Education Program (IEP) for their child, fearing stigmatization.

Dr. Rossi is initially inclined to insist on the IEP. But rather than cultivate conflict, she instead first employs Empowerment, reflecting on her own emotions and potential biases. She recognizes her frustration with parents who often resist early intervention and her bias toward immediate action based on her experience with her own child with special needs. She then acknowledges her tendency to push for extensive testing, which may not always be necessary. Dr. Rossi takes a deep breath, reminding herself to approach this case objectively.

Instead of immediately and forcefully advocating for an IEP, she practices active listening, hearing the parents out about their worries regarding their child being branded as "delayed" or even being bullied and shamed. She acknowledges their concerns, saying, "I understand your worries about labeling your child. It's natural to want to protect them."

Because she has effectively employed Empowerment, Acknowledgment, and adopted a Relational Mindset, both she and the parents are now less defensive, open to creative solutions, and willing to see things differently. Dr. Rossi then recasts the conversation by explaining how an IEP can be a roadmap for personalized learning and growth. She shares the story of another patient who thrived with early intervention. By creating a supportive, collaborative environment, Dr. Rossi capitalizes on the trust she has built with the parents. They ultimately agree to start with a less intensive support plan, with the understanding that they'll reassess in three months to determine if an IEP is needed.

In the exam room and clinical collaborations, healthcare professionals are called upon to negotiate treatment plans, facilitate patient-provider dialogue, and unite interprofessional perspectives. Utilizing the HEAR Approach™ can lead to successful outcomes where the needs and concerns of everyone are heard.

Example: The Boardroom (Business of Health Pillar)

When the Chief of Surgery advocates investing in new medical equipment during a budget negotiation, but the hospital President wants to keep funds in reserve for potential emergencies, the hospital Chief Fianancial Officier (CFO) is faced with navigating competing priorities.

Instead of immediately shutting down the debate and letting her boss (the President) get his way, the CFO decides to step back and empathize with the Chief of Surgery.

She actively listens to understand the clinical benefits and potential impact on patient outcomes. The CFO then validates the Chief of Surgery's perspective: "I appreciate your commitment to providing the best possible care for our patients. Your insights on how this equipment could improve surgical outcomes are valuable and compelling." At this juncture, most CFOs would then pivot to deliver the "bad news" that the President has other plans. Instead, the CFO presses forward, saying, "I'd like to work together to find funding for this purchase or look at some alternatives that align with our budget. Let's set up a task force."

By acknowledging the Chief of Surgery's viewpoint, the CFO sets the stage for a more collaborative discussion on finding a financially sustainable solution that aligns with the organization's mission. This could involve exploring alternative funding sources, phasing the investment over time, or finding ways to optimize the use of existing resources to free up funds for the new equipment. The CFO's approach demonstrates how Acknowledgment can lead to more creative and mutually beneficial solutions in financial negotiations.

Governing the organization's financial health involved negotiations about facilities, payer contracts, and, most of all budgets. The HEAR Approach™ can turn tense discussions into opportunities for innovative thinking that lead to long-term collaboration and mutual respect regardless of the ultimate outcome.

What HEAR Tools and Practices Look Like

The HEAR Approach™ provides a robust toolkit and innovative practices for navigating complex multiparty negotiations to achieve mutually beneficial outcomes. Its components are embedded in the different steps of the HEAR methodology, all aimed at enhancing healthcare negotiations. These tools and practices empower providers to skillfully negotiate across a variety of settings spanning patient care, regulatory frameworks, and healthcare policies, amplifying their effectiveness and impact.

Example: Cultivating Self-Awareness

Dr. Steif, a department head, wants to prepare for a negotiation to secure funding for a new research initiative he's excited about. Before doing so, he wants to ensure that he's on the strongest footing possible – not just in his arguments but also in his own emotional grounding.

The Empowerment stage of the HEAR Approach™ helps healthcare professionals develop the self-awareness needed to advocate with poise in high-stakes healthcare scenarios. One key practice is engaging in Internal Scans before critical negotiations by spending 5–10 minutes reflecting through prompts like:

- What are my core interests here? What's the bigger mission driving me?
- How am I currently feeling? What emotional influences could arise?
- What blind spots might I have? What potential triggers should I anticipate?
- What areas of knowledge am I lacking? How can I address these gaps?
- How will I respond to potential objections or a "no"?
- What alternative approaches or backup plans should I consider?

During his internal scan, Dr. Steif identifies a potential blind spot due to his limited understanding of the hospital's current financial situation. Recognizing his overconfidence in the project's merits had caused him to overlook potential budgetary concerns, he develops a backup plan for a scaled-down pilot study if full funding isn't approved – a constructive alternative to becoming frustrated and argumentative when faced with fiscal constraints.

By developing self-awareness and grounding through Empowerment practices like internal scans, healthcare providers elevate their ability to resolve conflicts, secure buy-in for key initiatives, and unite stakeholders around a shared vision of optimal patient care. This self-awareness not only improves negotiation skills but also enhances their overall effectiveness as healthcare leaders.

Example: Validating Sensibilities

A palliative care nurse practitioner discusses end-of-life care preferences with a patient's family members with conflicting opinions. Worried about the potential for escalating tensions, she wants to calm the waters and move individuals into a collaborative problem-solving mindset.

The Acknowledgment stage of the HEAR Approach™ equips healthcare professionals with tools to navigate healthcare's inherently diverse perspectives with Emotional Intelligence. One key practice is validating diverse perspectives. After giving each viewpoint a fair hearing, providers can neutralize potential defensiveness by verbalizing Acknowledgment of the underlying thoughts, emotions, and intentions – even if they disagree.

The nurse practitioner employs this technique when she says, "I understand this is an incredibly difficult and emotional situation for all of you. Your differing perspectives come from a place of deep care and concern for your loved one's well-being, even if you disagree on the best path forward." Acknowledging all sides makes each party less defensive and more open to collaboration. As a result, family members may begin to move toward listening to one another, opening the door for Recasting the debate to discover shared interests that may not have been apparent at the start, and setting the stage for more creative and mutually rewarding solutions.

Example: Brainstorming with Suspended Judgment

A community health center is struggling to improve patient access to mental health services due to limited resources and a shortage of mental health professionals. Stuck and feeling trapped, the center is seeking a process where seemingly intractable obstacles can be reimagined as opportunities for mutual-gain solutions.

The Recasting stage of the HEAR Approach™ empowers healthcare providers to transform conflicts into opportunities for collaborative innovation, respecting all stakeholder needs and leveraging insights gained through the Empowerment and Acknowledgment stages. One key practice involves brainstorming with suspended judgment. Doing so involves engaging all parties in brainstorming, guided by a framework that:

- Encourages an "everything is possible" mentality.
- Actively listens without initially judging any ideas proposed.
- Considers unorthodox perspectives that might otherwise be dismissed.
- Combines different ideas into innovative, integrated solutions.

Through Recasting the challenge as an opportunity to innovate and expand access, the health center team brainstormed creative solutions. They proposed implementing telehealth services to connect patients with remote mental health providers, while simultaneously collaborating with local schools and community organizations to provide mental health education and early intervention programs. The team also suggested training primary care providers to screen for and treat common mental health conditions, complemented by a partnership with a local university to develop a mental health provider training program and pipeline.

By suspending judgment and considering diverse perspectives, the team generated innovative solutions that addressed the underlying problem of access to mental health services in a resource-constrained environment. Not only did these multifaceted approaches address the immediate need for mental health services – they also targeted building long-term capacity.

Conclusion: Empowering Transformative Healthcare Negotiations

This initial exploration of the HEAR Approach™ reveals its powerful potential to navigate the delicate complexities of healthcare negotiations. By integrating the core tenets of Healthcare-Specific tailored strategies, Empowerment, Acknowledgment, and Recasting conflicts as opportunities, the HEAR Approach™ unlocks a comprehensive methodology to elevate the negotiation capabilities of healthcare professionals.

However, the HEAR Approach™ represents more than simply refining negotiation skills. The challenges inherent to healthcare negotiations have persisted for far too long – power struggles eroding trust, interdisciplinary conflicts hindering care continuity, and patient voices muffled by systemic inertia. It is a call to embrace a fundamentally new mindset focused on collaboration over confrontation, understanding over ego, and uniting diverse perspectives in service of a shared mission – delivering optimal patient care and healthcare outcomes.

Implementing the HEAR Approach™ requires the continuous iterative refinement of the mindset and method outlined above. However, the potential benefits are far-reaching: enhanced patient experiences, streamlined operational efficiency, fortified interprofessional partnerships, and a revitalized healthcare system equipped to address evolving challenges resourcefully. By embracing this method, healthcare professionals can drive transformative change, fostering a more responsive, collaborative, and patient-centered healthcare environment.

REFLECTION EXERCISE: APPLYING THE HEAR APPROACH™

Think about a specific situation you are facing or have faced recently that requires negotiation. How are you thinking about it? Where are you stuck?

Now think about the concepts related to the HEAR Approach™. What would change about your situation if you adopted a collaborative, empathetic approach that considers all parties' needs and could lead to better outcomes? How does identifying which pillar is involved change your understanding of stakeholders and their interests? How could what you read about Empowerment, Acknowledgment, and Recasting be employed to change your approach? Which tool or practice you've learned about in this chapter could assist you in reaching your goal?

Key Takeaways

1. Research shows that professionals who possess strong negotiation skills are better equipped to advocate for patient needs, secure crucial resources, and drive positive change within their organizations.
2. Conventional negotiation models operate on fundamentally misaligned principles with the adversarial positioning of parties and a winner-takes-all mindset.
3. Healthcare professionals can foster collaborative, patient-centric decision-making processes that lead to better outcomes and more efficient use of resources by mastering Healthcare-Specific negotiation strategies.
4. The HEAR Approach™ provides a comprehensive toolkit for healthcare professionals that empowers them to successfully navigate Healthcare-Specific negotiations.

Notes

1. Roger Fisher, William Ury, and Bruce Patton, *Getting to Yes: Negotiating Agreement without Giving In* (New York: Penguin Books, 2011).
2. Leonard J. Marcus, Barry C. Dorn, and Eric J. McNulty, *Renegotiating Health Care: Resolving Conflict to Build Collaboration* (San Francisco, MA: Jossey-Bass, 2011).
3. Jodi Halpern, *From Detached Concern to Empathy: Humanizing Medical Practice* (Oxford: Oxford University Press, 2001).
4. Kathleen G. Sebelius, "Transforming Health Care in America: A Call to Action," *New England Journal of Medicine* 361, no. 2 (2009): 109–111.
5. Anastakis, D. J. "Negotiation skills for physicians." *The American Journal of Surgery* 185, no. 1 (2003): 74–78.
6. Thomas H. Lee and Laura S. Kaiser, "Turning Value-Based Health Care into a Real Business Model," *Harvard Business Review*, October 8, 2015, https://hbr.org/2015/10/turning-value-based-health-care-into-a-real-business-model.
7. David A. Lax and James K. Sebenius, *3-D Negotiation: Powerful Tools to Change the Game in Your Most Important Deals* (Cambridge, MA: Harvard Business Review Press, 2006).
8. Daniel Goleman, Richard Boyatzis, and Annie McKee, *Primal Leadership: Unleashing the Power of Emotional Intelligence* (Cambridge, MA: Harvard Business Review Press, 2013).
9. Amy C. Edmondson, *The Fearless Organization: Creating Psychological Safety in the Workplace for Learning, Innovation, and Growth* (Hoboken, NJ: John Wiley & Sons, 2018).
10. Leonard J. Marcus, Barry C. Dorn, and Joseph M. Henderson, "Meta-Leadership: A Framework for Building Leadership Effectiveness," *National Preparedness Leadership Initiative*, Harvard School of Public Health, 2013.
11. Douglas Stone, Bruce Patton, and Sheila Heen, *Difficult Conversations: How to Discuss What Matters Most* (New York: Penguin Books, 2010).
12. Robert A. Baruch Bush and Joseph P. Folger, *The Promise of Mediation: The Transformative Approach to Conflict* (San Francisco, MA: Jossey-Bass, 2004).
13. William Ury, *Getting Past No: Negotiating in Difficult Situations* (New York: Bantam Books, 1991).
14. Lax and Sebenius, *3-D Negotiation.*

Chapter 2

The Relational Mindset

The Foundation of the HEAR Approach™

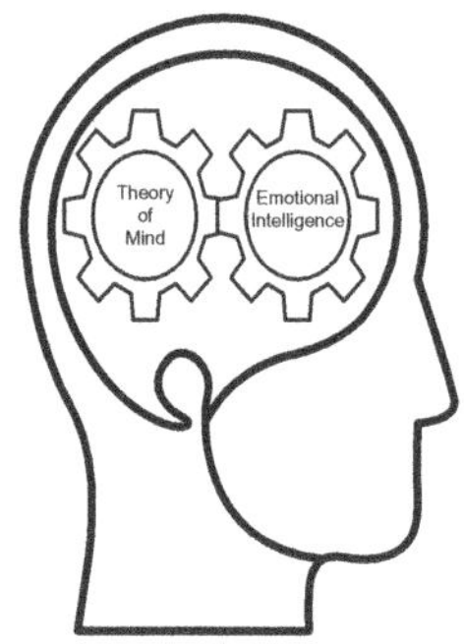

The quality of our relationships determines the quality of our lives.

– Esther Perel

DOI: 10.4324/9781003336013-3

Imagine you're a hospital administrator tasked with implementing a new electronic health record (EHR) system. You know that this transition will be challenging, disrupting established workflows and requiring extensive training. As you prepare for the crucial meeting with department heads, you take a deep breath, knowing that the success of this project hinges on your ability to navigate the complex web of concerns and resistance you're about to face. As you sit down to discuss the implementation with the heads of various departments, you can feel the tension in the room.

The head of surgery, Dr. Cataneo, has his arms crossed and a deep frown etched on his face. You can sense his concern about how this change will impact his team's daily operations and patient care. His reputation for perfectionism and efficiency is well-known throughout the hospital, and you anticipate that he'll be one of the toughest to convince. The lead nurse, Isabella, fidgets with her pen, clearly uneasy. You know she's worried about the learning curve for her staff and the potential for errors during the transition. Her eyes dart nervously around the room, silently communicating with other nursing staff representatives. The pharmacy manager, Mark, has a stack of papers in front of him, likely filled with questions about integrating the new system with existing medication management processes. You notice his fingers tapping rhythmically on the table, a telltale sign of his barely contained anxiety.

As you begin to discuss the implementation timeline and the benefits of the new system, you can see the resistance growing. The air in the room feels thick with apprehension, and you can almost hear the unspoken objections building. Dr. Cataneo soon interrupts, stating bluntly, "This is going to be a disaster. We don't have time for this kind of disruption." His words cut through the room like a scalpel, and you see several heads nodding in agreement. Isabella chimes in, "My nurses are already overwhelmed. How are we supposed to train everyone on a new system without compromising patient care"? Her voice wavers slightly, betraying the emotional toll this change is already taking on her team. Mark adds, "I have serious concerns about the compatibility of this system with our current processes. We can't afford any mistakes with medication management." He shuffles through his papers, pulling out a chart that illustrates the potential points of failure.

The meeting is quickly spiraling into a series of objections and complaints, with each department head focused on their own concerns and challenges. The cacophony of voices rises, with side conversations breaking out and frustrations mounting. You can feel the tension rising, and you know that if you don't find a way to bridge these divides, the EHR implementation could be doomed before it even begins. Your mind races, searching for a way to unify these disparate voices and channel their concerns into constructive dialogue…

As EHR implementations have rolled out across hospitals, the concerns raised above are not uncommon. How can healthcare professionals navigate these complex dynamics to achieve a successful outcome in the face of competing priorities, limited resources, and high stakes? The answer lies in adopting a Relational Mindset in healthcare negotiations – an approach that prioritizes building trust, understanding, and collaboration among all stakeholders.

Flaws in Transactional "Win-Lose" Approaches to Healthcare Negotiations

To begin to grasp the relational mindset, it's helpful to start by contrasting it with a transactional approach. A transactional mindset, as described by social psychologist Alan Fiske's "market pricing" model, sees interactions as discrete exchanges, with the goal of maximizing one's own benefit in each transaction.[1] This "win-lose" mentality prioritizes short-term gains at the expense of relationships. Research shows this outlook fails to account for the interdependent nature of organizational interactions, especially in healthcare settings where collaboration and long-term relationships are crucial.[2]

Many healthcare professionals inadvertently adopt transactional negotiation tactics ill-suited to their field's unique challenges. These approaches, often borrowed from business, law, or sales, frequently operate on principles that are fundamentally at odds with healthcare's core mission:

- An emphasis on maximizing individual or organizational gain, often at the expense of broader healthcare outcomes.
- A tendency to view negotiations as zero-sum games, where one party's gain is another's loss.
- A focus on short-term wins rather than sustainable, long-term solutions that benefit all stakeholders.
- A failure to adequately consider the ethical implications and potential impact on patient care.

These misaligned principles can lead to breakdowns in communication, erode trust between healthcare providers and institutions, and ultimately compromise patient care. As healthcare continues to evolve and face new challenges, it becomes increasingly clear that a more nuanced, relationally focused approach to negotiation is not just beneficial but essential for the field's continued progress and effectiveness.[3]

Defining the Relational Mindset

The Relational Mindset is a way of approaching interactions that prioritizes building and maintaining positive relationships. It recognizes that the quality of the relationships healthcare professionals cultivate directly impacts the quality of their lives, work, and patient outcomes. In contrast to the transactional mindset, a relational approach perceives interactions as part of an interconnected web. It acknowledges that today's engagement lays the foundation for future ones, and how we treat others has far-reaching consequences. This mindset seeks solutions benefiting all parties, fostering trust, collaboration, and long-term success.[4]

Pioneering researchers like Dr. Amy Edmondson, a professor at Harvard Business School, have demonstrated that adopting a relational mindset can transform professional interactions and collaboration by offering a more holistic and humanistic view of professional interactions.[5]

Dr. Edmondson's work on psychological safety and team learning highlights the importance of prioritizing interpersonal connections over individual competition. By fostering trust, understanding, and cooperation, healthcare professionals can create environments where people feel heard, valued, and respected. This relational approach leads to better communication, durable and doable agreements, more creative problem-solving, and, ultimately, better outcomes.[6]

The Relational Mindset underwriting this approach is rooted in the concept of relational coordination, which emphasizes the importance of shared goals, shared knowledge, and mutual respect in fostering effective collaboration. Dr. Jody Hoffer Gittell, a professor at Brandeis University, has conducted extensive research on relational coordination.[7] Her studies have shown that stronger relational coordination among healthcare providers leads to improved quality of care, reduced postoperative pain, and shorter hospital stays for patients.[8] This shift toward a more relational paradigm has the potential to address many of the systemic challenges facing modern healthcare, from burnout to fragmented care delivery. By prioritizing relationships and fostering trust, collaboration, and innovation, healthcare professionals can elevate standards of care and ultimately enhance the well-being of both patients and providers.

THE POWER OF A RELATIONAL MINDSET

But what does a Relational Mindset look like in practice? Let me share a personal story that illustrates the power of this approach. It's a chapter from my "lowlight reel," a moment that now feels more like a behind-the-scenes outtake than anything else.

Let me set the scene: a law firm conference room. I am with another second-year litigation associate, and we are both on pins and needles. The two of us were selected to work on a high-profile case that is going to trial. It's an opportunity any budding trial attorney would die for – the chance to second-chair an important trial. For young lawyers like us, this was a rare shot to gain courtroom experience and make a name for ourselves in the firm. We are both waiting to hear who the partner has selected. As she walks in with a sly smile on her face, she says, "My decision is… you two figure it out," and walks out of the room. Sitting there in stunned silence at this unexpected curveball, neither of us knew what to say. Then, our competitive instincts kicked in, and what could have been a collaborative moment turned into an all-out rivalry.

I won't go into all the details, but suffice it to say it got to the point where we were tallying up our wins like some kind of legal scoreboard – billable hours, depositions, motions – you name it. Looking back, the whole thing seems ridiculously competitive. As the comparisons intensified, I began to feel increasingly uncomfortable with the situation. I remember catching my reflection in the conference room window, and the absurdity of it all hit me like a ton of bricks.

That's when I decided to switch gears. I realized that our fierce competition might actually be detrimental to the case and our professional growth. I reached out to my colleague, offered a genuine apology for letting things spiral out of control, and asked to hear their side of the story. This move – out of left field for both of us – broke the ice. As we started actually listening to each other, not just hearing words but understanding intentions, we found common ground. It turned out our skills complemented each other in ways we'd been too blind to see.

So, we pitched an idea to our partner: instead of duking it out for the second chair, why not share it? Co-chair the trial, combine our forces, and maybe, just maybe, make this more about the client's win than our own. This shift from a *me-vs.-you* to an *us-for-them* approach wasn't just a game-changer for that trial; it reshaped how I view competition and collaboration in my professional life.

As much as I cringe at it, this experience taught me the power of a relational mindset. By shifting my focus from competition to collaboration, I achieved a better outcome, built a stronger working relationship, and contributed to a more positive organizational culture. This lesson has stayed with me throughout my career, influencing how I approach challenges and opportunities. It's a constant reminder that in any field, our greatest achievements often come not from outperforming others but from finding ways to work together toward shared goals.

Transitioning to a Relational Mindset in Healthcare

Healthcare professionals should adopt a relational mindset, shifting from an "I" focus to an inclusive "we" mentality. This approach centers on mutual understanding, shared success, cohesive teamwork, and true patient partnerships. Such a pivotal reframing catalyzes elevated care experiences and outcomes while also strengthening dynamics within healthcare teams and across departments.[9]

The benefits of the "We" mindset span everything from comprehensive patient care to cohesive, mission-aligned teams. When selecting medical devices like insulin pumps, healthcare providers should gather feedback from patient representatives and caregiver groups from the start. Studies show that involving patients and caregivers in these evaluations alongside providers significantly increases adherence and improves clinical outcomes.[10] The same is true when proposing new programs, such as a cardiovascular prevention initiative. Research indicates that higher levels of cooperative coordination between teams lead to lower hospital infections, readmissions, and mortality rates – even lower staff turnover, fostering a more cohesive, engaged workforce.[11] Healthcare leaders should engage administrators early from an inclusive "we" perspective to ensure priorities stay aligned across different service lines and eliminate operational silos.

Consider the dramatic differences between a transactional approach compared to a relational model when it comes to patient care:

> A hospital administration team, driven by a transactional mindset, implements a rigid, one-size-fits-all protocol for post-surgical pain management to standardize care and reduce costs. While this approach may improve efficiency metrics, it fails to account for patients' individual needs, preferences, and responses to pain management options. As a result, some patients experience inadequate pain relief or adverse side effects, leading to increased complications, prolonged recovery times, and lower patient satisfaction.
>
> In contrast, a relational approach recognizes that effective pain management requires a personalized, patient-centered approach. The administration encourages open communication between healthcare providers and patients, fostering a collaborative environment where patients actively participate in their pain management decisions. Providers take the time to understand each patient's unique needs, concerns, and preferences, tailoring pain management plans accordingly. Through this relational approach, patients receive individualized pain management that balances their specific needs with evidence-based practices. This leads to better pain control, fewer complications, and improved patient satisfaction.

By prioritizing patient engagement and shared decision-making, the relational mindset enhances trust, promotes better recovery outcomes, and strengthens the patient-provider relationship, ultimately contributing to higher quality care and a more positive healthcare experience.

But the benefits of a relational approach are not just limited to the Practice of Medicine and Delivery of Care pillars. The Business of Health pillar might seem to be an aspect of medicine where a transactional approach is not just accepted but encouraged. However, that pillar is an equal beneficiary of the relational mindset, as the following example illustrates:

> A hospital's purchasing department operates with a transactional mindset and focuses solely on securing the lowest prices for medical supplies, regardless of other factors. They frequently switch suppliers based on short-term cost savings without considering the long-term implications of these decisions. As a result, the hospital experiences inconsistent product quality, unreliable delivery, and

a lack of supplier support during critical situations, such as supply chain disruptions or product recalls. This transactional approach prioritizes immediate financial gains over the stability and quality of patient care.

In contrast, a relational approach recognizes the value of building long-term, mutually beneficial partnerships with suppliers. The purchasing department seeks to understand the suppliers' capabilities, expertise, and commitment to quality and innovation. They engage in open, transparent communication to establish shared goals and expectations. Rather than focusing solely on price, the hospital considers factors such as product quality, reliability, and the supplier's ability to provide ongoing support and collaboration. They invest in long-term contracts with suppliers who demonstrate a commitment to continuous improvement and align with the hospital's mission and values.

By adopting a relational approach, the hospital establishes stable, reliable supply chains that ensure consistent access to high-quality medical supplies. The collaborative nature of these supplier relationships fosters innovation, allowing the hospital to benefit from the latest advancements in medical technology and supplies. This, in turn, enhances patient care, improves operational efficiency, and reduces the risk of supply related issues impacting patient safety. The relational mindset creates a foundation for long-term, sustainable partnerships that prioritize the overall quality and continuity of healthcare delivery.

To embed inclusive "we" practices into daily healthcare workflows, organizations should adopt a range of practices. These include designating "Patient Voice" representatives to participate in procurement decisions and strategic initiative rollouts that impact patient care delivery. Regular interdepartmental collaborative meetings should be established, where clinical leads and administrators align priorities before finalizing decisions that span multiple areas. Organizations should also open channels for feedback and innovative ideas from all stakeholders – including front-line staff, patients, and community members – through various platforms such as online forums, surveys, town halls, and digital platforms. For major organization-wide initiatives like implementing a new EHR system, interdisciplinary task forces should be created with representatives from all impacted teams to ensure a cohesive implementation approach. Finally, to promote and reinforce a "we" culture, organizations should formally recognize and incentivize outstanding examples of interdepartmental collaboration and patient-inclusive practices. These strategies collectively work to foster a more inclusive, collaborative, and patient-centered healthcare environment.

By integrating the "we" mindset, healthcare organizations can nurture a cooperative culture that elevates patient care experiences, reduces preventable adverse events, boosts staff engagement and retention, and optimizes resource utilization – ultimately driving better population health outcomes.

Psychological Foundations of the Relational Mindset

In healthcare, the stakes in negotiations are often high, and the outcomes can profoundly impact people's lives. Adopting a relational mindset is essential for navigating these complex, emotionally charged situations with empathy and understanding. Whether discussing treatment options with a patient, coordinating care with colleagues, or making decisions about resource allocation, healthcare professionals benefit by focusing on optimizing collective benefit and viewing negotiations as collaborative opportunities where mutual gains and shared value creation are prioritized.

The Relational Mindset is rooted in two key psychological concepts: Emotional Intelligence (EI) and Theory of Mind (ToM). These concepts form a significant part of the psychological underpinnings that support developing and applying the relational mindset in healthcare negotiations.

Emotional Intelligence

Emotional Intelligence, a concept popularized by psychologist Daniel Goleman, refers to the ability to recognize, understand, and manage one's own emotions, as well as the emotions of others.[12] Pioneering researchers in the field of EI, such as Drs. Peter Salovey and John D. Mayer,[13] have emphasized the importance of EI in healthcare settings. In their seminal work published in the journal *Imagination, Cognition, and Personality*,[14] they defined EI as the ability to monitor one's own and others' feelings and emotions, to discriminate among them, and to use this information to guide one's thinking and actions.

Numerous studies demonstrate the tangible benefits of EI for healthcare professionals. Research has found that surgeons with higher EI exhibit better clinical performance and achieve superior patient outcomes.[15] Similarly, physicians with elevated EI levels tend to have higher patient satisfaction rates and more collaborative relationships with colleagues. By developing self-awareness, self-regulation, empathy, and social skills, healthcare providers can better navigate the emotionally complex landscapes they face daily, ultimately improving patient care and job satisfaction. Improving EI is a continuous process that is vital in the high-stakes, emotionally complex world of healthcare. Here are some targeted strategies and exercises to enhance each component of EI:

- **Boost Self-Awareness**: Healthcare professionals can practice daily mindfulness or meditation to heighten awareness of their emotional states. They can keep a journal detailing their emotions and reactions, especially in healthcare settings, to uncover patterns in how their emotions influence their professional behavior.
- **Cultivate Empathy**: Providers can engage in active listening during interactions, focusing on truly understanding the patient or colleague's perspective. They can participate in role-playing exercises during training sessions to improve their ability to empathize with different viewpoints and emotional experiences.
- **Regulate Emotions**: Healthcare professionals can adopt stress management techniques such as deep breathing or progressive muscle relaxation to maintain emotional equilibrium in challenging situations. Applying these techniques before and during high-pressure healthcare scenarios can support reasoned decision-making.
- **Enhance Social Skills**: Finally, healthcare providers can work on their communication skills by focusing on nonverbal cues, adjusting their tone of voice, and practicing attentive engagement. By engaging in exercises that constructively express their emotions, they can foster better understanding and collaboration in healthcare.

By committing to developing EI through the practical application of these strategies, healthcare professionals can equip themselves to provide more empathetic care, foster cohesive team dynamics, and approach pivotal negotiations with diplomacy. EI enables providers to cultivate an environment of emotional awareness and understanding, which is the bedrock of the relational mindset in healthcare.[16]

Theory of Mind

Theory of Mind involves the ability to understand that people have their own unique perspectives, thoughts, beliefs, and desires that may differ from our own. Developed by psychologists Josef Perner and Heinz Wimmer, ToM is about an individual's ability to put themselves in someone else's shoes to appreciate that person's subjective experience and point of view.[17] This concept enables people to understand and predict others' behaviors, thoughts, and emotions by recognizing that they have different mental states.

Extensive research has demonstrated the value of ToM in healthcare, showing its benefits for enhancing therapeutic relationships, improving patient satisfaction, increasing empathy and communication abilities, and ultimately leading to better quality of care.[18] Healthcare professionals can apply ToM daily to enhance patient-provider communication, foster multidisciplinary collaboration, and provide more personalized, tailored care:

- Consider a social worker collaborating with a patient's care team. By leveraging ToM skills, the social worker can better understand the perspectives and priorities of various team members – physicians focusing on clinical outcomes, nurses emphasizing daily care needs, and therapists addressing functional goals. This deeper appreciation allows the social worker to facilitate more comprehensive, patient-centered care plans that address all stakeholders' viewpoints.
- Imagine a pediatrician having a sensitive discussion with parents about their child's developmental delays. With strong ToM skills, the pediatrician can respond and validate the parents' emotional experiences, fears, and questions with empathy, creating a supportive environment for productive dialogue and shared decision-making.

In situations with opposing viewpoints, such as differing opinions among specialists on a treatment approach, ToM mastery enables rising above disagreements. It facilitates transcending divisiveness to find common ground and consensus by genuinely understanding each party's motivations and concerns.[19]

Honing ToM skills is essential for healthcare professionals operating in the emotionally charged and high-stakes healthcare environment. To gauge and refine ToM capacities, healthcare professionals can engage in the following reflective practices and targeted strategies:

1. **Predict and Analyze Reactions**: Healthcare professionals should reflect on instances when patients' or colleagues' responses deviated from expectations. They should analyze these situations to improve

their ability to anticipate others' perspectives and adjust their approach accordingly.

2. **Integrate Diverse Viewpoints**: During team decisions about patient care or departmental changes, practitioners should actively seek out and incorporate perspectives from various stakeholders. This practice enhances inclusive decision-making and broadens their understanding of different viewpoints.
3. **Identify and Respond to Emotional Cues**: Caregivers should focus on recognizing both verbal and nonverbal emotional signals in daily interactions. They should practice adjusting their approach to create a supportive environment, especially in emotionally charged situations like patients expressing fear about procedures.

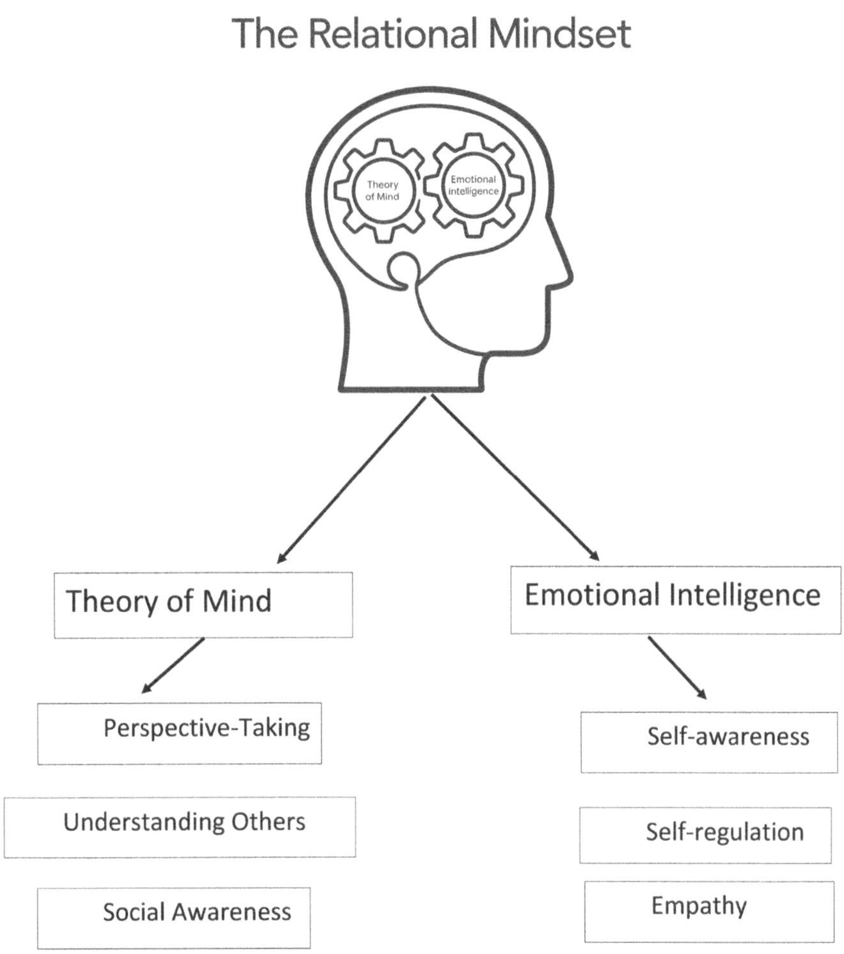

Figure 2.1 Relational Mindset diagram.

4. **Engage in Perspective-Taking Exercises**: Healthcare professionals should regularly participate in role-reversal exercises, diverse scenario role-plays, or perspective-taking journaling. These activities help develop empathy and a deeper understanding of others' motivations and life circumstances.
5. **Practice Active Listening and Validation**: During conversations, medical staff should concentrate on comprehending the speaker's full context and underlying perspectives. They should summarize and validate the speaker's viewpoint before responding, ensuring a complete understanding of their position.

By intentionally practicing strategies like these, providers strengthen their ability to step into others' subjective realities in healthcare's interpersonal environment. This enhances team decision-making, fortifies stakeholder communication, prevents conflict, and exemplifies the empathetic, patient-centered care critical to positive health outcomes.[20]

THEORY OF MIND ASSESSMENT

This assessment helps healthcare professionals evaluate their ability to understand and appreciate others' unique perspectives, thoughts, beliefs, and desires. It identifies areas for improvement in perspective-taking, empathetic communication, and cognitive flexibility. This assessment aligns with the ToM principles discussed above and can be used to enhance patient-provider communication, foster multidisciplinary collaboration, and provide more personalized care.

1. Perspective-Taking:
   - How well do I understand the unique experiences, beliefs, and motivations of stakeholders in healthcare situations?
   - What steps can I take to actively seek out and consider diverse viewpoints in team decisions and patient interactions?
   - How can I use perspective-taking to anticipate concerns and develop more inclusive solutions?
2. Empathetic Communication:
   - How effectively can I adapt my communication style to convey information and build understanding with different individuals?
   - What strategies can I employ to demonstrate genuine interest in and respect for others' perspectives?

- How can I use empathetic communication to foster collaboration and inclusivity in healthcare settings?

3. Cognitive Flexibility:
   - How well can I maintain an open and adaptable mindset in various healthcare scenarios?
   - What techniques can I use to question my own assumptions and biases and consider alternative viewpoints?
   - How can I leverage cognitive flexibility to generate creative, mutually beneficial solutions in complex healthcare situations?

Healthcare professionals should review their answers and consider specific steps they can take to enhance their ToM skills and address any limitations in understanding others' perspectives. They should also reflect on how they can apply these skills in daily practice to improve patient care, team collaboration, and overall healthcare outcomes. Regular engagement in perspective-taking exercises, active listening, and validation techniques can further strengthen their ability to navigate the complex interpersonal dynamics in healthcare settings.

Relational Mindset Tools and Practices: Empathy Mapping

There are a variety of tools and practices healthcare professionals should consider to assist in adopting a relational mindset. They should first and foremost use "I" statements when expressing personal needs and concerns. For instance, instead of saying, "You always dismiss my ideas," they should try, "I feel like my perspective isn't being fully considered." This approach helps avoid defensiveness and keeps the focus on finding mutually beneficial solutions. Additionally, healthcare professionals should strive to find common ground by looking for areas of agreement or shared interest, no matter how small. Highlighting these commonalities can build a sense of connection and cooperation, even amid disagreements. They should also be willing to compromise, recognizing that not every discussion will result in getting everything they want. The key is remaining open to finding a middle ground and considering creative solutions that meet everyone's core needs. These strategies collectively promote a more collaborative and productive process in healthcare decision-making and team interactions.

One of the most effective tools and practices for adopting a relational approach is the use of empathy mapping. This powerful strategy serves as a natural extension of the relational mindset, taking the concept of understanding others to a deeper level. In healthcare negotiations, empathy mapping helps professionals think more inclusively about "we" approaches and solutions. Using this structured approach allows providers to move beyond surface-level interactions and truly engage with the needs, concerns, and motivations of all parties involved in the healthcare process.

Empathy mapping involves creating a visual map to develop a deeper understanding of another person's thoughts, feelings, and experiences. By employing empathy mapping techniques, healthcare providers can enhance their perspective-taking abilities and foster more user-centered solutions in healthcare contexts. This practice allows them to better comprehend others' perspectives, demonstrate respect and empathy, and build rapport and trust – setting the stage for more collaborative and mutually beneficial solutions in healthcare negotiations.

Step-by-Step Empathy Mapping Guide

The following guide outlines a systematic empathy mapping procedure for healthcare professionals, providing a structured approach to enhance understanding and foster more patient-centered care:

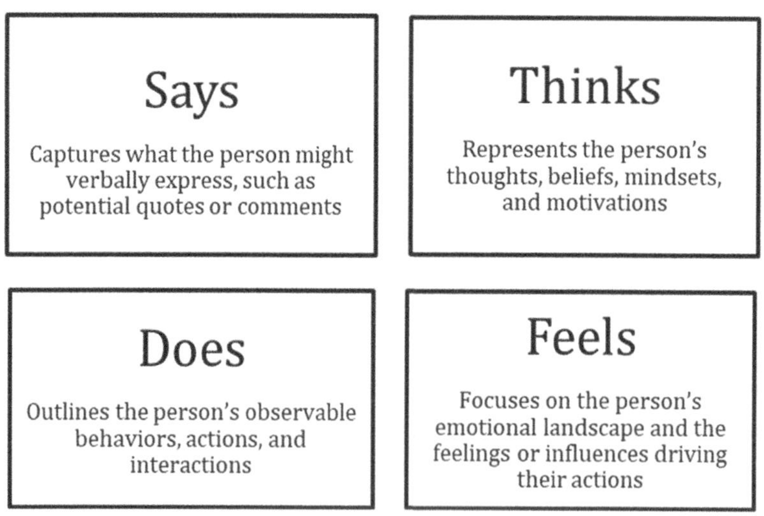

Figure 2.2 Empathy mapping guide.

1. Preparation:
   - Define the purpose of your empathy mapping exercise
   - Gather any existing data, research, or insights about the target person/group.
2. Identify the Subject:
   - Clearly define the person, group, or persona you need to empathize with.
   - Create a brief profile including demographics, background, and context.
3. Create the Empathy Map Canvas:
   - Prepare a visual space (physical or digital).
   - Draw the core four quadrants: Says, Thinks, Does, Feels.
4. Populate the Map:
   - For each section, consider the following:

Says

- Actual quotes or common phrases.
- Tone of voice and language used.
- Frequent topics of discussion.

Thinks

- Beliefs and values.
- Assumptions and biases.
- Hopes and fears.
- Decision-making processes.

Does

- Observable behaviors and actions.
- Daily routines and habits.
- Interactions with others and systems.
- Body language and nonverbal cues.

Feels

- Emotional states in different situations.
- Concerns and anxieties.
- Joys and frustrations.
- Attitudes toward specific topics.

5. Validate and Refine:
   - Observe person(s) or group and converse with them to gather information.
   - Update the map based on new insights and identify gaps in your understanding.
6. Apply Insights:
   - Use the empathy map to inform your negotiation tactics and communication approaches.
   - Use the map to align team members on user-centric goals and strategies.

While empathy mapping may appear difficult, with practice, it becomes a more intuitive and spontaneous process.

What Empathy Mapping Looks Like

Dr. Elena Rodriguez, an oncologist at a community hospital with 15 years of experience, is preparing for a multidisciplinary team meeting to discuss treatment options for Mrs. Sarah Thompson, a 58-year-old patient recently diagnosed with stage III breast cancer. Mrs. Thompson is a retired elementary school teacher and avid gardener whose diagnosis has deeply shaken her typically optimistic outlook on life. The meeting will include Dr. Paulos, a surgical oncologist; Dr. Liu, a radiation oncologist; Maria, a nurse navigator, and Mrs. Thompson's daughter, who is also her primary caregiver. Dr. Rodriguez has also invited Dr. Boyd, a psychiatrist with advanced training in psychosocial onocology, to join the meeting, recognizing the importance of addressing the patient's mental health during treatment.

Before the meeting, Dr. Rodriguez takes a few moments to mentally create empathy maps for each participant, drawing on her experience and previous interactions:

1. Surgical Oncologist Dr. Paulos
   - Says: "We should consider a mastectomy followed by reconstruction."
   - Thinks: "This approach gives us the best chance of removing all the cancer."
   - Does: Reviews imaging results, explains surgical options.
   - Feels: Confident in surgical skills, concerned about potential spread.

2. Radiation Oncologist Dr. Liu
   - Says: "I recommend a course of radiation therapy post-surgery."
   - Thinks: "We need to ensure we target any remaining cancer cells."
   - Does: Calculates optimal radiation dosage, discuss side effects.
   - Feels: Focused on precision, aware of the treatment's impact on the patient's life.
3. Nurse Navigator (Maria):
   - Says: "We need to consider Mrs. Thompson's overall well-being and support system."
   - Thinks: "How can we make this journey easier for the patient?"
   - Does: Coordinates appointments, provides educational resources
   - Feels: Empathetic toward patient's emotional state, dedicated to comprehensive care
4. Mrs. Thompson's Daughter (Lisa):
   - Says: "I'm worried about how my mom will cope with the treatment."
   - Thinks: "What if we're making the wrong decision?"
   - Does: Researches treatment options, supports mother emotionally.
   - Feels: Overwhelmed, protective, afraid of losing her mother.
5. Psycho-oncologist (Dr. Boyd):
   - Says: "We need to address Mrs. Thompson's emotional well-being throughout her treatment journey."
   - Thinks: "How can we help Mrs. Thompson maintain her mental health and cope with the challenges ahead?"
   - Does: Assesses patient's psychological state, provides coping strategies.
   - Feels: Committed to holistic patient care, aware of the psychological impact of cancer diagnosis and treatment.

By mentally preparing these empathy maps, Dr. Rodriguez can lead a more inclusive, patient-centered discussion that considers medical necessities alongside the patient's and family's emotional needs. This approach allows for better decision-making and helps build trust among the team and the patient's family.

Using the Empathy Map to Guide Negotiation Strategy and Communication

After creating and refining your empathy maps, the next crucial step is to apply these insights strategically in your negotiations. Here's how Dr. Rodriguez could use her empathy maps to guide her approach:

Tailor Communication and Build Rapport

The empathy map supports negotiation in the following ways:

- Use language and concepts that resonate with each stakeholder based on their "Thinks" and "Feels."
- Reflect the tone from the "Says" section to create understanding and connection.
- Adapt a communication style to best resonate with each stakeholder (e.g., use precise medical terminology with Dr. Paulos, focus on patient well-being with Maria, and employ clear, jargon-free explanations for Lisa).

Address Underlying Concerns and Emotions

- Proactively address unspoken concerns from the "Thinks" and "Feels" sections.
- Validate emotions identified in the "Feels" section to create a supportive atmosphere.
- Acknowledge specific concerns, such as Dr. Liu's focus on targeting remaining cancer cells, Maria's dedication to comprehensive care, and Lisa's fear of losing her mother.

Align Proposals with Motivations and Anticipate Reactions

- Frame proposals to align with each stakeholder's underlying motivations.
- Use the "Does" section to predict and prepare for potential reactions.
- Prepare counterarguments or adjustments based on anticipated responses (e.g., Dr. Paulos's potential emphasis on surgical approaches, Dr. Liu's focus on radiation therapy, and Lisa's questions about alternative treatment options).

Facilitate Collaboration and Integration

- Bridge perspectives by finding common ground between stakeholders with differing views.
- Use an understanding of each person's viewpoint to facilitate collaborative problem-solving.
- Ensure each team member's input is considered, from Dr. Paulos's surgical expertise to Maria's insights on patient support, and integrate them into a comprehensive treatment plan that addresses Lisa's concerns for her mother's overall well-being.

By systematically applying these strategies based on your empathy map, Dr. Rodriguez can navigate the negotiation more effectively, addressing both the logical and emotional aspects of the discussion.

During the meeting, Dr. Rodriguez used her empathy mapping insights to facilitate a collaborative discussion. She acknowledged each team member's expertise and concerns: "Dr. Paulos, I appreciate your focus on removing all the cancer. Dr. Liu, your point about targeting remaining cells is crucial. Maria, thank you for reminding us to consider Mrs. Thompson's overall well-being. Dr. Boyd, your insight into Mrs. Thompson's emotional state will be invaluable as we plan her treatment." She also addressed Lisa's concerns directly: "Lisa, I understand this is overwhelming. We're here to answer all your questions and ensure your mother receives the best possible care."

As a result of the empathy map, Dr. Rodriguez is also able to integrate the different perspectives of the individuals gathered at the meeting: "Let's discuss how we can combine surgical and radiation approaches while minimizing the impact on Mrs. Thompson's quality of life. Maria, what support services can we offer to help Mrs. Thompson through this process? Dr. Boyd, how can we incorporate psychological support at each stage of treatment?" She also encourages collaborative problem-solving: "Given Mrs. Thompson's specific case, what if we consider a lumpectomy followed by radiation instead of a full mastectomy? This might address our oncological concerns while being less invasive, allowing her to return to her garden sooner. Drs Paulos and Liu, what are your thoughts on this approach?"

Dr. Rodriguez concludes the meeting by summarizing the proposed treatment plan and next steps, ensuring that each team member's input has been considered and integrated. She scheduled a follow-up meeting with Mrs. Thompson and Lisa to present the team's recommendations, allowing time for questions and shared decision-making.

Overcoming Barriers to Adopting a Relational Mindset

While the benefits of a relational mindset over a transactional one are seemingly clear, implementing it in practice can be challenging within the fast-paced, high-pressure healthcare environment. Some common barriers include:

- **Ingrained Transactional Habits and Mindsets**: Healthcare professionals often have to make quick decisions and prioritize efficiency, which can lead to a more transactional approach.

- **Time and Resource Constraints**: Heavy workloads, short staffing, and limited resources can make it difficult for healthcare professionals to prioritize building relationships and engaging in more collaborative decision-making.
- **Hierarchical Structures and Power Dynamics**: The hierarchical nature of many healthcare organizations can hinder open communication and collaboration across different levels and disciplines.
- **Lack of Training and Support**: Many healthcare professionals may not have received formal training in relational skills or have access to ongoing support to develop these skills.

To overcome these barriers, healthcare organizations can create an environment that nurtures and sustains a relational mindset by addressing these barriers head-on and providing the necessary support and resources. Actions they can take include:

- **Providing Targeted Training and Coaching**: Offer or seek out training programs specifically designed for healthcare professionals, focusing on relational mindset principles and practices, such as empathy, active listening, and collaborative problem-solving.
- **Fostering a Culture of Psychological Safety**: Encourage open communication, value diverse perspectives, and create an environment where people feel safe speaking up, asking questions, and challenging the status quo.
- **Integrating Relational Skills into Performance Evaluations**: To signal the importance of these skills and incentivize their development, include metrics related to relational skills, such as teamwork, communication, and patient satisfaction, in performance evaluations.
- **Celebrating and Sharing Success Stories**: Highlight and share examples of how adopting a relational mindset have led to better patient outcomes, improved teamwork, and increased job satisfaction to inspire others to embrace this approach.

Junior staff members can actively develop their relational mindset skills by seeking out mentors and learning from them while sharing their own experiences with peers to foster a culture of continuous improvement.[21] Proposing and participating in "lunch and learn" sessions focused on relational mindset skills can provide valuable learning opportunities. During performance reviews, expressing interest in developing these skills and requesting specific training can help guide professional growth as well. Volunteering for interdisciplinary projects or committees offers practical experience in applying a relational mindset across different healthcare roles. Finally, maintaining a reflective journal allows junior staff to track their progress and insights, ensuring ongoing personal and professional development.[22] By taking these proactive steps, junior staff can contribute to and benefit from a more relational culture, regardless of their position in the organizational hierarchy.

Setting the Stage for Effective Healthcare Negotiations: Defining Your Purpose

Before entering any healthcare negotiation, it is crucial that healthcare professionals define their purpose through the lens of a relational mindset. This approach goes beyond merely stating their position; it involves articulating objectives while considering the broader context of relationships and shared goals in healthcare's interconnected ecosystem.

Healthcare providers, like Dr. Arora in the examples below, can define their purpose with a relational focus using the following steps.

1. Articulate the Core Objective: Clearly state what the negotiation aims to achieve, addressing both clinical and operational outcomes. Include both tangible outcomes and relationship-building goals.

   Example: Dr. Arora approached the meeting with this clearly defined purpose: "To secure $3.2 million in funding for a comprehensive home dialysis program and patient support system for end-stage renal disease patients who have limited access to in-center treatment, with the goal of improving quality of life while potentially reducing hospitalization rates and long-term treatment costs."
2. Aligning with Relational and Healthcare Goals: Reflect on how the purpose advances patient-centered care and improves health outcomes. Consider how it also supports operational efficiency and financial sustainability.

   Example: Dr. Arora evaluated how the home dialysis program aligned with these goals. The program expanded access to care for patients living in rural areas or with limited mobility, offered the potential to reduce emergency department visits and hospitalizations, and positioned the hospital as a leader in kidney care innovation – attracting more patients and strengthening partnerships with payer organizations.

3. Balancing Objective and Relational Outcomes: Define measurable success criteria in terms of clinical metrics (e.g., reduced complications), operational benchmarks (e.g., decreased hospitalization rates), and financial indicators (e.g., cost-effectiveness). Also, consider relational outcomes in terms of enhanced cross-disciplinary collaboration, strengthened partnerships, and improved patient and family engagement.

   Example: Dr. Arora's purpose statement also outlined specific outcomes: reducing hospitalization rates by 35%, improving patient-reported quality of life scores by 40%, and generating significant cost savings through prevention of complications. He also aimed to strengthen collaboration among the nephrology, nursing, patient education, and social work departments, and enhance partnerships with home health agencies and technology providers developing remote monitoring solutions.
4. Anticipating Others' Perspectives: Consider how the purpose aligns with or impacts stakeholders across the pillars (e.g., clinicians, care coordinators, and administrators). Prepare to articulate your purpose in ways that resonate with different healthcare pillars (Exam Room, Operating Room Boardroom).

   Example: Dr. Arora anticipated nephrologists' concerns about maintaining quality of care outside the clinical setting, nurses' interest in the training and support systems for patients, care coordinators' focus on integrating home dialysis into existing chronic care pathways, and administrators' interest in expanding their service area while balancing concerns about initial investment costs and reimbursement models.

When healthcare professionals define their purpose with a relational mindset, they create a strong foundation for applying the HEAR Approach™ in negotiations. This approach enables providers to move beyond rigid positions, opening up possibilities for creative problem-solving and mutually beneficial outcomes. A clearly defined purpose guides healthcare professionals in using Healthcare-Specific strategies and informs their Empowerment and Acknowledgment practices, ultimately providing a sound basis for Recasting as needed throughout the negotiation process.

Conclusion: Integrating the Relational Mindset with the HEAR Approach™

The relational mindset is a powerful tool for navigating the complex and often high-stakes world of healthcare negotiations. By prioritizing building and maintaining positive relationships, healthcare professionals can create an environment where trust, understanding, and collaboration flourish. They will become not only more effective negotiators but also more compassionate and impactful leaders, contributing to a healthcare system that prioritizes empathy, collaboration, and patient-centered care.

But cultivating a relational mindset requires practice and commitment. It involves taking the time to understand others' perspectives and being willing to find creative, integrative solutions that benefit all parties involved. Strategies like empathy mapping, discussed in this chapter, provide practical tools for developing and applying a relational mindset across various healthcare contexts.

While the relational mindset provides a crucial foundation, it is most effective when combined with structured negotiation techniques. This is where the HEAR Approach™ comes into play. Integrating the relational mindset with the HEAR Approach™ is crucial for effectively navigating complex negotiation situations. By combining the principles of the relational mindset with the practical strategies of the HEAR Approach™, healthcare professionals can enhance their ability to build trust, foster collaboration, and achieve mutually beneficial outcomes:

Healthcare-Specific Strategies: The relational mindset encourages healthcare professionals to tailor their negotiation strategies to the challenges and priorities of the healthcare sector. By leveraging their EI and ToM skills, they can better understand and address the unique emotional and interpersonal dynamics present in healthcare negotiations, ultimately leading to more effective and empathetic solutions.

Empowerment: Embracing a relational mindset empowers healthcare professionals to approach negotiations with greater self-awareness, EI, and confidence. By understanding and managing their own emotions and considering the perspectives of others through (ToM), they can communicate more effectively, build stronger relationships, and advocate for their needs and the needs of those they represent.

Acknowledgment: The relational mindset emphasizes the importance of acknowledging and validating the perspectives, concerns, and emotions of all parties involved in a negotiation. By actively listening, demonstrating empathy, and using their EI and ToM skills to understand and appreciate others' viewpoints, healthcare professionals can create an atmosphere of trust and respect, which is essential for successful negotiations.

Recasting: Integrating the relational mindset with the principle of Recasting allows healthcare professionals to reframe challenges as opportunities for collaboration and mutual benefit. By using their EI and ToM abilities to identify shared goals, interests, and underlying emotions, they can generate creative solutions that satisfy the needs of all stakeholders and promote a more collaborative healthcare environment.

By mastering these techniques and integrating them with the HEAR Approach™, healthcare professionals can foster stronger relationships, drive innovative solutions, and ultimately improve the quality of patient care.

Of course, integrating the relational mindset with the HEAR Approach™ can present challenges in healthcare settings. Common obstacles include time constraints in fast-paced environments, ingrained habits favoring more transactional or hierarchical approaches, and resistance from negotiation counterparts who prefer traditional, position-based tactics. These challenges can make it difficult for healthcare professionals to adopt and consistently apply a relational mindset in their negotiations and interactions.

To overcome these challenges, healthcare professionals should be persistent and lead by example, consistently modeling the principles of the relational mindset and the HEAR Approach™, even in the face of resistance or setbacks. Over time, this persistence can demonstrate the value of this approach to others, potentially increasing receptivity and adoption across the healthcare environment. They can start small by applying the relational mindset and HEAR strategies in lower-stakes negotiations, gradually building up to more complex situations as their comfort and confidence grow. Seeking training and support through workshops, seminars, or coaching sessions focused on developing relational negotiation skills can enhance proficiency and confidence in this approach. Perhaps most importantly, they can master the HEAR Framework unpacked in Chapters 3 through 6.

REFLECTION EXERCISE: ASSESSING AND STRENGTHENING YOUR EMOTIONAL INTELLIGENCE

To understand your EI capabilities and identify areas for improvement, consider reflecting on the following aspects of your healthcare interactions.

1. **Self-awareness**: Recognize and understand your emotions during healthcare interactions. How do they influence your decisions, actions, and interactions with patients and colleagues?
2. **Empathy**: Evaluate your ability to accurately perceive and understand the emotions of others. How effectively do you read emotional cues and genuinely empathize with patients' and team members' experiences and concerns?
3. **Emotion Management**: Assess how well you manage your own emotions and help others manage theirs, especially in high-stress or emotionally charged situations.

As you progress through your day-to-day work, make a conscious effort to apply the strategies you've learned and document your experiences by journaling about them. This practice will help you develop a more nuanced understanding of your EI in various healthcare contexts.

Key Takeaways

1. Adopting a relational mindset in healthcare negotiations leads to more sustainable outcomes, stronger professional relationships, and improved patient care by prioritizing long-term collaborative partnerships over short-term gains.
2. Emotional Intelligence and ToM skills are crucial for healthcare professionals to effectively manage complex interpersonal dynamics and navigate high-stakes negotiations in medical settings.
3. Techniques such as empathy mapping and active listening enable healthcare professionals to gain deeper insights into stakeholders' perspectives, fostering trust and facilitating mutually beneficial solutions.
4. Integrating the relational mindset with the HEAR Approach™ creates a powerful framework for healthcare negotiations, combining empathetic understanding with structured problem-solving to achieve optimal results for all parties involved.

Notes

1. Alan P. Fiske, "The Four Elementary Forms of Sociality: Framework for a Unified Theory of Social Relations," *Psychological Review* 99, no. 4 (1992): 689–723.
2. Jody Hoffer Gittell, *High Performance Healthcare: Using the Power of Relationships to Achieve Quality, Efficiency and Resilience* (New York: McGraw-Hill, 2009).
3. Leonard J. Marcus, Barry C. Dorn, and Joseph M. Henderson, "Meta-Leadership: A Framework for Building Leadership Effectiveness," *National Preparedness Leadership Initiative*, Harvard School of Public Health (2013).
4. Roger Fisher, William Ury, and Bruce Patton, *Getting to Yes: Negotiating Agreement without Giving In* (New York: Penguin Books, 2011).
5. Amy C. Edmondson, *The Fearless Organization: Creating Psychological Safety in the Workplace for Learning, Innovation, and Growth* (Hoboken, NJ: John Wiley & Sons, 2018).
6. Amy C. Edmondson, "Psychological Safety and Learning Behavior in Work Teams," *Administrative Science Quarterly* 44, no. 2 (1999): 350–383.
7. Jody Hoffer Gittell, "Coordinating Mechanisms in Care Provider Groups: Relational Coordination as a Mediator and Input Uncertainty as a Moderator of Performance Effects," *Management Science* 48, no. 11 (2002): 1408–1426.
8. Jody Hoffer Gittell et al., "Impact of Relational Coordination on Quality of Care, Postoperative Pain and Functioning, and Length of Stay: A Nine-Hospital Study of Surgical Patients," *Medical Care* 38, no. 8 (2000): 807–819.
9. Amy C. Edmondson, *Teaming: How Organizations Learn, Innovate, and Compete in the Knowledge Economy* (San Francisco, CA: Jossey-Bass, 2012).
10. Yael Rotbain et al., "Insulin Pump Preferences among Patients and Health Care Professionals: A Discrete-Choice Experiment Approach," *Journal of Diabetes Science and Technology* 13, no. 4 (2019): 776–783.
11. Gittell et al., "Impact of Relational Coordination."
12. Daniel Goleman, *Emotional Intelligence: Why It Can Matter More Than IQ* (New York: Bantam Books, 1995).
13. Peter Salovey and John D. Mayer, "Emotional Intelligence," *Imagination, Cognition and Personality* 9, no. 3 (1990): 185–211.
14. Salovey and Mayer, "Emotional Intelligence."
15. Arora Sonal, Hutan Ashrafian, Rachel Davis, Thanos Athanasiou, Ara Darzi, and Nick Sevdalis, "Emotional Intelligence in Medicine: A Systematic Review through the Context of the ACGME Competencies," *Medical Education* 44, no. 8 (2010): 749–764.
16. For more detailed guidance on implementing these strategies, please refer to the following sources, which provide in-depth information and additional exercises to further develop your Emotional Intelligence in healthcare settings: Reuven Bar-On and James Parker, *The Handbook of Emotional Intelligence: Theory, Development, Assessment, and Application at Home, School, and in the*

Workplace (New York: Jossey-Bass, 2000); Travis Bradberry and Jean Greaves, *Emotional Intelligence 2.0* (New York: TalentSmart, 2009); Cary Cherniss and Daniel Goleman, *The Emotionally Intelligent Workplace: How to Select for, Measure, and Improve Emotional Intelligence in Individuals, Groups, and Organizations* (New York: Jossey-Bass, 2001); Steven Stein and Howard Book, *The EQ Edge: Emotional Intelligence and Your Success* (New York: John Wiley & Sons, 2011).

17. Josef Perner and Heinz Wimmer, "'John Thinks That Mary Thinks That...': Attribution of Second-Order Beliefs by 5- to 10-Year-Old Children," *Journal of Experimental Child Psychology* 39, no. 3 (1985): 437–471.
18. Anat Perry and Simone Shamay-Tsoory, "Understanding Emotional and Cognitive Empathy: A Neuropsychological Perspective," in *Understanding Other Minds: Perspectives from Developmental Social Neuroscience*, eds. Simon Baron-Cohen, Helen Tager-Flusberg, and Michael Lombardo (Oxford: Oxford University Press, 2013), 178–194.
19. Kimberly A. Schonert-Reichl, Veronica Smith, Anat Zaidman-Zait, and Clyde Hertzman, "Promoting Children's Prosocial Behaviors in School: Impact of the 'Roots of Empathy' Program on the Social and Emotional Competence of School-Aged Children," *School Mental Health* 4, no. 1 (2012): 1–21.
20. Helen Riess, "The Science of Empathy," *Journal of Patient Experience* 4, no. 2 (2017): 74–77.
21. David A. Kolb, *Experiential Learning: Experience as the Source of Learning and Development* (Upper Saddle River, NJ: Pearson Education, 2015).
22. Jennifer A. Moon, *Learning Journals: A Handbook for Reflective Practice and Professional Development* (London: Routledge, 2006).

Chapter 3

Mastering Multifaceted Negotiations in and Across Healthcare's Three Pillars

Good medicine also means being able to listen and understand the economic, social, and emotional context in which people live.

– **Paul Farmer**

DOI: 10.4324/9781003336013-4

In the mid-2010s, the Comprehensive Cancer Care Institute (CCCI) of Western Plains State University launched a multi-billion-dollar expansion project called "The Next Frontier."[1] This bold initiative sought to transform the institute's capabilities, research trajectories, and treatment technologies, positioning CCCI at the forefront of cancer care innovation. The ambitious project sought to double the institute's patient capacity, introduce cutting-edge proton therapy facilities, and establish a state-of-the-art genomics research center.

Dr. Emily Wilson, CCCI's Chief of Oncology, was a central figure in this endeavor. As a respected clinician and leader, her primary goal was to ensure that the expanded facilities delivered unparalleled cancer care. However, Dr. Wilson quickly realized that achieving this vision would require skillful navigation of the complex interconnections between medical excellence, operational efficiency, and financial sustainability – the three pillars upon which CCCI's success rested. She found herself grappling with questions like how to balance the acquisition of cutting-edge medical equipment with the need for additional staff and the financial constraints of the project.

Jacob Thompson, the Chief Operating Officer (COO), collaborated closely with Dr. Wilson. Thompson managed the expansion's operational intricacies, optimizing patient flow and resource allocation across departments. His challenge was to ensure that the new facilities would not only accommodate more patients but also streamline processes to reduce wait times and improve overall efficiency. Working alongside them was Angela Reynolds, the Chief Financial Officer, (CFO), who shouldered the crucial task of securing funding and negotiating with investors, donors, and insurance providers to ensure the project's fiscal viability. Reynolds faced the daunting task of balancing the massive upfront costs with projected long-term returns, all while navigating the multifaceted landscape of healthcare reimbursement.

As the expansion gained momentum, Dr. Wilson found herself in the middle of challenging negotiations. She needed to advocate forcefully for the cancer institute's clinical needs, carefully consider the operational concerns raised by Thompson, and navigate the financial implications highlighted by Reynolds. Balancing these competing priorities was no simple feat, but critical to the project's ultimate success. For instance, when discussing the implementation of a new robotic surgery system, Dr. Wilson had to weigh its potential to improve patient outcomes against Thompson's concerns about training staff and integrating it into existing workflows, all while considering Reynolds's analysis of return on investment (ROI).

The fate of the expansion hinged on Dr. Wilson, Thompson, and Reynolds's ability to work collaboratively and bridge the needs of the three pillars of healthcare. Only by finding a balance between clinical excellence, operational efficiency, and financial sustainability could they hope to realize the transformative potential of "The Next Frontier" of cancer care. This often meant making difficult compromises, such as phasing the introduction of new technologies to allow for gradual training and integration, or redesigning patient care protocols to maximize the use of expensive new equipment.

The CCCI expansion highlights how negotiations in healthcare are inherently interconnected across the Practice of Medicine, Delivery of Care, and Business of Health pillars. Whether implementing new clinical protocols that impact operations and budgets, redesigning care processes to enhance workflow and resource utilization, or undertaking facility expansions that require aligning medical, operational, and financial strategies, healthcare professionals must adeptly recognize and navigate the interplay across the three domains. Each key decision reverberates through this integrated ecosystem. The ability to skillfully bridge priorities and forge collaborative solutions benefiting patients, providers, and the organization is paramount for catalyzing meaningful progress in healthcare delivery. A comprehensive, trilingual negotiation approach that harmonizes clinical, operational, and business perspectives becomes essential.

Understanding the Interplay of Medicine, Care Delivery, and Business

Effective negotiation in healthcare extends beyond isolated decisions or actions. It requires a deep understanding of the three fundamental pillars that form the foundation of the healthcare system: The Practice of Medicine (Operating Room), the Delivery of Care (Exam Room), and the Business of Health (Boardroom). Each pillar presents unique challenges and opportunities that require tailored negotiation strategies.

The HEAR Approach™ provides a comprehensive framework encompassing Healthcare-Specific Strategies, Empowerment, Acknowledgment, and Recasting. This robust methodology equips practitioners with the tools to navigate complex healthcare negotiations while maintaining a relational mindset. The first of these elements is the focus of this chapter, examining how such strategies can enhance understanding of effective negotiation within and across the three pillars. Healthcare professionals, whether nurses advocating for patient-centric policies, pharmacists navigating medication protocols, or administrators shaping care standards, engage in critical negotiations within their domains. However, the impact of these negotiations often extends beyond their immediate roles, influencing the broader healthcare landscape.

This chapter explores the skills and strategies needed to effectively manage negotiations across the nuanced landscapes of medicine, care delivery, and the business of health. It explores the importance of developing mastery of "trilingual" negotiation skills – the ability to communicate fluently in the languages of medicine, care delivery, and the business of health – which are vital in the multifaceted healthcare ecosystem.

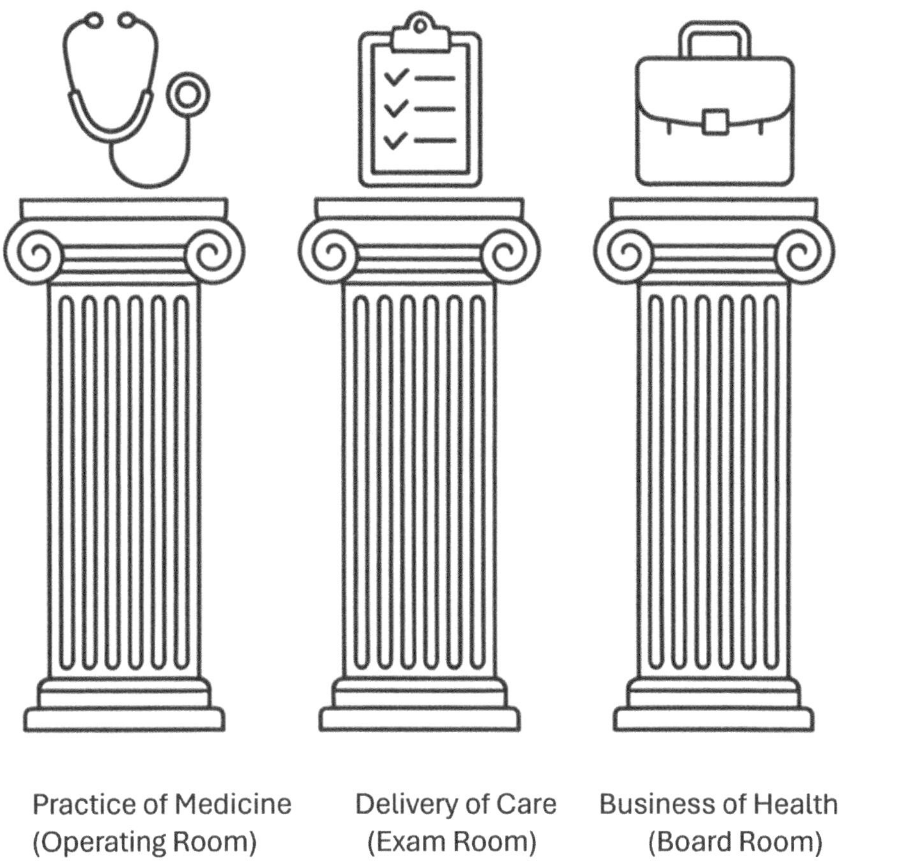

Figure 3.1 Healthcare's Three Pillars.

The Practice of Medicine in the Operating Room: Where Clinical Expertise Meets Compassionate Care

The Practice of Medicine represents the confluence of clinical expertise, patient-centered care, and strategic decision-making. This pillar embodies the essence of healthcare provision – diagnosing, treating, and managing patient health and well-being. In this domain, practitioners apply their hard-earned medical knowledge, clinical skills, and problem-solving abilities to make a tangible difference in patients' lives.

The Practice of Medicine extends beyond mere medical interventions; it involves navigating the complex intersectionality of clinical judgment, patient preferences, and evidence-based practice. Every patient interaction, from routine check-ups to critical care decisions, entails a delicate negotiation. Healthcare providers must balance their clinical expertise with each patient's unique needs, values, and circumstances, ensuring that the care provided aligns with individual goals and priorities.

The Practice of Medicine focuses on clinical decision-making and patient outcomes driven by direct medical expertise, while the Delivery of Care emphasizes the systems, processes, and coordination needed to implement those decisions effectively. Although these areas intersect – both rely on clinical proficiency and patient-centered communication – they address distinct aspects of healthcare. Acknowledging this overlap is key to understanding how negotiation plays a role across the broader healthcare ecosystem.

Effective negotiation within the Practice of Medicine demands a multifaceted skill set. Practitioners must adeptly communicate complex medical information in an understandable manner to patients and families, actively listen to their concerns and questions, and collaborate with interdisciplinary teams to develop comprehensive care plans. Additionally, healthcare providers need to advocate for their patients, whether by securing access to necessary treatments or navigating the intricacies of insurance coverage.

Here is just a sample of the kinds of challenges providers frequently encounter that require adept negotiation skills:

Coordinated Triage and Care Planning in the Chaotic Emergency Department: An intense shift in the overcrowded emergency department entails a constant influx of ambulances, an overflowing waiting room, and existing patients requiring continuous monitoring amid the commotion. A 62-year-old patient presents with concerning chest pain and shortness of breath. An emergency medicine resident must swiftly coordinate with the triage nurse, consult the cardiology attending on testing and treatment options, collaborate with the pharmacist on potential medication interactions, and keep the patient's primary care physician informed. Despite the frenetic pace, the resident strives to maintain clear communication, actively listening to all viewpoints. Navigating the added complexity of potentially differing perspectives from the attending, the resident adeptly builds consensus. Through this process, the team develops a shared understanding, enabling them to craft a comprehensive plan that addresses the patient's immediate needs while considering long-term implications.

Advocating for Innovative Treatment Access: A dedicated neurologist is treating Sandra, a 38-year-old battling aggressive relapsing-remitting multiple sclerosis. When a groundbreaking disease-modifying therapy hits the market, it shows incredible promise in clinical trials, significantly slowing disease progression and reducing relapses. There's just one problem: the price tag is astronomical, and Sandra's insurance company denies coverage. Unwilling to give up, the physician rolls up her sleeves and engages in data-driven negotiations with the insurer. The neurologist builds a compelling case, highlighting how this innovative treatment could be quite literally transformative for Sandra, preserving her function and independence for years to come. Armed with rock-solid clinical evidence, the physician persists in these efforts. After several rounds of negotiations, this tenacity pays off, securing coverage of this cutting-edge therapy for Sandra.

Orchestrating Seamless Interprofessional Coordination: The lead nurse practitioner on a primary care team is tasked with managing Patrick, a 57-year-old with multiple chronic conditions, including diabetes, hypertension, and depression. Caring for Patrick requires an intricate collaboration among the nurse practitioner, the primary physician, endocrinology, cardiology, behavioral health, physical therapists, and other allied professionals. This role demands deft navigation of the interprofessional landscape, ensuring clear role delineation while fostering open communication. Orchestrating Patrick's care plan requires finesse in reconciling evidence-based practices with personal preferences, financial constraints, and occasionally divergent specialist recommendations. Skillful negotiation fosters mutual respect and coordinated care planning, enabling the team's patient-centered approach tailored to Patrick's specific needs and priorities.

These real-world examples from healthcare professionals illustrate the diverse negotiations integral to medical practice in daily operations. Refining negotiation skills optimizes patient interactions, interdisciplinary collaboration, and advocacy for innovative care options. By cultivating trusted relationships and fostering teamwork, providers can engage in patient-centered negotiations that pave the way for optimal health outcomes. Research reinforces that prioritizing open communication and involving patients in shared decision-making correlates with increased satisfaction and treatment adherence.[2] Honing negotiation capabilities within medical practice through the HEAR Approach's™ principles elevates a practitioner's ability to navigate the complexities of clinical decision-making.

The Delivery of Care in the Exam Room: Orchestrating Patient-Centered Care Experiences

While the Practice of Medicine concentrates on clinical decision-making, the Delivery of Care pillar focuses on the operational aspects that shape patient care experiences. In this domain, healthcare professionals navigate intricate processes and systems, ensuring seamless, efficient, and patient-centric service delivery.

The Delivery of Care realm centers on the hands-on activities involved in diagnosing, treating, and educating patients. Here, practitioners apply their medical knowledge to address individual needs, treatment options, and educational strategies directly impacting patient health and well-being. At its core, Delivery of Care requires blending scientific expertise with a deep understanding of patients as individuals, combining clinical proficiency and personalized care in each interaction.

Excelling in this area relies in part on the ability to negotiate a multitude of factors that directly shape the patient experience. This includes tailoring treatment regimens to individual lifestyles and preferences, collaboratively navigating operational protocols while advocating for patient needs, and orchestrating seamless interdepartmental coordination. In short, this pillar demands a delicate equilibrium of clinical expertise, empathetic communication, and situational adaptability.

Healthcare professionals across the Delivery of Care continuum shared the following real-world scenarios that capture the intricate negotiations at the heart of providing patient-centric experiences:

Medication Adherence Collaboration: A clinical pharmacist reviewing Mrs. Diallo's chart observes an elderly patient consistently missing doses of her hypertension medication. During their consultation, Mrs. Diallo expresses concerns about the cost of the prescription and her complex regimen's manageability. The pharmacist collaborates with her primary care physician, skillfully negotiating a simplified, more affordable plan aligning with her needs and preferences. This process involves exploring generic alternatives, discussing potential combination medications, and considering extended-release formulations to reduce dosing frequency. Through active listening, patient advocacy, and creative problem-solving, the pharmacist improves Mrs. Diallo's adherence and overall health outcomes.

Orchestrating Integrated Interdisciplinary Care: An attending hospitalist overseeing Ms. Gonzalez's care recognizes that her multiple chronic conditions and recent falls necessitate a comprehensive approach. The hospitalist assembles an interdisciplinary team – physical therapists, occupational therapists, social workers, and geriatric specialists – to discuss her care. In these collaborative meetings, each professional contributes their perspectives and priorities, which can lead to differing recommendations. The hospitalist skillfully facilitates these discussions, encouraging active listening, validating each viewpoint's merits, and guiding the group toward an integrated, patient-centered care plan. This approach fosters a cohesive, coordinated strategy that optimizes Ms. Gonzalez's quality of life.

Compassionate End-of-Life Transition Planning: A palliative care nurse practitioner works with Mr. Aoki, a terminally ill patient with advanced cancer, as his condition declines. Differing opinions emerge among Mr. Aoki's family regarding appropriate interventions and care options. The nurse practitioner navigates these emotionally charged conversations with empathy and practiced negotiation skills. He provides a safe environment for expressing fears and concerns, actively listening to each perspective. Through skillful guidance, the practitioner helps the family reach a shared understanding by honoring Mr. Aoki's wishes, facilitating decisions focused on his comfort and preserving dignity in his final days.

These examples from healthcare professionals illustrate the diverse negotiations integral to delivering patient-centric care in daily practice. Refining negotiation skills proves vital for advocating for patients, facilitating complex team decisions, and ensuring that operational choices consistently prioritize individual well-being.

Research extensively highlights how effective communication and interprofessional collaboration directly enhance patient outcomes, boost efficiency, and optimize resource utilization.[3] By developing strong negotiation abilities within this pillar, healthcare providers foster cohesive teamwork, seamless care coordination, and a steadfast focus on delivering patient-centric experiences within operational realities.

The Business of Health in the Boardroom: Navigating Healthcare's Economic Landscape

Within the Business of Health domain, skilled negotiation is essential across a variety of roles and responsibilities, including:

- Hospital administrators negotiating budgets and resource allocation.
- Healthcare executives partnering with insurers and pharmaceutical companies.
- Financial officers managing capital investments in medical technology.
- Compliance officers navigating regulatory requirements and policy changes.
- Human resource managers addressing staffing needs and compensation packages.

These scenarios highlight the necessity of carefully balancing financial considerations with the commitment to delivering high-quality patient care. Applying well-crafted negotiation strategies becomes critical for ensuring that economic factors align with the core mission of enhancing healthcare accessibility, outcomes, and long-term sustainability.

Research underscores the importance of engaging diverse stakeholders, grounding decisions in evidence, and upholding a steadfast patient-centric approach when allocating resources or shaping policies.[4] By strengthening negotiation abilities and gaining a comprehensive understanding of healthcare's interconnected pillars, healthcare leaders are equipped to navigate complex fiscal and administrative challenges while staying true to the principles of equitable, high-caliber care delivery.

Within the Business of Health pillar, professionals navigate complex negotiations daily. The following real-world scenarios illustrate the nuanced decision-making at the heart of balancing financial considerations with quality care:

Funding Community Health Outreach: Public health officials often face the challenge of securing funding for crucial community programs like mental health support. To make a compelling case, they need to present data on community needs and potential impacts while keeping funders' priorities in mind. Winning strategies highlight relatable success stories, key demographic insights, and a clear connection between the program's goals and the funders' mission. Through compelling storytelling and data visualization, officials can inspire funders to invest in these vital initiatives by illustrating the community's needs and the program's potential impact.

Securing Research Funding for Medical Innovations: In today's competitive research landscape, securing grants for groundbreaking projects like new diagnostic tools requires more than just scientific expertise – it demands skilled negotiation. Savvy investigators must not only showcase their scientific expertise but also articulate the potential for clinical breakthroughs and long-term economic benefits in a way that captures funders' imaginations. Success hinges on demonstrating how innovation can dramatically improve patient care while delivering sustainable value – tapping into funders' desires for impactful, cost-effective advancements. By painting a vivid picture of the future their research could create, investigators can turn their scientific visions into funded realities.

Forging Strategic Partnerships for Health Technology: When negotiating with tech companies for cutting-edge patient data systems, IT leaders and administrators face a complex challenge. They must balance priorities around data security, system functionality, and budget constraints. The goal is to focus on technological solutions that measurably improve care delivery, strengthen data protection, and align with financial realities. Success lies in selecting systems that not only boast impressive features but also genuinely enhance patient care, support healthcare providers, and maintain fiscal responsibility. By keeping these objectives at the forefront, healthcare leaders can effectively navigate the high-stakes landscape of health technology procurement.

These examples highlight the critical nature of fiscal and administrative negotiations within the Business of Health sector. Each decision impacts the delicate balance between financial viability and quality care delivery. Mastering effective negotiation strategies and tactics is crucial for harmonizing economic factors with the mission of optimizing healthcare access, upholding quality standards, and developing sustainable care models. Skilled negotiators navigate financial realities while staying true to patient-centric principles, forging a path that provides tangible benefits to both individuals and communities.

The Ever-Present Cost Consideration Across Healthcare

No matter which arena healthcare professionals operate within, cost factors cast a long shadow over virtually every negotiation. Mastering healthcare negotiations requires recognizing that cost implications inevitably shape the process and ultimate outcomes. Whether discussing experimental treatment paths with patient families, advocating for infrastructure upgrades, or negotiating supply contracts, healthcare providers must balance financial realities with the core mission of providing high-quality, patient-centered care. This demands a nuanced understanding of how cost considerations intersect with clinical decision-making, operational efficiency, and strategic planning.

Consider physicians exploring clinical trial options for a patient. They may find themselves weighing the potential benefits of a cutting-edge therapy against steep out-of-pocket costs for the family. Their ability to convincingly articulate the treatment's value – in terms of improved quality of life and long-term cost-effectiveness – becomes key in making it an accessible option. Similarly, a facilities manager lobbying for an overhaul of an aging hospital wing needs to build a strong case. They must show how an updated environment enhances patient safety, infection control, and operational flow, demonstrating how the renovation expenses pay off through improved metrics and throughput over time.

The skilled healthcare negotiator excels at crafting creative solutions that optimize resource utilization for maximum patient benefit while ensuring the organization's financial viability. They have the communication skills to guide stakeholders toward well-informed decisions that balance quality care with operational sustainability. This delicate balancing act requires a bird's-eye view of healthcare's interconnected pillars. For instance, introducing a new medical device isn't just about the technology – it may trigger a domino effect of staff training programs and updated security protocols, touching on care delivery and business operations. Similarly, evolving healthcare legislation can ripple through clinical practices, reimbursement models, and organizational policies.

As seen in the following examples, the cost factor plays a critical role across the three healthcare pillars, shaping the approach to negotiations:

Practice of Medicine: When determining a treatment plan for a patient with rheumatoid arthritis, a rheumatologist must prioritize clinical effectiveness while considering a range of factors that impact the patient's ability to adhere to the prescribed regimen. They should recommend the most clinically effective treatment plan while also understanding the patient's financial situation to ensure that options are accessible and sustainable, facilitating adherence and long-term success. This process involves comparing potential outcomes and side effects across therapeutic options and coordinating with the specialty pharmacy regarding costs and insurance coverage. Additionally, the rheumatologist may explore cost-saving strategies such as patient assistance programs, generic alternatives, or step therapy approaches when appropriate. Ongoing monitoring of both the treatment's efficacy and its financial sustainability for the patient is crucial, as changes in insurance coverage or the patient's economic situation may necessitate adjustments to the treatment plan over time. This inclusive and empathetic process ensures an informed, shared decision aligning medical and personal factors.

Delivery of Care: A nurse educator implementing a fall prevention program might be tempted to focus solely on the long-term potential savings from reduced fall-related incidents and associated healthcare costs, ignoring the need to fit the initial investment in training within budgetary limits. But doing so reveals the need to take a multi-pronged approach, which might involve surveying nursing staff on preferred learning formats, negotiating with content providers for cost-effective materials, and exploring partnerships with other units to share resources. The educator should analyze delivery models, weigh program costs against engagement metrics, and advocate for an approach that maximizes skill reinforcement while respecting financial constraints. Cost-saving strategies may include developing in-house training materials, utilizing free online resources, or implementing a train-the-trainer model to reduce ongoing expenses. Regular cost-benefit analyses and budget reviews ensure the program remains financially sustainable while meeting its educational objectives.

Business of Health: At the opposite end of the spectrum from the Delivery of Care example, when considering an investment in telehealth capabilities, healthcare IT leaders need to evaluate total long-term value, not just upfront costs. They should diligently research potential efficiencies in care delivery, specialist access expansion, and revenue generation from new reimbursement models while negotiating service pricing models and staggered rollout phases to assess impact before full-scale commitment. Their goal ought to be an innovative yet sustainable solution to amplify the organization's clinical expertise while optimizing economic performance. Healthcare IT leaders should factor in projected cost savings from reduced in-person visits and improved chronic disease management and consider tiered pricing structures based on usage volume or outcomes achieved, aligning vendor incentives with organizational goals. These decision-makers should explore partnership opportunities with other healthcare organizations to distribute costs and maximize resource utilization. IT leaders must conduct financial reviews to ensure ongoing alignment with both clinical and fiscal objectives.

In healthcare negotiations, cost management extends far beyond mere budgeting – it involves achieving harmony between controlling expenses and maximizing the value of patient care and organizational operations. Navigating this balance through strategic, evidence-driven negotiation is critical for institutional sustainability and achieving the core mission.

The Interconnectedness of Healthcare Pillars

The Practice of Medicine, the Delivery of Care, and the Business of Health are inherently interdependent, with decisions and actions in one pillar often having significant ripple effects across the others. Consider what happens with the implementation of a new patient engagement technology:

- Clinical staff must assess the potential impact on patient care and workflows (Practice of Medicine).
- Administrators must evaluate the implications for staff training and patient experience (Delivery of Care).

- Finance professionals must consider the costs and return on investment (Business of Health).

Introducing a new treatment protocol in the Practice of Medicine may require additional staff training and equipment upgrades in the Delivery of Care, which in turn impacts resource allocation decisions in the Business of Health. Conversely, changes in reimbursement policies or contractual agreements in the Business of Health can influence clinical practices and care delivery models in the Practice of Medicine and Delivery of Care. By understanding and communicating the interconnected implications across these pillars, stakeholders can reach well-informed decisions that benefit the organization as a whole. But navigating these complex interconnections requires a unique set of "trilingual" negotiation skills.

The HEAR Approach™ offers a guide for applying trilingual negotiation skills in an integrated manner:

- Healthcare-Specific Strategies embracing a holistic perspective: Considering the broader context and interconnections between pillars.
- Empowerment that prioritizes an empathetic approach: Tailoring communication to different stakeholders' needs and priorities.
- Acknowledgment that reflects an adaptive mindset: Adjusting strategies based on evolving circumstances and new information.
- Recasting with a results-oriented focus: Driving outcomes that optimize value across all pillars.

By combining these elements, healthcare professionals can effectively navigate the complexities of interconnected negotiations and make decisions that benefit the organization and its stakeholders.

Mastering Trilingual Negotiation Skills

Developing trilingual negotiation capabilities means understanding and communicating effectively across the distinct contexts and priorities found in the Practice of Medicine, Delivery of Care, and Business of Health. This approach goes beyond utilizing universal language; instead, it requires adaptive communication, tailoring styles and content to each specific pillar and stakeholder. Healthcare professionals need to become fluent in the unique "languages" of clinical practice, patient care delivery, and healthcare business, adapting their message to resonate with each audience's particular concerns and objectives.

Honing these cross-pillar skills requires continuous learning, adaptability, and collaboration among different healthcare disciplines. Providers must develop the ability to "code-switch" between pillars, translating concepts and priorities from one domain to another to facilitate understanding and agreement. This cross-pillar translation could mean explaining financial concepts to clinicians in terms of patient outcomes or conveying clinical needs to administrators in terms of operational efficiency and cost-effectiveness. Strategic framing becomes crucial, presenting ideas in ways that resonate with each pillar's objectives while maintaining a holistic perspective that considers impacts across all three pillars in decision-making.

Research consistently points to the benefits of effective communication and interprofessional teamwork.[5] Studies show that open communication between physicians and nurses leads to better outcomes, such as fewer hospital-acquired infections and lower readmission rates.[6] Moreover, negotiated care planning processes that involve all stakeholders result in improved treatment adherence and higher patient satisfaction.[7] These processes often require stakeholder empathy, understanding, and validating diverse viewpoints and priorities to foster collaborative problem-solving that addresses concerns across pillars.[8]

As healthcare professionals strengthen their trilingual negotiation abilities, they become better equipped to bridge gaps between healthcare's interconnected pillars. An integrated approach enhances care coordination, reduces operational silos, and fosters collaborative, evidence-based decision-making – key factors in delivering high-quality patient care. This allows providers fluent in the language of trilingual negotiation to drive positive outcomes benefiting patients, providers, and the healthcare organization as a whole. Achieving this balance often requires navigating the delicate balance between financial realities and patient care priorities, as well as addressing conflicts that arise from different pillars' perspectives.

Healthcare Negotiation Mapping Tool to Trilingual Negotiations

The Healthcare Negotiation Mapping Tool originated from collaborations with professionals across the Practice of Medicine, Delivery of Care, and Business of Health pillars. A critical insight emerged from these conversations: framing and communicating issues often proved more challenging in negotiations than the substantive aspects themselves, especially when engaging colleagues from different healthcare sectors. This underscored the importance of effective communication and negotiation skills when navigating the diverse perspectives within the healthcare landscape. Studies reinforce how framing profoundly impacts decision-making processes, risk perceptions, negotiation outcomes, and interpersonal trust.[9]

The development of the tool was an iterative process, informed by healthcare professionals' experiences and validated through their daily application. Users reported heightened effectiveness, particularly in cross-pillar negotiations, attesting to its value in bridging this complex ecosystem.

At its core, the tool provides a structured approach to identifying key stakeholders, understanding their priorities across the three pillars, and tailoring negotiation strategies accordingly. The integrated chart synthesizes these crucial elements, guiding healthcare professionals to consider interconnected impacts and leverage tailored communication skills. By methodically working through the steps of the chart, providers can develop comprehensive strategies that account for the healthcare landscape's intricacies.

Pillar The three main areas of the healthcare system	**Key Stakeholders** The primary individuals or groups involved in negotiations within each pillar	**Negotiation Focus** The main topics, issues, or goals that are typically the subject of negotiations within each pillar	**Trilingual Skills** The unique communication and negotiation skills required to effectively engage with stakeholders across different pillars	**Interconnectedness Insights** The key considerations regarding how actions and decisions within one pillar can impact and influence others
Practice of Medicine **(Operating Room)**	Physicians, Surgeons, Anesthesiologists, Nurses, Allied Health	Treatment options, Clinical protocols, Patient care standards, Team dynamics	Clinical justification, Patient advocacy, Evidence-based negotiation, Conflict resolution	Decisions here shape care delivery's efficiency and effectiveness, influencing organizational policies and resource distribution
Delivery of Care **(Exam Room)**	Nurses, Care Coordinators, Social Workers, Patient Navigators, Healthcare Administrators	Care coordination strategies, Patient flow optimization, Resource Management, Team communication	Operational logistics, Patient experience balance, Cross-disciplinary collaboration	Directly affects clinical practice and financial sustainability, requiring compliance with evolving healthcare regulations
Business of Health **(Board Room)**	Executives, Financial Officers, Policymakers, Insurance Payers, Healthcare Suppliers	Financial planning, Resource allocation, Strategic partnership development, Policy adherence	Financial acumen, Value proposition communication, Navigating reimbursement models, Stakeholder engagement	Sets the operational approach, affecting clinical practices and care delivery strategies and aligning them with overarching patient care priorities

Figure 3.2 Healthcare Negotiation Mapping Tool.

Applying the Healthcare Negotiation Mapping Tool

The Healthcare Negotiation Mapping Tool outlines four easy-to-follow steps for healthcare professionals to identify stakeholders, understand priorities across the three pillars, and tailor their negotiation approach. Providers begin by selecting the primary pillar (Practice of Medicine, Delivery of Care, or Business of Health) for the negotiation and then move through the row as follows:

1. Pinpoint key stakeholders using the "Key Stakeholders" column.
2. Identify core issues by reviewing the "Negotiation Focus" options.
3. Assess crucial communication capabilities using the "Trilingual Skills" section.
4. Recognize potential cross-pillar impacts using "Interconnectedness Insights."

By methodically working through this framework, providers can develop strategies attuned to the healthcare landscape's nuances.

The Healthcare Negotiation Mapping Tool serves as a foundational tool that we will revisit and expand upon in Part II of this book, where it informs the development of the Trilingual Planner – a comprehensive framework for managing negotiations that span all three healthcare pillars simultaneously. For now, let's examine how the guide can be applied to a specific healthcare negotiation scenario.

To see the benefits of using the Healthcare Negotiation Mapping Tool, consider a hospital administrator from the Delivery of Care pillar negotiating with physicians in the Practice of Medicine to implement a new care coordination protocol to reduce readmission rates, which impacts the Business of Health. The hospital faces financial penalties due to high readmission numbers, so the administrator believes enhancing care coordination is crucial.

Using the guide, the administrator can:

1. Identify Key Stakeholders and their Priorities:
   - Recognize the need to communicate the protocol's operational benefits (Delivery of Care priority).
   - Address physicians' concerns over impacts on clinical decision-making and workload (Practice of Medicine priority).

2. Focus on Negotiation Focal Points Across Pillars:
   - Highlight how reducing readmissions through improved coordination creates financial upsides (Business of Health priority).
   - Stress how reducing readmissions aligns with providing high-quality, cost-effective organizational care (Practice of Medicine and Delivery of Care priorities).
3. Apply Trilingual Skills to Tailor Communication:
   - Use operational efficiency language when discussing with administrators (Delivery of Care).
   - Employ clinical outcome terminology when addressing physicians (Practice of Medicine).
   - Utilize financial impact language when communicating with executives (Business of Health).
4. Develop a Collaborative Approach (Interconnectedness Insights):
   - Create a cross-pillar task force that engages physicians in the design and rollout, fostering buy-in (Practice of Medicine).
   - Engage nursing staff and care coordinators (Delivery of Care) who can support implementation, offer insights, and troubleshoot challenges.
   - Ensure a comprehensive, balanced strategy that addresses concerns from all pillars, including financial considerations (Business of Health).

The tool helps the administrator anticipate obstacles like physician resistance in viewing the protocol as a burden that infringes on clinical autonomy. Armed with this awareness, they can proactively address concerns, increasing the likelihood of successful negotiation and buy-in. For example, the administrator may facilitate discussions exploring ways the protocol could streamline workflows while enhancing clinical handoffs and patient monitoring. They could share data demonstrating how preventing readmissions enhances patient outcomes and organizational metrics tied to value-based reimbursement models.

By integrating insights from all three pillars uncovered through the Healthcare Negotiation Mapping Tool, the administrator builds an interdisciplinary coalition aligned around a unified, patient-centric goal of delivering higher-value care through optimized coordination.

THE HEALTHCARE NEGOTIATION MAPPING TOOL IN ACTION:

THE NEXT FRONTIER EXPANSION AT CCCI

To illustrate the Healthcare Negotiation Mapping Tool in action in the real world, consider how Dr. Emily Wilson, Chief of Oncology, utilized it to strategize the Next Frontier Expansion at CCCI. The first step she took was to identify key stakeholders across the three pillars. Using the tool's framework, she mapped out key figures in the Practice of Medicine, including her oncology clinical team, surgical, radiation, and other specialty physicians, as well as nurses, pharmacists, and therapists. For Delivery of Care, she identified nursing leadership and frontline staff, care coordinators, patient navigators, and operations staff. In the Business of Health pillar, she noted the finance team led by the university's CFO, legal/compliance departments, insurance providers, and potential investors.

With this comprehensive stakeholder mapping, Dr. Wilson ensured no critical perspectives were missed. Next, she assessed the core negotiation focus for each group through their respective pillar lenses. For the Practice of Medicine, the focus was on ensuring cutting-edge cancer capabilities and adhering to the latest treatment protocols. The Delivery of Care priorities centered on optimizing patient flow, care experiences, and resource utilization. The Business of Health focus was on securing funding, managing budgets, and ensuring long-term financial viability. By pinpointing these distinct priorities, Dr. Wilson could tailor her negotiation strategies accordingly.

The next step guided Dr. Wilson in approaching negotiations with crucial "trilingual" communication skills in mind. For clinical discussions, she prioritized articulating improvements to patient outcomes and research opportunities. With operations teams, she focused on efficient care coordination and facility optimization. In financial negotiations, she led with projected ROI, cost savings via better outcomes, and reputational benefits as a premier cancer center. Throughout negotiations, Dr. Wilson consistently consulted the Interconnectedness Insights portion of the tool, recognizing how new treatment protocols affected staffing and budgets, while facility layouts influenced patient flow and care experiences. By proactively accounting for these interconnected impacts, she avoided potential bottlenecks or resource conflicts.

As a result of using the tool, a comprehensive cross-training initiative was developed, allowing oncology nurses to upskill on the latest protocols and providing clinicians with deeper operational and financial context. The tool kept Dr. Wilson operating with a panoramic view, preventing isolated decision-making and fostering an integrated, patient-centric approach. It helped her anticipate challenges, facilitate collaboration, and implement cohesive strategies balancing clinical excellence, operational efficiency, and economic sustainability. The result was a cutting-edge cancer center delivering exceptional, streamlined care through innovative, value-based models.

Conclusion: The Value of Healthcare-Specific Negotiation Strategies

A fundamental insight of this chapter is how mastering negotiation in the healthcare field requires a deep understanding of the interconnected nature of the Practice of Medicine, the Delivery of Care, and the Business of Health. The Healthcare Negotiation Mapping Tool serves as a valuable resource for assisting in navigating these complexities. By methodically identifying key stakeholders, understanding their unique priorities, and tailoring communication through trilingual negotiation skills, healthcare professionals can bridge gaps and foster true collaboration.

As you progress through the HEAR Approach™ and deepen your grasp of Emotional Intelligence, strategic framing, and cross-pillar dynamics, the Healthcare Negotiation Mapping Tool's utility will increase. In offering healthcare-specific negotiation strategies, it embraces a new mindset focused on collaboration over confrontation, understanding over ego, and uniting diverse perspectives in service of optimal patient care.

Implementing this approach requires continuous refinement, but the potential benefits are far-reaching: enhanced patient experiences, streamlined operational efficiency, fortified interprofessional partnerships, and a revitalized healthcare system equipped to address evolving challenges. By integrating the guide's principles with the HEAR Approach™, healthcare professionals can drive transformative change, fostering a more responsive, collaborative, and patient-centered healthcare environment.

REFLECTION EXERCISE: ACTIVATING THE HEALTHCARE NEGOTIATION MAPPING TOOL IN THE CONTEXT OF HEAR

Think of a recent or upcoming negotiation in your healthcare role. Take 15 minutes to apply the Healthcare Negotiation Mapping Tool to this situation.

Now identify one specific strategy or insight from this chapter that you could apply to enhance your approach to this negotiation. How might it change the outcome?

Finally, consider how applying the HEAR Approach™ might change your perspective:

- How could empathy and acknowledgment improve your understanding of other stakeholders' positions?
- In what ways could you recast potential conflicts as opportunities for collaboration?
- How might empowering other stakeholders lead to more innovative solutions?

By practicing this structured reflection, you'll develop greater fluency in applying these concepts to real-world scenarios, positioning yourself for more collaborative, dynamic negotiations attuned to healthcare's complex ecosystem.

Key Takeaways

1. Effective healthcare negotiations require a profound understanding of the interconnections between the Practice of Medicine, Delivery of Care, and Business of Health pillars, enabling professionals to navigate complex scenarios with a holistic perspective.
2. Cost considerations permeate virtually every healthcare negotiation, demanding that professionals balance financial realities with the core mission of providing high-quality, patient-centered care across all three pillars.
3. The Healthcare Negotiation Mapping Tool provides a structured approach for professionals to systematically analyze stakeholders,

priorities, and potential impacts across pillars, enhancing their ability to achieve optimal outcomes in complex healthcare negotiations.

4. Mastering trilingual negotiation skills, including fluency in the distinct languages of medicine, care delivery, and the business of healthcare, is crucial for bridging diverse perspectives and facilitating mutually beneficial solutions in healthcare negotiations.

Notes

1. The following scenario is based on a real-life multi-billion dollar expansion undertaken by a major university. While the characters and specific negotiations are fictionalized accounts, the core challenges and stakeholder dynamics reflect the realities that this and other healthcare institutions face when embarking on large-scale projects.
2. Glyn Elwyn et al., "Shared Decision Making: A Model for Clinical Practice," *Journal of General Internal Medicine* 27, no. 10 (2012): 1361–1367, https://doi.org/10.1007/s11606-012-2077-6.
3. Merrick Zwarenstein, Joanne Goldman, and Scott Reeves, "Interprofessional Collaboration: Effects of Practice-Based Interventions on Professional Practice and Healthcare Outcomes," *Cochrane Database of Systematic Reviews* 3 (2009): CD000072, https://doi.org/10.1002/14651858.CD000072.pub2
4. John P. Kotter and Leonard A. Schlesinger, "Choosing Strategies for Change," *Harvard Business Review* 86, no. 7/8 (2008): 130–139.
5. Zwarenstein et al., "Interprofessional Collaboration."
6. Linda H. Aiken, Jeannie P. Cimiotti, Douglas M. Sloane, Herbert L. Smith, Linda Flynn, and Donna F. Neff, "Effects of Nurse Staffing and Nurse Education on Patient Deaths in Hospitals with Different Nurse Work Environments," *Medical Care* 49, no. 12 (2011): 1047–1053, https://doi.org/10.1097/MLR.0b013e3182330b6e.
7. Elwyn et al., "Shared Decision Making."
8. Jody Hoffer Gittell, "Relationships between Service Providers and Their Impact on Customers," *Journal of Service Research* 4, no. 4 (2002): 299–311, https://doi.org/10.1177/1094670502004004007.
9. Amos Tversky and Daniel Kahneman, "The Framing of Decisions and the Psychology of Choice," *Science* 211, no. 4481 (1981): 453–458, https://doi.org/10.1126/science.7455683.

Chapter 4

Empowerment

Embracing Vulnerability, Seeking Knowledge, and Advocating Boldly

Empowerment comes from within and is often born out of vulnerability.

– **Brené Brown**

DOI: 10.4324/9781003336013-5

Dr. Nadine Burke Harris had always been driven to help children. As a young pediatrician in San Francisco's Bayview-Hunters Point neighborhood, she witnessed firsthand the harsh realities of childhood adversity and trauma. Many of her patients came from disadvantaged backgrounds, grappling with poverty, violence, and neglect.[1] The weight of their struggles often felt overwhelming, leaving Dr. Burke Harris questioning her ability to make a lasting impact. Despite pouring her heart into each case, she frequently felt frustrated, as if she wasn't truly making a difference in these kids' lives. This sense of helplessness in the face of complex systemic barriers is one countless healthcare professionals can relate to when confronting seemingly insurmountable challenges.

However, Dr. Burke Harris refused to give in to despair. One day, while reviewing the records of a particularly challenging case, she noticed a pattern – the child's health issues seemed directly linked to their exposure to adverse childhood experiences (ACEs) – traumatic events such as abuse, neglect, household dysfunction, or exposure to violence that can have lasting negative effects on health and well-being. This realization was a game-changer, sparking a journey of self-discovery that would transform her approach to pediatric care.[2]

Determined to find innovative ways to serve her young patients better, Dr. Burke Harris began to seek out new approaches and perspectives. She immersed herself in ACEs research, attended conferences, and connected with experts. This deep dive equipped her with compelling data and insights she could use to persuade skeptical colleagues and policymakers. By participating in conferences, she not only refined her ability to articulate complex ideas clearly and persuasively but also expanded her professional network, building alliances with like-minded advocates. Through this process, she gained a nuanced understanding of healthcare policy and practice while cultivating the strategic mindset essential for effective negotiation in healthcare.

As her grasp of the details around ACEs deepened, so did her sense of confidence and empowerment. Dr. Burke Harris began to see herself not just as a physician but as an advocate and change-maker. She learned to leverage her unique perspective and experiences, turning what she once perceived as limitations into powerful tools for advocacy. By validating her emotions, clarifying her goals, and anticipating potential roadblocks, she found the strength to have tough conversations with stakeholders at all levels, from parents to policymakers.

Dr. Burke Harris started incorporating ACE screening into her practice, tailoring treatment plans accordingly. Each small victory reinforced her belief in her ability to effect change. Her growing confidence prepared her for the difficult negotiations ahead: convincing hospital administrators to implement ACE screening, persuading fellow pediatricians to adopt trauma-informed care practices, and ultimately, advocating for state-level policy changes. Her goal was clear: to transform pediatric care to address the impact of childhood adversity.

Dr. Burke Harris' journey of empowerment didn't just change her own practice – it inspired others. Her innovative, evidence-based approach quickly made her a leader in pediatric medicine. She founded the Center for Youth Wellness and played a pivotal role in California legislation, allocating $95 million for ACE screening and treatment. Through her example, she empowered countless other healthcare professionals to advocate for change, creating a ripple effect that continues to transform pediatric care across the country.

Dr. Burke Harris' transformative story exemplifies how embracing vulnerability, seeking knowledge, and advocating boldly can profoundly impact patient care and negotiation effectiveness. Turning inward and recognizing how her background shaped her perspective led her to align personal growth with self-awareness and Emotional Intelligence. Her purposeful action embodied the mindset and behaviors needed to navigate healthcare's emotional landscapes and high-stakes negotiations. Dr. Burke' Harris' journey demonstrates how developing clarity, confidence, and a solutions-focused mindset can drive positive change in even the most challenging healthcare environments.

The Essence of Self-Empowerment in Healthcare Negotiations

Self-empowerment, the second foundational element of the HEAR Approach™, equips providers with vital tools for navigating patient care scenarios, interdisciplinary collaborations, and organizational decision-making within healthcare's emotionally intense and high-stakes settings. At its core, self-empowerment involves cultivating an astute awareness of one's emotions, priorities, and potential obstacles. This capacity is indispensable when negotiating the inherently charged atmosphere of healthcare interactions.

Healthcare professionals often find themselves in tense discussions with patients' families about end-of-life care decisions or negotiating with the administration for additional staffing to ensure patient safety. Their ability to remain grounded, focused, and self-aware is tested in these moments. Self-empowerment enables them to navigate these challenging situations with greater ease and confidence, ultimately leading to better outcomes for patients and the organization as a whole.

Research consistently shows that by cultivating self-empowerment, negotiators can enhance their overall effectiveness in healthcare settings.[3] They become better equipped to maintain emotional balance in high-pressure situations, allowing for more effective thinking and decision-making.[4] Self-empowered healthcare professionals can articulate their positions and rationales more clearly, ensuring their perspectives are well understood. Additionally, they develop the capacity to listen actively to others without feeling threatened, fostering more open and productive dialogues.[5] This heightened self-awareness and confidence enable providers to more readily identify shared goals and common ground among diverse stakeholders. Ultimately, self-empowerment clears the ground for healthcare professionals to propose innovative solutions that benefit all parties, leading to more successful negotiations and improved outcomes.[6]

The power of self-empowerment lies in three key elements: validation, acknowledgment, and self-awareness.

Validation involves healthcare providers accepting and embracing their emotions without judgment, which is particularly important in the emotionally charged world of healthcare. By allowing themselves to experience feelings authentically, they can manage stress more effectively and enhance the genuineness of their interactions with patients, families, and colleagues. For example, a nurse might feel frustrated after a difficult shift with multiple high-needs patients. Instead of suppressing these feelings, they could acknowledge their frustration, perhaps by journaling or discussing it with a trusted colleague. This validation allows them to process the emotion healthily, reducing burnout risk and enabling them to approach their next shift with renewed empathy and energy.

Acknowledgment entails healthcare professionals recognizing and being open about their underlying interests and goals in a negotiation. It's important to reflect honestly on what's truly driving them – whether it's a commitment to improving patient outcomes, a desire to mitigate organizational risk, or enhancing their professional reputation. When they acknowledge these motivating factors, they can thoughtfully align their negotiation approach to advance those priorities more purposefully and effectively. For instance, a department head advocating for new equipment might realize their motivation stems from both a desire to improve patient care and a wish to make their department more competitive. By acknowledging both factors, they can craft a more compelling proposal that addresses both clinical benefits and the hospital's strategic positioning, potentially increasing their chances of success.

Self-awareness lies at the heart of empowerment. It involves healthcare professionals reflectively identifying their innate strengths, potential blind spots, and emotional triggers. This could mean recognizing tendencies like becoming defensive when their leadership decisions face scrutiny or acknowledging discomfort with confrontation. For instance, a healthcare administrator leading a team discussion on updating facility policies might anticipate feeling flustered if colleagues push back strongly. Self-awareness would allow them to proactively employ tactics to manage that reaction productively. Healthcare professionals can address challenges with greater poise and clarity by continuously monitoring their inner landscape during negotiations.

Dr. Toby Cosgrove, former CEO of the Cleveland Clinic, exemplified this kind of self-empowerment during contentious healthcare reform negotiations.[7] In a pivotal meeting with government officials and insurance representatives, Dr. Cosgrove remained calm and open-minded despite conflicting interests. He actively listened to all parties, acknowledged their concerns, and proposed innovative solutions that addressed multiple stakeholders' needs. This self-aware approach enabled him to build trust among conflicting parties, ultimately leading to a compromise that improved patient care while managing costs.

Mastering self-empowerment is essential for navigating healthcare's complex and high-stakes negotiation settings, where the goal is not to "win" but to achieve the best possible outcome for all stakeholders – especially patients. It allows negotiators to prioritize shared goals, build trust, and create mutually beneficial solutions in a composed and solution-focused manner that enhances patient care and organizational effectiveness.

Strategies for Achieving Self-Empowerment

Healthcare professionals interact with diverse stakeholders, each with their own perspectives and priorities to consider. Embodying self-empowerment principles allows them to approach these interactions with a clear mind, emotional balance, and a collaborative problem-solving orientation.[8] Meta-analyses demonstrate that Emotional Intelligence, a key component of self-empowerment, is positively associated with improved communication, collaboration, and problem-solving among healthcare teams.[9] When providers are self-aware and emotionally centered, they possess the confidence and security to consider others' viewpoints without feeling threatened and can more readily embrace a relational, collaborative outlook.[10] Achieving self-empowerment, therefore, is critical in healthcare negotiations.

The RESET technique is one of the most powerful tools available to healthcare professionals. It is a effective tool for managing emotional challenges during healthcare negotiations. This method consists of five steps: Recognize, Evaluate, Step Back, Empathize, and Transform. When faced with a triggering situation, practitioners should first recognize their emotional response, then evaluate its intensity. Next, they step back mentally to gain perspective, followed by empathizing with all parties involved. Finally, they transform the situation by choosing a constructive response.

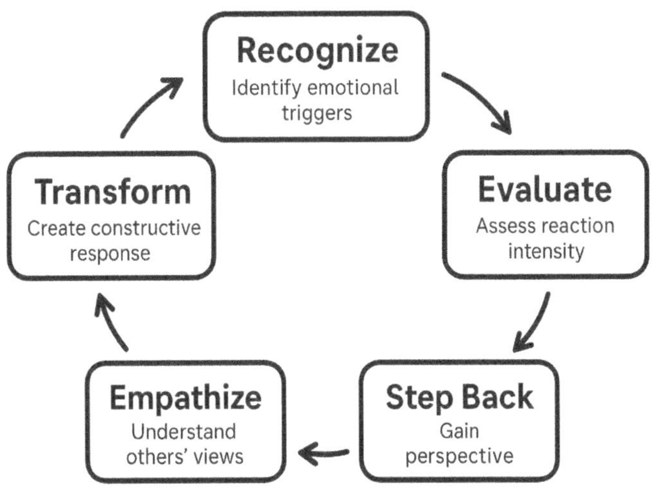

Figure 4.1 The RESET technique for managing emotional challenges in healthcare negotiations.

This figure illustrates the five-step RESET method (Recognize, Evaluate, Step Back, Empathize, Transform) that healthcare professionals can use to manage emotional responses during challenging negotiations. The circular flow illustrates how practitioners can recognize their emotional triggers, assess the intensity of their reaction, step back to gain perspective, empathize with all parties involved, and ultimately transform the situation by choosing a constructive response.

For example, consider Dr. Kavitha Nallathambi, a seasoned oncologist, in a tense budget meeting with the hospital's financial officer. When the officer questions the need for an expensive new treatment protocol, Dr. Nallathambi feels her frustration rising. Applying the RESET technique, she first *recognizes* her emotional trigger ("I'm feeling defensive about my proposal"). She then *evaluates* the intensity of her reaction, realizing it's rooted in her passion for patient care. Taking a mental *step back*, Dr. Nallathambi pauses to consider the broader context. She *empathizes* with the financial officer's responsibility to manage limited resources. Finally, she *transforms* her initial defensive reaction into a constructive response: "I understand your concerns about the cost. Let's review the long-term patient outcomes and potential cost savings this treatment could provide. I believe you'll see it as an investment in both patient care and hospital efficiency."

Regular practice of the RESET technique can develop greater Emotional Intelligence and resilience. Over time, this approach will enhance practitioners' ability to maintain composure and navigate complex healthcare negotiations more effectively, ultimately leading to better outcomes for all stakeholders involved.

The following practices and techniques can aid healthcare professionals in cultivating self-empowerment in the context of the HEAR Framework:

- **Intention Setting**: Before each negotiation or important interaction, negotiators can clarify their goals and core values to anchor themselves in their purpose. They should take a few minutes to write down specific objectives and the principles guiding their approach. This practice helps maintain focus and integrity during challenging discussions, ensuring actions align with professional ethics and personal values.
- **Reflective Journaling**: Healthcare professionals should regularly document their experiences, emotions, and decision-making processes to identify patterns and areas for growth. They should set aside time each week to write about significant interactions, noting emotional responses and outcomes. Periodically reviewing these entries can help recognize personal growth, recurring challenges, and potential areas for professional development.

- **Self-Compassion Practice**: Healthcare professionals should develop a kind and understanding attitude toward themselves, especially when facing challenges or setbacks. They should implement a daily self-compassion ritual, such as reciting positive affirmations or acknowledging personal efforts regardless of outcomes. This practice can help maintain resilience in the face of healthcare's inherent challenges and prevent burnout by fostering a balanced perspective on personal and professional experiences.
- **Physical Preparation**: Negotiators should recognize the mind-body connection by maintaining good sleep habits and regular exercise to support mental clarity and emotional resilience. They should establish a consistent sleep schedule and incorporate physical activity into their daily routine, even if it's just a short walk. These habits can significantly improve energy levels, cognitive function, and stress management capabilities in demanding healthcare environments.

Some activities include reaching out and working with others to hone self-empowerment skills:

- **Mentorship**: Seeking guidance from experienced leaders offers healthcare professionals valuable insights into complex negotiations and builds confidence. Regular check-ins with a trusted mentor provide opportunities to discuss upcoming challenges and reflect on past experiences, offering perspective to navigate the nuances of healthcare leadership and negotiation more effectively.
- **Support Network Building**: It is crucial to cultivate relationships with like-minded professionals for mutual support and encouragement. Attending healthcare conferences, joining professional associations, and participating in online forums allow practitioners to connect with peers facing similar challenges. Regular interaction with this network provides emotional support, practical advice, and opportunities for collaboration.
- **Emotional Intelligence Training**: Investing in workshops or courses helps healthcare professionals enhance their ability to recognize and manage emotions while refining communication skills. Role-playing challenging healthcare scenarios with colleagues, followed by a debrief to discuss emotional responses, communication effectiveness, and areas for improvement, ensures these skills are practiced and integrated effectively.

Last but not least, healthcare practitioners should consider meditation or developing a *Mindfulness Practice* to cultivate emotional balance and presence. They can start with short, daily guided meditation or deep breathing exercises, gradually increasing the duration over time. Regular practice can enhance focus, reduce stress, and improve decision-making abilities in high-pressure healthcare situations. There are several resources that they can look into for more details. Five resources I recommend include the following:

- *Mindful Medicine: 40 Simple Practices to Help Healthcare Professionals Heal Burnout and Reconnect to Purpose* by Jan Chozen Bays (2022).
- *The Mindful Healthcare Professional: A Guide to Compassionate Care* by Carmelina D'Arro (2023).
- *Mindful MD: 6 Ways Mindfulness Restores Your Autonomy and Cures Healthcare Burnout* by Gail Gazelle (2023).
- *Mindfulness in Medicine: An Evidence-Based Approach*, edited by Patricia A. Kinser and Sian Cotton (2023).
- *The Mindful Nurse: Using the Power of Mindfulness and Compassion to Help You Thrive in Your Work* by Carmel Sheridan (2021).

Adopting a comprehensive approach toward developing self-empowerment fosters a culture of continuous learning and helps healthcare professionals navigate complex interpersonal dynamics more skillfully.

EMPOWERMENT STRATEGIES ACROSS HEALTHCARE ROLES

For advanced practice providers, empowerment strategies include:

- Using internal scans before difficult patient interactions or team meetings.
- Applying RESET when dealing with challenging patients or family members.
- Negotiating for improved staffing ratios or resource allocation using data and patient outcomes.

For administrators, empowerment strategies include:

- Conducting bias awareness exercises before making hiring or policy decisions.

- Using the Healthcare Negotiation Mapping Tool when planning facility changes or budget allocations.
- Intentionally choosing communication styles in staff meetings and performance reviews.

For specialists, empowerment strategies include:

- Employing internal scans before interdisciplinary team meetings to clarify goals and potential biases.
- Using RESET when collaborating with colleagues who have differing treatment approaches.
- Negotiating for new equipment or research funding using evidence-based proposals and cost-benefit analyses.

For general practitioners, empowerment strategies include:

- Applying bias awareness techniques when diagnosing patients from diverse backgrounds.
- Using Internal Scans before patient consultations to ensure a clear, focused mindset.
- Negotiating with insurance companies using patient case studies and treatment efficacy data to advocate for patient needs.

By tailoring these strategies to their specific roles, healthcare professionals can enhance their effectiveness and job satisfaction while improving patient care.

Achieving Internal Clarity: The Keystone to Effective Negotiation

Self-empowerment is a cornerstone of effective negotiation in healthcare settings, providing professionals with the internal resources necessary to navigate complex interactions successfully. This idea goes beyond mere tactical preparation, delving into the realm of personal development and Emotional Intelligence. By focusing on self-empowerment, healthcare professionals can cultivate a state of internal clarity and emotional balance that significantly enhances their negotiation capabilities.

This inner work is vital for negotiating effectively in healthcare settings. When healthcare professionals enter negotiations internally conflicted – grappling with intangible insecurities, lingering trust issues, or emotional residue from prior interactions – securing a favorable resolution becomes challenging. Subconscious drives for validation, unresolved anxieties, or self-doubts can cloud their judgment and decision-making abilities.

These inner tensions act as invisible weights, hindering the capacity to stay fully present and engage with clarity. By proactively implementing empowerment strategies, healthcare professionals can holistically prepare their minds, emotions, and spirits – not just their bargaining tactics. It's about entering every interaction with an unencumbered mindset, poised to navigate complexities with poise and effectiveness.

Embodying empowerment in healthcare negotiations thus transcends merely securing an agreement. It fundamentally reframes how professionals engage throughout the entire experience, nurturing an "our" perspective over individual interests alone. Self-awareness and emotional centeredness enable providers to more readily embrace a relational, collaborative outlook. This shift occurs because self-empowerment provides the confidence and security to consider others' viewpoints without feeling threatened.

By achieving internal alignment and emotional buoyancy, healthcare providers create space for interactions that are more productive and personally fulfilling for all involved. By prioritizing internal clarity, healthcare professionals begin every negotiation from a position of poise and presence rather than reacting to subconscious triggers. This cultivates mutual trust and respect, creating space for collaborative, innovative problem-solving.

THE VALUE OF INTERNAL CLARITY FOR EMPOWERED HEALTHCARE NEGOTIATIONS: A PHARMACEUTICAL CASE STUDY

The sterile conference room felt like a battleground to Kevin. As a clinical research associate leading a groundbreaking cancer therapy study, he knew the next hour could determine the fate of years of painstaking work. Across the polished table sat a team of pharmaceutical executives, their sharp suits and calculating gazes starkly contrasting with Kevin's world of lab coats and clinical trials. His jaw tightened as he imagined the executives questioning his authority or dismissing his expertise in favor of their bottom-line priorities.

Kevin's mind churned with doubts: Would they see him as competent enough to lead such a high-stakes project? Could he stand firm without appearing combative or losing their respect? The stakes felt monumental – countless patients' futures depended on the outcome of this potential partnership. Kevin realized that to champion his research effectively, he needed more than impeccable data and determination; he needed to project a confident and composed presence while managing his own insecurities.

Kevin implemented several strategies to align and empower his mind, emotions, and purpose before engaging with potential pharmaceutical partners. First, he clarified his core priorities: accelerating access to innovative treatments while upholding the highest standards of scientific integrity. Through reflection, Kevin identified specific concerns, such as the fear of appearing indecisive under pressure or being dismissed by assertive corporate stakeholders. To address these concerns, he practiced visualization exercises, rehearsed key points of the negotiation, and engaged in mindfulness techniques to ground himself in self-assurance.

These preparatory steps paid off when Kevin entered the room. When a pharmaceutical executive proposed an accelerated timeline that risked undermining the study's integrity, Kevin's internal clarity allowed him to respond with calm authority rather than defensiveness. He firmly but respectfully explained the scientific rationale for his timeline, backing his position with compelling data. Kevin's steady demeanor enabled him to propose a phased approach: delivering preliminary results early while maintaining the rigor of the full study. This compromise satisfied the executive's urgency while protecting the integrity of the research, demonstrating how self-empowerment can lead to balanced and innovative solutions.

Kevin's composed and confident approach also earned the trust of the pharmaceutical team. They began to see him not just as another researcher pitching a project but as a capable and reliable partner. Kevin's approachable demeanor during budget discussions encouraged one executive to disclose internal concerns about cost pressures. This transparency created an opportunity to collaborate on cost-effective strategies that preserved the study's quality. His ability to maintain control over his emotions and perspective fostered a more constructive and mutually respectful negotiation environment.

Ultimately, Kevin's self-empowerment contributed to a favorable agreement that included:

- A timeline balancing speed with scientific rigor.
- A budget fully funding necessary resources.
- A collaborative oversight committee respecting both parties' interests.
- Provisions for sharing preliminary findings without compromising the full study.

This outcome benefited not only Kevin and the pharmaceutical company but also the patients who would rely on the results of a rigorously conducted study of this groundbreaking cancer therapy.

Enhancing Negotiation Effectiveness: A Guide for Internal Scans

A healthcare professional's thorough internal preparation is invaluable for optimal performance in high-stakes negotiations. One powerful technique for achieving clarity on goals, strategies, and tactics is conducting a comprehensive Internal Scan. This – reflective, structured process aligns mental, emotional, and professional perspectives and cultivates a clear and focused mindset primed for effective negotiations. This process seamlessly bridges introspective self-exploration with the pragmatic application of negotiation principles.

Here's a step-by-step explanation of how healthcare professionals can conduct an empowering internal scan:

1. **Set Aside Quiet Time for Reflection**: A peaceful, distraction-free environment allows negotiators to fully focus on their thoughts and emotions. Techniques like deep breathing, meditation, or mindfulness exercises can be used to center and ground oneself. This dedicated time for reflection allows the negotiator to clear their mind and approach the upcoming negotiation with a calm, focused demeanor.
2. **Acknowledge and Label Emotions**: The professional should identify and acknowledge their emotional state, whether it's anxiety, enthusiasm, or apprehension. Being specific in labeling emotions helps gain a clear understanding of their nature and intensity. This emotional awareness serves as a foundation for effective self-regulation during the negotiation process.

3. **Reflect on Professional Goals and Accomplishments**: The negotiator should consider how the goals for the negotiation align with broader professional goals and long-term objectives. Reviewing a negotiation journal can help reflect on past successes and accomplishments. This reflection process enables the negotiator to maintain a strategic perspective and ensure that each negotiation contributes to their overall professional development.
4. **Anticipate Potential Triggers and Plan Constructive Responses**: Identifying potential emotional triggers that might arise during the negotiation allows negotiators to prepare responses and tailor their communication to the partner's preferences. Techniques like mirroring, labeling, and active listening can be employed to build rapport and address concerns effectively. "If-then" planning helps prepare for different scenarios, allowing for adept responses to various situations. This comprehensive preparation enhances the negotiator's ability to navigate complex healthcare discussions with confidence and flexibility.
5. **Rehearse the Negotiation**: The negotiator should mentally simulate the negotiation setting, conversation flow, and responses to various scenarios. Practicing out loud and considering role-playing with a trusted colleague or mentor can be beneficial. This rehearsal process helps build confidence and refine communication skills, leading to a more polished and effective negotiation performance.
6. **Continuously Monitor and Adjust During the Negotiation**: It's crucial to remain attentive to one's emotional state and biases throughout the negotiation. The negotiator should be prepared to adjust their strategy in real-time based on the dynamics and the counterpart's responses. This ongoing self-awareness and flexibility allow the negotiator to maintain composure and make strategic adjustments as the negotiation unfolds.
7. **Reflect Post-Negotiation**: After the negotiation, the professional should identify what worked well, the challenges faced, and areas for improvement. Engaging in continuous learning and skill development is essential. This post-negotiation reflection is a critical step in the ongoing process of refining negotiation skills and strategies, ensuring continuous growth and improvement over time.

Conducting internal scans is a fundamental aspect of empowerment that lies at the core of the HEAR Approach's™ philosophy. This iterative practice of self-reflection and growth enables negotiators to take control of their internal narratives and transform potential vulnerabilities into sources of strength. As a result of this process, professionals approach negotiations with heightened clarity and a sharper sense of purpose, ensuring their decisions stem from well-informed intentions rather than impulsive emotional responses.

The Pervasive Influence of Biases in Healthcare Negotiation

While self-empowerment and internal reflection lay a solid foundation for empowerment, it's essential to also consider how to navigate the external factors that shape negotiation experiences in healthcare. A sense of empowerment isn't just a product of one's inner world; it's also profoundly influenced by others' perceptions and how their biases and assumptions can color one's self-image.

Biases are inherent tendencies that shape perceptions, decisions, and behaviors in subtle yet powerful ways. Within the complex healthcare arena, biases can stem from diverse sources – differences in professional backgrounds, hierarchical roles, personal experiences, and unconscious stereotypes or assumptions related to gender, race, ethnicity, and culture.[11] Numerous research studies have demonstrated how these biases permeate every aspect of the healthcare ecosystem, influencing clinical decision-making, policy development, team dynamics, and the very culture of healthcare organizations.[12]

Unchecked biases can lead to disparities in medical treatment, compromised patient health outcomes, and strained interprofessional collaboration.[13] For example, a physician might inadvertently discount a nurse's valuable clinical insights due to an ingrained hierarchical bias, or a board member with a business background might discredit a doctor's request for new medical technology, assuming the doctor doesn't understand the financial implications. Such biases can breed communication breakdowns, erode trust, and undermine a cohesive, inclusive environment for optimal patient care.

However, by cultivating self-awareness and actively identifying and dismantling personal biases, healthcare professionals can approach negotiations with empowerment, openness, and genuine curiosity about different perspectives. This self-reflective mindset is crucial to navigating the diverse backgrounds and viewpoints inherent in the healthcare landscape. Understanding one's biases paves the way for more empathetic, productive, and transformative discussions that ultimately benefit patients, providers, and the healthcare system.

Overcoming Biases and Assumptions

Healthcare professionals can use the empowerment techniques and internal clarity practices described above to check themselves for bias. One effective method is structured self-reflection, which involves regularly examining personal biases through guided journaling or facilitated peer discussions. Professionals can set aside dedicated time each week to reflect on patient interactions, treatment decisions, or team dynamics. Using prompts such as "What assumptions did I make about this patient?" or "How might my background influence my approach to this case?" can help uncover hidden biases. Healthcare providers can enhance their self-awareness and improve decision-making by documenting insights and tracking progress over time.

Another powerful tool is active listening training. This involves developing advanced listening skills through specialized workshops and daily practice. Techniques such as mirroring, summarizing, and asking clarifying questions can be particularly effective. Healthcare professionals can also implement a "teach-back" method in patient interactions, where patients explain their understanding of diagnoses or treatment plans. This approach not only ensures mutual comprehension but also builds trust, particularly with diverse patient populations. By honing these skills, healthcare providers can better recognize and mitigate the impact of their biases in negotiations and daily interactions.

While developing awareness about personal biases is crucial, implementing effective mitigation strategies within healthcare organizations presents substantial challenges. Research consistently highlights several obstacles to progress in this area, ranging from deeply ingrained thought patterns and resistance to change from leaders to organizational inertia and a lack of robust support systems and accountability.[14]

However, studies also demonstrate the remarkable positive impacts when healthcare institutions proactively confront biases head-on. For example, a landmark study in the *Journal of General Internal Medicine* found hospitals with comprehensive programs enhancing cultural competency and addressing implicit biases experienced significant improvements in patient satisfaction, treatment adherence, and health outcomes across diverse populations.[15]

Healthcare professionals who adopt an empowered mindset can arm themselves with practical strategies, like the following, to assist their institutions in addressing systemic biases and assumptions:

- **Inclusive Decision-Making Process**: Establish a formal protocol for incorporating diverse viewpoints in clinical and administrative decisions. Create multidisciplinary teams that include representatives from various specialties, experience levels, and cultural backgrounds. Implement a structured decision-making framework, such as the DECIDE model (Define, Examine, Consider, Identify, Determine, Evaluate), ensuring all voices are heard and considered.
- **Assertive Communication Training**: Launch workshops focusing on assertive communication techniques, emphasizing the use of "I" statements. Practice formulating responses to challenging situations, such as "I've noticed a pattern in our treatment approach that might be influenced by unconscious bias. Can we discuss this?" Role-play these scenarios with colleagues to build confidence in addressing sensitive topics.
- **Data-Driven Bias Recognition**: Implement a system for collecting and analyzing patient care data to identify potential biases in treatment decisions or outcomes. Regularly review metrics such as treatment disparities, patient satisfaction scores, and health outcomes across different demographic groups. Use this data to facilitate evidence-based discussions about bias and track the effectiveness of bias mitigation efforts.
- **Comprehensive Bias and Cultural Competency Curriculum**: Develop an ongoing, multi-tiered education program addressing bias and cultural competency. Include mandatory foundational training for all staff, advanced modules for leadership, and specialty-specific courses. Incorporate case studies, interactive simulations, and regular refresher sessions to ensure continuous learning and application of concepts.
- **Bias Intervention Protocol**: Establish a clear, step-by-step process for addressing observed biases in real-time. Train staff on respectful intervention techniques and create a supportive environment where calling out potential biases is encouraged and valued. Implement a non-punitive reporting system to track interventions and identify areas needing additional support or training.
- **Cross-Cultural Mentorship Program**: Create a structured mentorship program pairing healthcare professionals with mentors from different cultural or professional backgrounds. Set specific goals for these relationships, such as expanding cultural knowledge, challenging assumptions, and developing more inclusive practices. Regular check-ins and guided reflections can maximize the impact of these partnerships.

- **Bias-Conscious Quality Improvement**: Integrate bias awareness into existing quality improvement processes. When reviewing adverse events or near-misses, include assessing how biases might have contributed to the situation. Develop action plans that address both systemic issues and potential biases, ensuring a comprehensive approach to patient safety and care quality.
- **Patient Feedback Integration**: Implement a robust system for collecting and acting on diverse patient feedback. Use culturally appropriate surveys, focus groups, and community advisory boards to gather insights on perceived biases or disparities in care. Regularly share this feedback with staff and involve patients in developing solutions, fostering a culture of accountability and continuous improvement.

These strategies provide a comprehensive approach to navigating biases in healthcare settings, offering practical, actionable steps that can be implemented by empowered individuals at the organizational level. Consistently applying these strategies, proactively addressing challenges, and fostering an inclusive culture allow biases and assumptions to be effectively navigated, leading to improved patient care, staff satisfaction, and better healthcare negotiation outcomes.

The Hurdles Biases Pose

The case of Dr. Priya Modi, a skilled internist at a regional medical center, vividly illustrates how biases and assumptions can impact healthcare negotiations and patient care. As Dr. Modi settled into her new role, she encountered several instances where these issues hindered effective communication and collaboration:

Patient Care Assumptions: During morning rounds, Dr. Modi suggested a novel treatment approach for a chronic obstructive pulmonary disease patient. Some staff members, especially those with more experience, resisted her new ideas and approaches. One such senior physician, Dr. Johnson, dismissively responded to her suggestion, saying, "Dr. Modi, I appreciate your enthusiasm, but we've treated this condition the same way for years. It's worked just fine."

Professional Hierarchy Beliefs: In a team meeting, Dr. Modi proposed a collaborative care plan involving nursing staff and physical therapists. But an underlying assumption within the organization was that physicians should hold all the decision-making power, permitting the valuable insights of other healthcare team members to be discounted. The Nurse Manager, Thompson, responded to Dr. Modi's suggestion by saying, "I know you're new here, but physicians usually just give orders. Let's not complicate things."

Cultural Insensitivity: Some staff lacked cultural competency, failing to recognize the importance of considering patients' diverse backgrounds in providing comprehensive care. When discussing treatment options for Mr. Patel, a 65-year-old Hindu patient with diabetes, Dr. Modi suggested a diet plan that accommodated his vegetarian lifestyle and proposed scheduling his insulin doses around his daily prayer times. But a colleague, Dr. Davis, remarked, "I didn't see why we needed to cater to every cultural whim. Medicine is medicine, regardless of background."

Gender Stereotypes and Microaggressions: Despite her qualifications and expertise, Dr. Modi encountered gender bias that subtly undermined her professional credibility. In a department meeting, Dr. Modi presented a well-researched proposal for a new quality improvement initiative. As she concluded, a senior administrator, Dr. Simmons, smirked, "Well, looks like we've got a real go-getter here." Without inviting questions from others, he stood up and dismissively said, "We'll take this under advisement," as he left the room.

Crafting an Empowered Response

Dr. Modi recognized that addressing these challenges would require a strategic approach. She turned to the Healthcare Negotiation Mapping Tool introduced in Chapter 3, which provided a framework for identifying key stakeholders, understanding their interests, and developing strategies for effective negotiation. The tool was particularly useful in helping Dr. Modi map out the various perspectives and priorities of her colleagues, administrators, and patients, allowing her to craft targeted approaches for each group.

Dr. Modi pursued a multipronged approach to addressing the issue of bias within her organization:

Leading by Example: In her interactions with patients and colleagues, Dr. Modi modeled inclusive, respectful, and collaborative communication. When negotiating treatment plans, she actively sought input from all team members, demonstrating the value of diverse perspectives in decision-making.

Reframing Conversations: When faced with biased comments, Dr. Modi skillfully reframed the conversation to focus on shared goals. For example, when Dr. Davis questioned accommodating cultural preferences, she responded, "By considering our patients' cultural backgrounds, we can build trust and negotiate treatment plans that they're more likely to adhere to, ultimately improving outcomes."

Building Alliances: Dr. Modi identified allies who shared her commitment to inclusivity and collaboration and engaged them in discussions about negotiating change within the hospital's power structures. In meetings with hospital administration, Dr. Modi presented compelling data and narratives demonstrating the benefits of unbiased hiring practices and equitable career advancement opportunities, highlighting how these changes would enhance patient care and staff satisfaction.

Raising Awareness and Celebrating Successes: Dr. Modi organized workshops on implicit bias, cultural competency, and interprofessional collaboration. As positive changes like collaborative negotiations took root, Dr. Modi publicly acknowledged the contributions of staff members who championed inclusivity and a supportive workplace culture.

Dr. Modi gradually transformed the culture at her regional medical center, and her journey showcases how individual action, grounded in effective negotiation techniques, can confront biases, foster understanding, and drive meaningful change in healthcare settings.

EMPOWERMENT STRATEGIES IN VIRTUAL HEALTHCARE NEGOTIATIONS

As virtual meetings become increasingly common in healthcare, it's crucial to adapt empowerment strategies for remote settings. Practices such as these can go a long way to improving communication when negotiating:

1. **Enhanced Internal Scans**:
   - Before virtual negotiations, conduct a more thorough internal scan, considering potential distractions in your environment.
   - Set intentions for maintaining focus and presence despite the physical distance.

2. **Virtual RESET**:
   - Be more deliberate in applying the RESET technique, as emotional cues can be harder to read online.
   - Use the chat function or reaction buttons to signal when you need a moment to reset.
3. **Digital Body Language**:
   - Pay extra attention to your facial expressions and tone of voice.
   - Use hand gestures deliberately to emphasize points, ensuring they're visible on camera.
4. **Tech-Enhanced Collaboration**:
   - Utilize screen sharing to present data or visual aids effectively.
   - Use digital whiteboards for collaborative problem-solving during negotiations.
5. **Virtual Bias Awareness**:
   - Be mindful of potential biases related to technology comfort levels or home office environments.
   - Ensure equal speaking time and participation opportunities for all attendees.
6. **Building Virtual Rapport**:
   - Allow time for an informal chat before diving into negotiations to build a connection.
   - Use breakout rooms for smaller group discussions to foster more intimate conversations.

By adapting empowerment strategies to virtual settings, healthcare professionals can maintain effective negotiations regardless of physical distance.

The Need in Practice to Continuously Adjust for Empowerment

Healthcare professionals increasingly find themselves in complex scenarios requiring them to adjust their emotional stance within negotiations. Preparation is key to success in these scenarios, but true empowerment transcends thorough preparation; it's about the ongoing practice of recalibrating emotional states throughout the negotiation process. This idea is backed by the rigorous findings of cognitive neuroscience research, which underscores the critical role that continuous emotional monitoring plays in effective decision-making.[16]

Nurse Sojka's experience at a community hospital as she prepares for a crucial negotiation with the administration about implementing a new patient safety protocol illustrates the practical, continuous application of self-empowerment strategies. It offers a powerful example of how self-empowerment can transform personal and professional outcomes in healthcare negotiations.

Unpacking Emotions and Personal Biases: In the quiet of the nurses' lounge, Sojka prepares for her upcoming meeting with hospital administration. A mix of determination and apprehension washes over her as she reflects on past interactions. Recognizing the importance of addressing her internal biases, she takes a moment to identify them:

- **Age Bias**: As a younger nurse, she worries that older administrators might not take her seriously.
- **Gender Bias**: She recalls male administrators giving more weight to her male colleagues' opinions in previous meetings.
- **Experience Bias**: Despite her expertise in patient safety, her relatively short tenure sometimes makes her doubt her ability to influence hospital-wide policies.

A memory surfaces of Mr. Martinez, an administrator, questioning her expertise in a previous meeting. His words echo in her mind: "Nurse Sojka, are you sure you've considered all the factors here? You've only been here for a few years, and this is a complex issue."

Sojka often wonders, "Am I just looking for validation? Or am I still bothered by that staffing level discussion from last time?" She recognizes that it is crucial to separate these personal feelings from her professional objectives.

Clarifying True Interests in the Negotiation: Refocusing on her core goals, Sojka realizes that while part of her seeks recognition, her primary objective is implementing a protocol that significantly enhances patient safety. "What do I actually want to achieve in this meeting?" she asks herself, distinguishing between her need for personal validation and the practical outcomes of the negotiation.

Anticipating Triggers and Crafting Responses: Anticipating potential challenges, Sojka prepares for questions about implementation costs and staff training requirements. She envisions Mr. Martinez questioning the protocol's necessity and mentally rehearses her responses. "They're just doing their job," she reminds herself. "It's not about me or my skills. Stay focused on why this protocol matters for our patients." This mental preparation is crucial for keeping the discussion centered on patient safety benefits rather than allowing it to be derailed by her insecurities.

Applying an Internal Scan to Stay Centered During Negotiation: As Sojka enters the meeting room, she feels a sense of calm preparedness washover her. The administrator begins to raise their concerns, and Sojka listens attentively, providing well-thought-out responses. Throughout the discussion, she remains acutely aware of her emotional state, performing regular internal scans to ensure her replies stem from her commitment to patient safety rather than personal insecurities or a need for validation.

As the negotiation progresses, a pivotal moment arises that puts Sojka's composure to the test. Mr. Martinez, his voice tinged with skepticism, questions the cost-effectiveness of the new patient safety protocol, suggesting it might be an unnecessary financial burden on the hospital. Feeling a surge of defensiveness, Sojka swiftly recognizes the need to apply the RESET method:

- **Recognize**: She acknowledges the emotional trigger. "Ugh, he's questioning my judgment again," she thinks, feeling a familiar frustration rising.
- **Evaluate**: She evaluates why this comment bothers her. "It's like he doesn't trust my expertise. Does he think I haven't considered the costs?"
- **Step Back**: Sojka takes a moment to mentally step back from the situation, taking a deep breath to distance herself from her immediate emotional reaction.
- **Empathize**: She tries to empathize with Mr. Martinez's perspective, reminding herself, "He's just doing his job, making sure we're using resources wisely. It's not personal."
- **Transform**: Finally, Sojka transforms her initial reaction into a constructive response: "Mr. Martinez, I appreciate your concern about costs. Let's review the data on how this protocol can improve patient outcomes and reduce costs associated with hospital-acquired infections. I believe the evidence will demonstrate that this is a strategic investment in our patients' safety and well-being."

Through her careful internal preparation and deft application of RESET in real-time, Sojka navigates the negotiation with remarkable poise. She successfully avoids letting personal insecurities derail the discussion, instead fostering an atmosphere of openness and collaboration. Her empathy and professionalism demonstrate the administration's appreciation for her well-crafted proposal.

This scenario illustrates the power of self-empowerment strategies in high-stakes healthcare negotiations. Techniques such as internal scans, trigger anticipation, and emotional management prove instrumental in enabling healthcare professionals to navigate complex discussions effectively. By proactively addressing her biases, honing in on her true objectives, and skillfully employing methods like RESET, Sojka successfully championed patient-centric solutions while nurturing collaborative, solution-oriented dynamics.

The results of this negotiation stand in stark contrast to Sojka's previous experiences. Her adept management of emotions and biases allows her to present her case with newfound clarity and conviction, paving the way for a productive discussion about implementing the safety protocol. The administration, visibly impressed by her preparedness and professionalism, agrees to launch a pilot program to test the protocol's effectiveness. This triumph not only marks a significant step forward for patient safety but also serves as a powerful affirmation of Sojka's ability to effect positive change within the hospital, boosting her confidence in her leadership capabilities.

EMOTIONAL INTELLIGENCE ASSESSMENT

The assessment helps healthcare professionals evaluate their ability to recognize, understand, and manage their own emotions and those of others while identifying areas for improvement in self-awareness, empathy, and emotional regulation. This assessment aligns with the self-empowerment strategies discussed in this chapter and can be used as part of an internal scan before engaging in healthcare negotiations.

1. Self-Awareness:
   - How well do I understand my emotions and their potential impact on this negotiation?
   - What are my strengths and limitations in managing my emotions during high-stakes discussions?
   - How can I maintain a clear and focused mindset throughout the negotiation?

2. Self-Regulation:
   - What strategies can I use to manage my emotional responses and maintain composure during challenging moments?
   - How can I adapt my communication style to effectively convey my message and maintain a professional demeanor?
   - What techniques can I use to stay grounded and make well-informed decisions, even in emotionally charged situations?
3. Empathy:
   - How well do I understand and consider other stakeholders' emotions, needs, and perspectives in this negotiation?
   - What steps can I take to actively listen and demonstrate genuine understanding and concern for others' viewpoints?
   - How can I use empathy to build trust, rapport, and a more collaborative negotiation environment?
4. Relationship Management:
   - How can I effectively navigate the interpersonal dynamics and potential conflicts during this negotiation?
   - What strategies can I use to foster open, honest, and respectful communication among all parties?
   - How can I leverage my Emotional Intelligence to build stronger, more productive relationships with my negotiation counterparts?

Healthcare professionals should review their answers and consider what specific steps they can take to leverage their strengths in Emotional Intelligence and address their limitations during negotiations. They should also consider how they can apply the RESET technique (Recognize, Evaluate, Step Back, Empathize, and Transform) in conjunction with their Emotional Intelligence skills to navigate challenging moments during healthcare negotiations.

Conclusion: The Necessity for Empowerment

Empowerment is a transformative force that can reshape healthcare negotiations, fostering a more compassionate, collaborative, and patient-centric approach to care. This chapter explores the power of empowerment in healthcare negotiations, illustrating how self-awareness,

Emotional Intelligence, and strategic action can lead to meaningful change. Healthcare professionals can use introspection to build the courage to challenge their own biases and those around them. Recognizing and addressing biases and assumptions is a critical step in becoming a powerful advocate for change.

The HEAR Approach™, emphasizing self-reflection, active listening, and strategic communication, provides a roadmap for cultivating empowerment in healthcare negotiations. By integrating these principles into daily practice, individuals can navigate complex challenges with greater clarity, empathy, and effectiveness. However, empowerment is not a one-time achievement but an ongoing journey. Continuous learning, self-discovery, and advocacy for systemic change are crucial for maintaining empowerment in the ever-evolving healthcare landscape.

This approach was successful for Dr. Rajesh, a physician administrator who recognized that several external biases would impact an upcoming decision to invest in new diagnostic equipment for the cardiac care unit. Ahead of the committee meeting, he consciously sought perspectives from colleagues across different roles, experience levels, and backgrounds. During the discussions, he listened intently, asked questions to fully understand each viewpoint, and provided data-driven feedback when pushing back on assumptions about technology costs or clinical utility. His empowered stance enabled him to persuade his colleagues to invest in the equipment he sought.

Embracing the lessons of empowerment enables individuals to be agents of positive change in their negotiations and the healthcare system as a whole. While the path may be challenging, the rewards of taking an empowered stance are immeasurable.

REFLECTION EXERCISE: MOVING TOWARD AN EMPOWERED STANCE

Take a moment to consider what internal conflicts or self-doubts might be affecting your negotiation effectiveness. How could addressing these improve your ability to engage in healthcare negotiations?

Next, examine your own biases and assumptions, and consider how they may impact your approach to negotiations. Identify any biases held by others that may have influenced the process or outcome. Then, determine specific steps you can take to challenge and overcome these biases.

- Consider conducting an internal scan before your next negotiation. How might this awareness influence your approach?
- Contemplate using the RESET framework in an upcoming negotiation. How does this structured approach change your perspective on the situation and potential outcomes?

By engaging with these reflective questions, you can deepen your understanding of empowerment and its application in your own healthcare negotiation practice. Remember, the journey to empowerment is ongoing, but every step brings you closer to becoming a more effective, compassionate, and transformative healthcare professional.

Key Takeaways

1. Self-empowerment in healthcare negotiations involves developing acute self-awareness, Emotional Intelligence, and the ability to maintain composure under pressure, enabling clearer thinking and more effective decision-making.
2. Empowered negotiators prioritize shared goals and patient outcomes, fostering trust and collaborative problem-solving across diverse stakeholder groups in complex healthcare settings.
3. Mastering self-empowerment allows healthcare professionals to approach negotiations with poise and presence, creating space for more productive and fulfilling interactions that enhance both patient care and organizational effectiveness.
4. Actively identifying and addressing personal biases is crucial for healthcare negotiators, promoting empathy, openness, and genuine curiosity about diverse perspectives, ultimately leading to more transformative discussions and outcomes.

Notes

1. Nadine Burke Harris, *The Deepest Well: Healing the Long-Term Effects of Childhood Adversity* (New York: Houghton Mifflin Harcourt, 2018), 15–20.
2. Burke Harris, *The Deepest Well*, 30–35.

3. Marc A. Zimmerman, "Psychological Empowerment: Issues and Illustrations," *American Journal of Community Psychology* 23, no. 5 (1995): 581–599.
4. Elizabeth A. Phelps, Karolina M. Lempert, and Peter Sokol-Hessner, "Emotion and Decision Making: Multiple Modulatory Neural Circuits," *Annual Review of Neuroscience* 37 (2014): 263–287.
5. Carl R. Rogers and Richard E. Farson, "Active Listening," in *Communicating in Business Today*, ed. R. G. Newman, M. A. Danziger, and M. Cohen (Lexington, MA: D.C. Heath, 1987), 1–5.
6. Leigh L. Thompson, *The Mind and Heart of the Negotiator*, 2nd ed. (Upper Saddle River, NJ: Prentice Hall, 2001), 176–180.
7. Toby Cosgrove, *The Cleveland Clinic Way: Lessons in Excellence from One of the World's Leading Healthcare Organizations* (New York: McGraw-Hill Education, 2014), 145–150.
8. Jody Hoffer Gittell, *High Performance Healthcare: Using the Power of Relationships to Achieve Quality, Efficiency and Resilience* (New York: McGraw-Hill, 2009), 35–40.
9. Carolyn M. Youssef and Fred Luthans, "An Integrated Model of Psychological Capital in the Workplace," in *Oxford Handbook of Positive Psychology and Work*, eds. P. Alex Linley, Susan Harrington, and Nicola Garcea (New York: Oxford University Press, 2010), 579–588.
10. Daniel Goleman, Richard E. Boyatzis, and Annie McKee, *Primal Leadership: Unleashing the Power of Emotional Intelligence* (Boston, MA: Harvard Business Review Press, 2013), 55–60.
11. Anthony G. Greenwald and Mahzarin R. Banaji, "Implicit Social Cognition: Attitudes, Self-Esteem, and Stereotypes," *Psychological Review* 102, no. 1 (1995): 4–27.
12. John F. Dovidio and Susan T. Fiske, "Under the Radar: How Unexamined Biases in Decision-Making Processes in Clinical Interactions Can Contribute to Health Care Disparities," *American Journal of Public Health* 102, no. 5 (2012): 945–952.
13. Janice A. Sabin, Brian A. Nosek, Anthony G. Greenwald, and Frederick P. Rivara, "Physicians' Implicit and Explicit Attitudes about Race by MD Race, Ethnicity, and Gender," *Journal of Health Care for the Poor and Underserved* 20, no. 3 (2009): 896–913.
14. Katerina Bezrukova, Chester S. Spell, Jamie L. Perry, and Karen A. Jehn, "A Meta-Analytical Integration of over 40 Years of Research on Diversity Training Evaluation," *Psychological Bulletin* 142, no. 11 (2016): 1227–1274.
15. Elizabeth N. Chapman, Anna Kaatz, and Molly Carnes, "Physicians and Implicit Bias: How Doctors May Unwittingly Perpetuate Health Care Disparities," *Journal of General Internal Medicine* 28, no. 11 (2013): 1504–1510.
16. Antoine Bechara, Hanna Damasio, and Antonio R. Damasio, "Emotion, Decision Making and the Orbitofrontal Cortex," *Cerebral Cortex* 10, no. 3 (2000): 295–307.

Chapter 5

Acknowledgment

A Catalyst for Mutual Understanding and Shared Goals

The most basic of all human needs is the need to understand and be understood.

– Ralph Nichols

DOI: 10.4324/9781003336013-6

Derek Reese, an experienced Medicare negotiator, is preparing for a pivotal meeting with Robert Thompson, an executive from the pharmaceutical company that produces Revlimid, a critical but extremely expensive therapy for multiple myeloma patients. Joining them is Lisa Maher, a passionate patient advocate who has witnessed firsthand the devastating financial toll that Revlimid's high costs have taken on families desperate to access this life-saving treatment.

As a sophisticated negotiator, Derek understands the critical importance of creating an environment where all parties feel heard and understood. He recognizes that without this foundation of mutual respect and acknowledgment, even the most logical arguments may fall on deaf ears. Drawing from his years of experience, Derek appreciates that genuine dialogue and sustainable solutions emerge only when each stakeholder feels their perspective is truly valued and considered.

As Derek anticipates the meeting, he recognizes the entrenched perspectives that both Robert and Lisa bring to the table. Robert's firm has invested heavily in Revlimid's development, with research and development costs exceeding $1 billion over the past decade. The company argues that the high prices are necessary to recoup these investments and fund future research into life-saving therapies. There are also concerns about the potential impact on the firm's stock price and investor confidence if Medicare successfully negotiates a significant price reduction.

Derek makes a mental note to acknowledge the company's substantial investment and the risks they've taken in bringing Revlimid to market. He understands that validating these concerns doesn't mean agreeing with them but rather creating a space where Robert feels his perspective is genuinely considered.

On the other side of the table, Lisa brings a perspective shaped by years of advocacy work. She has stood alongside countless families grappling with the brutal reality of Revlimid's price tag, watching as life-saving treatment becomes a source of financial ruin. Many patients have been forced to choose between paying for their medication and covering basic living expenses, with some even resorting to rationing their pills or forgoing treatment altogether. Lisa has seen patients deplete their life savings, take on substantial debt, and face bankruptcy in their efforts to afford this essential medication.

Derek recognizes the deep emotional undercurrents in Lisa's advocacy. He resolves to actively encourage Lisa's narrative, recognizing that these compelling personal accounts are not just anecdotes but vital evidence of the human cost of high drug prices. He also understands that integrating this lived experience into the discussion is essential for crafting a solution that genuinely addresses patient needs and promotes equitable access to life-saving treatments.

Derek knows that these deeply held positions could quickly derail the negotiation into a heated and unproductive debate. However, he grasps that by employing the transformative principles of Acknowledgment – actively listening for underlying motivations, validating diverse perspectives, and addressing emotional undercurrents through empathetic engagement – he has the power to steer the conversation toward a more collaborative and value-driven outcome.

He begins the discussion by thanking both Robert and Lisa for their participation, acknowledging the importance of their unique perspectives on this complex issue. "Before we dive into the numbers," Derek says, "I'd like to hear from each of you about what you hope to achieve today. What are your primary concerns, and what do you see as the ideal outcome of our discussion?"

By opening the conversation with this invitation for shared understanding, Derek sets the tone for a dialogue rooted in mutual respect and acknowledgment. He knows that through active listening, validating concerns, and demonstrating empathy, he can help break down the barriers between these seemingly opposing viewpoints and encourage innovative problem-solving that addresses both the need for continued pharmaceutical innovation and improved patient access to life-saving treatments.

The Power of Acknowledgment: A Catalyst for Collaborative Healthcare Negotiations

Acknowledgment is a powerful catalyst for fostering more collaborative and value-driven healthcare negotiations. It is nothing less than the act of recognizing and validating the thoughts, feelings, and perspectives of others. As defined by conflict resolution expert William Ury, Acknowledgment involves "giving the other side the feeling that they have been heard, respected, and understood."[1] However, Acknowledgment goes beyond merely recognizing stated positions and involves a holistic mindset focused on building mutual understanding and trust among negotiating parties.[2]

The process of Acknowledgment involves healthcare professionals actively listening to understand the underlying motivations, concerns, and emotions that drive each party's position, even if they don't necessarily agree. When providers take the time to truly listen and validate the concerns and perspectives of others, they create a foundation for collaborative problem-solving. Acknowledgment, therefore, plays a crucial role in optimizing healthcare negotiations.

The impact of Acknowledgment on healthcare negotiations cannot be understated. When healthcare professionals feel heard and understood, they're less likely to become defensive or entrenched in their positions. Studies have shown that healthcare executives who employ acknowledgment strategies like appreciation and perspective-taking experience higher levels of stakeholder engagement and organizational buy-in when implementing new initiatives.[3] This is particularly important in healthcare, where the stakes are high and patient care is impacted.

A TRANSFORMATIVE APPROACH: UMASS MEMORIAL HEALTH'S SUCCESS STORY

Eric Dickson, MD, the President of UMass Memorial Health, has made Acknowledgment a cornerstone of his leadership approach. Under Dr. Dickson's Acknowledgment-centered leadership, UMass Memorial Health has experienced notable institutional improvements. UMass Memorial Health was recognized by Forbes as a "Best-in-State Employer," reflecting strong staff engagement and the successful implementation of system-wide initiatives.[4] Dr. Dickson's emphasis on thought diversity and innovative approaches to patient care has contributed to improvements in healthcare delivery at UMass Memorial Health.[5] These improvements demonstrate how an Acknowledgment-focused approach can create a more engaged workforce, improve operational efficiency, and enhance patient care.

Under Dr. Dickson's guidance, the multi-hospital system has undergone a significant cultural shift by prioritizing active listening, validating diverse viewpoints from staff and patients, and engaging in solutions-oriented dialogue that remains grounded in the organization's core mission.[6] As a result, he has created an environment where innovative solutions can flourish and where the organization can adapt more readily to changing healthcare demands. His leadership exemplifies the tangible benefits of incorporating Acknowledgment into healthcare negotiations and decision-making processes.

The UMass Memorial Health experience also highlights the long-term benefits of an Acknowledgment-centered approach. While the immediate improvements in labor relations and patient satisfaction are noteworthy, the cultural shift toward greater collaboration and shared purpose has the potential to drive sustained excellence in healthcare delivery.[7] A study by the Advisory Board Company found that healthcare organizations prioritizing accountability, open communication, and mutual understanding experienced 38% higher rates of successful initiative implementation and 27% improved patient satisfaction metrics.[8]

By fostering a culture of trust, healthcare organizations can break down barriers, encourage innovation, and drive meaningful change that ultimately benefits all stakeholders, from patients and staff to the broader community. The success at UMass Memorial Health serves as a compelling example for other healthcare systems seeking to improve their negotiation processes and organizational culture.

Enhancing Healthcare Outcomes and Patient Satisfaction

Acknowledgment is a transformative tool in healthcare negotiations, and its impact extends far beyond the negotiating table. When healthcare professionals take the time to listen, validate concerns, and demonstrate empathy, they create an environment that fosters trust, collaboration, and ultimately, better patient care.

Research has consistently shown that physicians who excel in empathy, a key component of Acknowledgment, have patients with significantly better clinical outcomes. For instance, diabetic patients of highly empathetic physicians are more likely to have well-controlled hemoglobin A1c levels, a crucial indicator of diabetes management.[9] A systematic review and meta-analysis found that the patient-clinician relationship has a significant effect on healthcare outcomes.[10] Another comprehensive analysis revealed that higher levels of physician empathy were associated with improved patient outcomes, including reduced pain, better quality of life, and increased patient satisfaction.[11]

Empathy and effective communication in healthcare settings have been shown to have significant positive impacts on patient outcomes and satisfaction. A systematic review and meta-analysis published in PLOS ONE found that the patient-clinician relationship has a small but statistically significant effect on healthcare outcomes.[12] This suggests that when patients perceive their healthcare providers as more empathetic and understanding, they are more likely to be satisfied with their care and potentially more adherent to treatment plans.

The benefits of effective communication extend to healthcare teams as well. A study highlighted the importance of clear communication in surgical teams, noting that interruptions and miscommunications can lead to errors.[13] By consistently applying strategies that enhance empathy and communication, healthcare professionals may contribute to a more collaborative and patient-centered healthcare system overall. These findings highlight the profound impact that Acknowledgment can have on tangible health outcomes and institutional culture, underscoring the need for healthcare professionals to master these skills.

Overcoming Common Barriers to Acknowledgment

Acknowledgment techniques have the power to revolutionize healthcare professionals' approach to healthcare negotiations. By fostering empathy, mutual understanding, and a focus on shared goals, these strategies pave the way for more collaborative and patient-centered outcomes.

However, it's essential to consider potential counterarguments and alternative perspectives. Some may argue that Acknowledgment techniques can be time-consuming and challenging to implement in fast-paced, high-pressure healthcare environments. In emergency situations or crises that demand quick decision-making, there may be limited opportunities for extensive dialogue and perspective-taking. Others may question the effectiveness of Acknowledgment strategies when dealing with parties who have deeply entrenched positions or a history of conflict. In long-standing disputes or situations involving power imbalances, such as those between providers and insurance companies, some may view Acknowledgment as an idealistic approach that fails to address underlying systemic issues. Factors such as organizational culture, resource constraints, and regulatory pressures can limit the effectiveness of these strategies in certain contexts.

Despite these potential counterarguments, it's crucial for healthcare providers to recognize the value of Acknowledgment, even in challenging negotiation scenarios. By recognizing the underlying concerns, emotions, and perspectives of all parties, healthcare professionals create a more productive dialogue and lay the foundation for future collaboration. It's important to note that Acknowledgment doesn't necessarily mean agreeing with or capitulating to the other party's position; rather, it's about creating a space for mutual understanding and respect.

While Acknowledgment techniques may require an initial investment of time and effort, they can ultimately lead to more efficient and sustainable outcomes in the long run. By fostering trust, reducing defensive reactions, and promoting creative problem-solving, Acknowledgment helps healthcare providers navigate complex negotiations more effectively.

While the benefits of Acknowledgment are clear, healthcare professionals often face barriers to its implementation in high-stress environments. Here are strategies to overcome common challenges:

Time Constraints

- Practice "micro-acknowledgments" – brief, focused moments of validation.
- Integrate Acknowledgment into existing workflows, such as during handovers or rounds.

Emotional Exhaustion

- Implement self-care practices to maintain emotional reserves.
- Use peer support systems to share the emotional load.

Hierarchical Structures

- Encourage leadership to model Acknowledgment behaviors.
- Implement "psychological safety" initiatives to promote open communication.

Cultural and Language Barriers

- Provide cultural competency training.
- Use professional interpreters and culturally adapted Acknowledgment techniques.

Resistance to Change

- Highlight success stories and positive outcomes from Acknowledgment practices.
- Offer ongoing training and support to reinforce new habits.

By proactively addressing these barriers, healthcare organizations can create an environment where Acknowledgment becomes an integral part of daily practice.

Putting Acknowledgment into Practice: Active Listening as a Catalyst for Mutual Understanding

In healthcare, prioritizing Acknowledgment – truly listening, validating, and empathizing – can transform negotiations and, in turn, transform patient lives. To incorporate Acknowledgment into healthcare negotiations, healthcare professionals should start with active listening. When healthcare providers negotiate a treatment plan with a patient, they should take the time to fully understand the patient's perspectives, fears, and priorities. Acknowledging patients' concerns and demonstrating empathy build trust and create a collaborative environment that facilitates shared decision-making.

The same principles apply when healthcare professionals negotiate with colleagues or administrators. By actively listening to diverse perspectives, acknowledging the challenges faced by different stakeholders, and seeking to find common ground, healthcare providers can achieve more effective and satisfying negotiation outcomes.

Active Listening involves fully engaging with and understanding the speaker through practices like maintaining open body language, rephrasing their points, and asking clarifying questions. When people feel truly heard, they become more open to creative problem-solving. As a result, active listening short-circuits the miscommunication and defensive reactions that often derail negotiations. By creating a space where all parties feel their viewpoints are valued, healthcare providers can facilitate more productive and collaborative discussions, even in challenging negotiation scenarios. By showing regard for diverse perspectives, healthcare professionals can powerfully foster an atmosphere of mutual understanding.

Refining active listening skills elevates healthcare providers' effectiveness by:

1. Strengthening Acknowledgment abilities and enhancing overall negotiation prowess.
2. Reinforcing a patient-centric mindset through greater stakeholder understanding.
3. Improving teamwork and interdisciplinary collaboration by validating diverse expertise.
4. Reducing miscommunication risks that could impact patient safety.
5. Demonstrating Emotional Intelligence to build meaningful patient-provider rapport.

Imagine a physician leading an interdisciplinary team meeting to discuss a complex patient's care plan. Tensions are high as the team tries to align the priorities of nurses, therapists, social workers, and administrative staff. By leveraging active listening strategies, the physician can create an environment where all perspectives are genuinely acknowledged:

Encouraging Non-Verbals: The physician's attentive posture, nodding, and eye contact validate the concerns raised by the nursing staff. "I can see this is a significant issue for your team," the physician might say, leaning forward and maintaining eye contact. "Please, tell me more about your concerns." This open body language prompts them to share more openly.

Reflective Paraphrasing: The lead therapist expresses doubts about the feasibility of the proposed care plan. The physician pauses and rephrases their point, "So, what I'm hearing is that you're concerned about the patient's ability to adhere to this plan, given their current functional status. Is that correct?" This shows the physician understands their perspective before presenting clinical recommendations.

Empathetic Language: The social worker shares their apprehension about the patient's discharge plan. The physician responds with empathy: "I understand your concern. Ensuring a safe and supportive discharge is a top priority for all of us. It's a complex situation, and I appreciate you bringing this to the team's attention." This acknowledgment builds rapport and shows that the physician values their input.

Summarizing Key Points: Throughout the meeting, the physician periodically recaps the dialogue. "Let me summarize what we've discussed so far. The nursing staff has raised concerns about the patient's daily care needs, the therapist has questioned the feasibility of the proposed plan, and the social worker has highlighted potential challenges with the discharge process. Did I capture everything accurately?" This ensures all contributions have been fully heard and integrated before proposing a path forward.

Maintaining Inclusive Flow: If the social worker and therapist's viewpoints seem at odds, the physician might re-center the discussion. "I appreciate both of your perspectives on this issue. While we may have different approaches, I believe we all share the same goal of maximizing the patient's quality of life. Can we explore how we might find a solution that addresses both the social and functional aspects of the patient's care?"

By practicing these active listening techniques, healthcare professionals create an environment where people feel their viewpoints are genuinely understood and valued. This culture of mutual acknowledgment paves the way for more collaborative, productive negotiations and sustainable solutions.

Active Listening thus serves as the cornerstone of Acknowledgment in negotiations. Beyond simply hearing words, active listening reflects fully engaging with the speaker's message, understanding their underlying motivations, and responding in a way that demonstrates genuine comprehension and respect.

Understanding Multiple Selves in Negotiations

As healthcare professionals cultivate their active listening skills, they will find that these skills are closely intertwined with the concept of navigating multiple selves in negotiation. By fully engaging with and seeking to understand their counterparts' perspectives, healthcare providers create an environment where different aspects of identity can emerge and be acknowledged. Active listening lays the foundation for recognizing and adapting to the complex identities and motivations at play in healthcare negotiations.

In healthcare negotiations, recognizing the concept of Multiple Selves is crucial. Stakeholders often present different aspects of themselves depending on the context:

- External Self: The professional role (e.g., a surgeon focusing on clinical outcomes).

- Internal Self: Personal values and motivations (e.g., a nurse's passion for patient care).
- Vulnerable Self: Underlying fears or insecurities (e.g., an administrator's anxiety about being perceived as prioritizing cost savings over patient care during budget discussions).

The External Self represents the most visible, surface-level stance centered around one's professional role and objectives. Healthcare professionals may see a surgeon prioritizing optimal clinical outcomes, an administrator concentrating on budgetary constraints, or a policy analyst fixating on legislative alignments. Cues include heavy reliance on technical jargon, frequent referencing of guidelines/policies, and role-specific priorities taking obvious precedence.

In contrast, *the Internal Self* reflects deeper personal core values, ingrained philosophies, and inherent biases that often underpin someone's interests and motivations. Healthcare providers might see this layer emerge through a clinical pharmacist's impassioned advocacy for medication safety protocols born of a patient-centric philosophy or a healthcare consultant who leans heavily on personal experiences that fundamentally shaped their perspectives on ethical care delivery.

The Vulnerable Self represents the most profound yet well-guarded dimension: the core fears, insecurities, and emotional scars harbored from past experiences that still loom large. Perhaps it's a new nurse manager's prickly defensiveness when their leadership capabilities are questioned or a seasoned paramedic's apprehension toward revising triage protocols, still haunted by the anxieties of a mass casualty event they responded to years ago.

The Multiple Selves concept takes on deeper significance when viewed through the lens of interest-based negotiation principles outlined in seminal works like *Getting to Yes* by Roger Fisher and William Ury. This paradigm encourages moving beyond stated positions ("I want X") to uncover the underlying interests ("I want X because…"), the core motivations and drivers beneath someone's stance. By identifying which "self" is prominent, healthcare professionals can tailor their communication approach.

In any negotiation, healthcare providers may encounter situations where their counterpart's behavior or communication style suddenly shifts. This phenomenon can also be explained by the "Multiple Selves" theory, which suggests that individuals have different aspects of their identity that can be "triggered" and come to the fore in various situations. According to

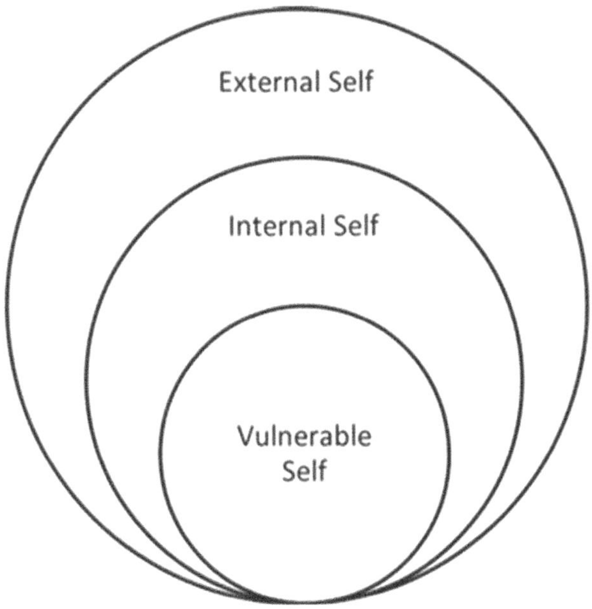

Figure 5.1 Multiple selves in negotiations.

psychologists, different "selves" emerge based on factors such as social roles, emotional states, or environmental cues.[14] For instance, a healthcare professional might exhibit a more authoritative "clinical self" in patient consultations while displaying a more collaborative "team member self" when interacting with colleagues during interdisciplinary meetings.

Healthcare professionals need to navigate diverse selves among their colleagues, patients, and other stakeholders, requiring advanced Emotional Intelligence and adaptability. Recent research in healthcare management and negotiations suggests that Emotional Intelligence and adaptability play crucial roles in effective leadership within healthcare settings. A chapter in *The Academic Medicine Starter Kit: Timeless Tips & Guidance for Early-Career Faculty Members* discusses strategies for effective negotiations in healthcare settings, emphasizing the importance of these skills in achieving successful outcomes.[15] A similar study published in the *Harvard Negotiation Law Review* found that negotiators who acknowledge their counterparts' multiple selves achieve more successful and mutually satisfactory outcomes.[16]

Adapting to these Multiple Selves is crucial for effective negotiation, as miscommunication can carry serious risks to patient safety, outcomes, and organizational effectiveness. Failing to acknowledge these different personas can lead to premature position-taking and missed opportunities for collaborative problem-solving. Conversely, recognizing what's happening and acknowledging the needs of the particular self can lead to positive outcomes, as the following scenario illustrates:

> Dr. Sarah Chi, the CFO of Metro General Hospital, is negotiating a budget allocation with Dr. Mark Scott, the head of the physical therapy department. This annual meeting is crucial for determining resource allocation and setting performance goals for the upcoming fiscal year.
>
> Dr. Scott, a passionate advocate for patient care, initially approached the discussion from a patient-centric perspective. He presents a compelling case for increased funding, highlighting the growing demand for rehabilitation services due to an aging population and the rise in sports-related injuries among younger patients. He emphasizes the potential to improve patient outcomes and reduce hospital readmissions through enhanced rehabilitation programs.
>
> However, the conversation takes a turn when Dr. Chi brings up the department's efficiency metrics, which show a lower patient turnover rate compared to similar-sized hospitals in the region. This shift in focus causes Dr. Scott to become defensive, moving away from his patient-centered approach to a more self-protective stance.
>
> Dr. Scott begins to justify his team's performance, citing the complexity of the cases they handle and the personalized care they provide. He argues that their approach, while potentially slower, leads to better long-term outcomes and higher patient satisfaction scores. His body language becomes more closed off, and his tone grows increasingly tense.
>
> Recognizing this emotional shift, Dr. Chi must navigate the conversation carefully to maintain a productive dialogue. She acknowledges Dr. Scott's dedication to patient care and his team's expertise, validating his perspective before addressing the efficiency concerns. She might say something like, "Mark, I appreciate your team's commitment to providing personalized care. It's clear that patient outcomes are at the forefront of your mind, which is exactly what we want to see."
>
> To steer the conversation back to a collaborative exploration of solutions, Dr. Chi could then propose a joint analysis of the data.

She might suggest, "Let's look at these metrics together and see if we can identify any areas where we can streamline processes without compromising the quality of care. Your insights into the day-to-day operations will be invaluable in this process."

By taking this approach, Dr. Chi accomplishes several things:

1. She diffuses the defensiveness by showing respect for Dr. Scott's expertise and priorities.
2. She reframes the discussion from a confrontational "justification" to a collaborative "problem-solving" exercise.
3. She demonstrates a willingness to understand the nuances of the physical therapy department's operations.
4. She keeps the focus on the shared goal of providing excellent patient care while maintaining financial sustainability.

As the conversation progresses, they might explore various options, such as:

- Implementing new technologies to streamline administrative tasks, freeing up more time for patient care.
- Analyzing patient flow to identify bottlenecks in the rehabilitation process.
- Considering a hybrid model that allows for both intensive, personalized care and more routine, streamlined treatments based on individual patient needs.
- Exploring partnerships with local sports clubs or senior living facilities to create preventive programs that could reduce the strain on the hospital's resources in the long-term.

Throughout this process, Dr. Chi continues to use Emotional Intelligence to gauge Scott reactions and adjust her approach accordingly. She remains open to his ideas and concerns, fostering an atmosphere of mutual respect and shared purpose.

By the end of the meeting, even if they haven't resolved all issues, they have laid the groundwork for ongoing collaboration. They agree to form a joint task force of finance team members and physical therapists to dive more deeply into the data and develop actionable strategies for the coming year.

Identifying Multiple Selves: A Step-by-Step Guide

Recognizing the different selves at play in a negotiation is crucial for effective communication and problem-solving. Healthcare professionals can use this step-by-step guide to identify the multiple selves of their negotiation counterparts:

1. **Observe Verbal and Non-verbal Cues**: Paying attention to a counterpart's language, tone, and body language is essential. Shifts in communication style, such as changes in formality, emotional expression, or focus on specific issues, can provide valuable insights.
2. **Listen for Underlying Interests**: Moving beyond surface-level positions helps uncover the motivations driving a counterpart's behavior. Open-ended questions and active listening techniques can reveal these underlying interests and concerns.
3. **Identify the External Self**: Signs of a counterpart's professional role, responsibilities, and objectives often emerge through their emphasis on authority, expertise, or organizational priorities. Recognizing these cues is key.
4. **Recognize the Internal Self**: Moments when a counterpart expresses personal values, beliefs, or experiences are important to notice. Anecdotes, emotional responses, or references to individual goals often highlight this aspect.
5. **Detect the Vulnerable Self**: Paying close attention to signs of fears, insecurities, or challenges can be crucial. Defensive behaviors, hesitation, or expressions of concern about potential risks often indicate vulnerability.

Navigating Multiple Selves: Strategies for Adaptation

Chris Voss' best seller *Never Split the Difference* has helped mainstream these interest-based approaches by providing accessible strategies for dismantling the "illusion of control" that positional bargaining creates.[17] As Voss emphasizes, true mastery lies in overcoming the unproductive psychological dynamics that defensive posturing inevitably triggers.

Providers can put these insights to work in healthcare negotiations. Once healthcare professionals have identified the different selves at play, they can use these strategies to adapt their negotiation approach:

1. **Tailor Communication**: Adjusting language, tone, and focus ensures alignment with the identified dominant self. Professional jargon and data work well for engaging the External Self, while more personal and empathetic language resonates with the Internal Self.
2. **Validate and Acknowledge**: Demonstrating understanding and respect for each person's perspectives fosters trust. Acknowledgment statements (e.g., "I hear what you're saying…") effectively validate others' experiences.
3. **Reframe the Negotiation**: Helping counterparts shift between selves by reframing the discussion around underlying interests creates clarity. Highlighting how proposed solutions align with professional objectives, personal values, or vulnerabilities facilitates agreement.
4. **Build Trust and Rapport**: Engaging with each self in a genuine and empathetic manner fosters a sense of connection. Sharing personal experiences and vulnerabilities when appropriate can encourage openness and collaboration.
5. **Maintain Flexibility**: Remaining attuned to shifts in a counterpart's dominant self throughout the negotiation is essential. Adapting strategies as these changes occur ensures an effective and responsive approach.

By following this step-by-step guide and implementing these adaptation strategies, providers can more effectively navigate the complex dynamics of multiple selves in healthcare negotiations. This enhanced understanding and flexibility will lead to more productive and mutually beneficial outcomes.

Applying the HEAR Approach™ to Navigate Multiple Selves

The HEAR Approach™ provides a comprehensive framework for recognizing and consciously engaging these multifaceted selves in negotiations. Empowerment strategies equip healthcare providers to clarify and remain anchored in their interests and philosophies rooted in their Internal Self, even amid positional posturing. Acknowledgment then guides healthcare professionals in validating the Internal Selves of others while creating a safe space for Vulnerable Selves to emerge without judgment. Mastering this interplay between examining one's own self while deftly navigating that of their counterparts is the essence of transformative healthcare negotiation.

Grounded in the HEAR Approach's™ transformative principles of Empowerment and Acknowledgment, healthcare professionals can approach every negotiation with a collaborative, patient-centric focus. By embracing these concepts as foundational practices, healthcare providers align themselves with the relational mindset's emphasis on interpersonal connections and shared goals. This elevates healthcare negotiations from mere transactions into meaningful, emotionally intelligent dialogues guided by empathy and respect, ultimately leading to outcomes that provide value for all stakeholders involved.

When navigating the different selves that can emerge during healthcare negotiations, the Healthcare Negotiation Mapping Tool (Chapter 3) and Empathy Mapping (Chapter 2) can be powerful aids for recognizing which self is most prominently displayed and for tailoring the healthcare provider's approach accordingly.

Connecting with the External Self: Healthcare professionals can use data, recent case studies, and expert guidelines to validate their professional realities and role-based priorities. When negotiating with an administrator, they should highlight how their proposal aligns with goals like cost savings and operational efficiencies. For policy negotiations, healthcare providers should clearly link their position to overarching legislative mandates or organizational directives.

Engaging the Internal Self: Healthcare professionals can start by using Empathy Mapping to identify their counterparts' core emotional drivers, personal philosophies, and motivating values regarding patient care. For example, they may explore a nurse's passion for holistic patient experience and staff well-being through reflective questions. With a healthcare consultant, they can relate their perspective to real-world experiences they believe may have shaped the consultant's patient-centric mindset. Healthcare providers can use personal stories and analogies that resonate with their counterparts' underlying motivations to build rapport.

Creating Safety for Vulnerability: Healthcare professionals can use a blend of verbal and non-verbal techniques to signal a judgment-free collaborative zone. They should use open body language, make eye contact, and speak in a calm, reassuring tone. For physicians, they can reframe the discussion to focus on how proposed changes enhance their abilities to provide exceptional care. With residents or newer staff, healthcare providers can offer reassurance that new protocols optimize patient safety and care quality.

The Healthcare Negotiation Mapping Tool also helps anticipate potential self-shifts in counterparts based on their stakeholder group. A physician leading a clinical discussion may start from their External role, focusing on medical evidence. However, when family impact arises, they may pivot to a more emotive, nurturing Internal Self. Similarly, a CFO negotiating budgets will initially embody their external fiscal stewardship role, but mentions of staff/care quality could reveal a Vulnerable Self concerned about institutional reputation and ethics.

To sustain an empathetic cadence, healthcare professionals can use active listening and the Empathy Mapping's "Values/Feelings" quadrant to consistently validate the fluctuating selves as they arise. They should make validation an active process, verbally mirroring the language, tone, and context that aligns with each emerging self. If clashing selves create tensions, healthcare providers can reframe the negotiation's purpose as a united, patient-centered mission. They should ask thoughtful questions that demonstrate curiosity about personal experiences shaping their counterparts' perspectives. By adapting these empathetic acknowledgment techniques as emotional contexts shift, healthcare professionals can facilitate collaborative problem-solving focused on ethical resolutions and optimizing care.

Transformative Mediation Principles: Fostering Collaborative Healthcare Negotiations

The Acknowledgment stage of HEAR aligns closely with the transformative mediation concepts pioneered by Joseph Folger and Robert A. Baruch Bush in their book *The Promise of Mediation: The Transformative Approach to Conflict*.[18] This model emphasizes empowering all parties involved and fostering mutual recognition of differing perspectives, complementing the Relational Mindset and Empowerment approach discussed earlier in Chapters 2 and 4.[19]

Transformative Mediation is a conflict resolution model that empowers each party while cultivating an environment where diverse viewpoints, emotions, and needs can be openly expressed. By proactively acknowledging and validating everyone's unique experiences, Transformative Mediation aims to decrease defensive tendencies, transform relationships, and create collaborative discussions oriented around mutual understanding and constructive change.

This approach dovetails with the Relational Mindset, which encourages healthcare professionals to approach negotiations with an "us" rather than "me" perspective. This means viewing negotiations as opportunities to build productive, long-term relationships that go beyond mere transactions. The transformative principles of Empowerment and Acknowledgment provide a powerful framework for implementing this mindset in practice.

Empowerment, rooted in self-awareness, involves clarifying objectives and cultivating a sense of confidence as healthcare providers enter negotiations. When they have a grounded presence and self-assuredness, healthcare professionals can advocate for their priorities while remaining open to joint problem-solving. Building upon this foundation of Empowerment, acknowledgment expands on this foundation by extending that openness to others, actively seeking to understand and validate their viewpoints, motivations, and contexts. This creates a climate of mutual respect, allowing participants to become less reactive and more solutions-oriented – even if they ultimately disagree.

To illustrate this, imagine a medical director proposing a new quality improvement initiative. By opening the conversation with an Acknowledgment of the various stakeholders' perspectives, such as the IT department's concerns about system integration or the finance team's questions about resource allocation, the medical director sets a tone of respect that fosters an open-minded atmosphere conducive to creative problem-solving. This approach encourages all parties to work collaboratively toward the common goal of enhancing patient care and organizational performance.

By integrating these principles, the HEAR Approach™ provides a practical framework for applying Acknowledgment in healthcare negotiations. This grounding in transformative mediation illustrates how acknowledgment strategies and techniques are founded on a proven, evidence-based approach to conflict resolution.

Connecting the Puzzle Pieces of Acknowledgment Through Appreciative Inquiry

Appreciative Inquiry is a powerful approach that shifts the focus of negotiations from problem-solving to opportunity amplification. It involves identifying and building upon existing strengths, successes, and shared aspirations rather than fixating on problems or constraints.[20] Research in positive psychology demonstrates the benefits of this constructive, opportunity-focused approach for driving more creative solutions. A study by Gervase Bushe, a professor at Simon Fraser University, found that Appreciative Inquiry-based interventions in organizations led to increased collaboration, innovation, and employee engagement.[21] By focusing on strengths and possibilities, Appreciative Inquiry creates a generative space where new ideas and solutions can emerge.

Applying Appreciative Inquiry in Healthcare

Appreciative Inquiry in healthcare negotiations follows a structured "4-D" process centering on Discovering, Dreaming, Designing, and Delivering. In the Discovery phase, negotiators identify what works well in the current system, such as recognizing efficient interdepartmental collaboration in emergency care. The Dream phase involves envisioning potential improvements or expansions, like applying this collaboration model to chronic care management. During the Design phase, participants plan how to achieve these envisioned improvements, such as outlining steps to implement cross-functional teams for diabetes care. Finally, the Deliver phase focuses on implementing the plan and monitoring outcomes, like tracking patient outcomes and staff satisfaction. By following these steps, healthcare professionals can shift negotiations from problem-solving to opportunity creation, fostering a more positive and collaborative environment.

A deeper dive into Appreciative Inquiry reveals key steps involved in implementing the 4-D approach:

1. **Identifying Strengths and Successes**: Before entering a negotiation, healthcare providers should take time to reflect on instances when the team or organization demonstrated resilience, creativity, or flexibility in delivering optimal patient care or achieving operational goals. For example, they might highlight how the staff efficiently handled a surge in patient volume during a crisis or how a cross-functional team successfully implemented a new care protocol. They might verbalize the strengths using language like the following: "Let's start by acknowledging the incredible work our team did during the recent flu outbreak. Despite the high patient volume, everyone came together to ensure that our patients received the best possible care. The collaboration between nursing, physicians, and support staff was truly remarkable. We can build on that spirit of teamwork as we discuss how to improve our surge capacity plan."
2. **Validate Personal and Professional Motivations**: Healthcare professionals should recognize and appreciate each party's perspectives,

investments, and professional pride. They should seek to understand their underlying motivations and values and find ways to align them with the overall goals of the negotiation. Administrators could acknowledge and give voice to these sentiments by saying things like, "As physicians, your top priority is providing the best care for your patients. We understand that you have concerns about how this new electronic health record system might impact your workflow. Let's explore how we can leverage this technology to enhance patient care while ensuring that it supports your clinical practice."

3. **Engage in Future-Focused Visioning**: Rather than dwelling on past problems or current constraints, healthcare providers should shift the conversation toward envisioning a desired future state. They should encourage participants to imagine what success would look like and what steps they can take to achieve it. When addressing a team, they might say: "Let's imagine it's a year from now, and our community health outreach program has exceeded all expectations. What would that look like? What kind of impact would we be having on the lives of our patients and the broader community? We can work backward from that vision and identify the resources and partnerships we need to make it a reality."
4. **Highlight Role-Specific Contributions**: Healthcare professionals should acknowledge and celebrate how each party's unique expertise and contributions have led to past successes. They should emphasize the importance of ongoing involvement in co-creating solutions and achieving shared goals. It's important to specifically call out the roles different individuals and groups can play in the implementation of the new approach: "The physical therapy department has played a critical role in improving patient outcomes and reducing readmission rates. Their innovative approach to rehabilitation has set a new standard of care. As we discuss expanding our services, we want to ensure that we're leveraging their expertise and insights throughout the planning process."

In healthcare negotiations, Appreciative Inquiry provides a pathway for transforming potentially negative dynamics into future-focused, cooperative discussions united around the shared mission of delivering exceptional patient care. For example, when negotiating a staffing plan with a hospital's finance department, healthcare providers can use Appreciative Inquiry to focus on past successes and highlight the positive impact of adequate staffing on patient outcomes and staff morale. This approach shifts the conversation from a purely financial perspective to one that acknowledges the value of investing in human resources.

Healthcare professionals can also use Appreciative Inquiry to encourage participants to explore what's currently working well to help envision a desired future and co-create solutions that leverage their collective potential. For example, when Summa Health, a nonprofit health system in Ohio, used Appreciative Inquiry to engage stakeholders in strategic planning, they were able to identify innovative opportunities for growth and improvement stemming from current practices. By appreciating their strengths and envisioning a desired future instead of focusing on problems, Summa Health developed a comprehensive plan that ultimately enhanced patient care, improved operational efficiency, and strengthened community partnerships.

By consistently applying these Appreciative Inquiry strategies, healthcare professionals can create a more positive, collaborative, and solutions-oriented environment in their healthcare negotiations. Mastering the appreciative mindset takes practice, but the benefits – increased trust, creativity, and shared commitment to patient care – are well worth the effort.

ACKNOWLEDGMENT: NEGOTIATIING A COMMUNITY HEALTH OUTREACH PROGRAM

The impact of Acknowledgment and the effectiveness of the various strategies noted above were clearly demonstrated in a negotiation over implementing a new community health outreach program focused on mental health and substance abuse prevention. Alicia Thompson, a social worker at Riverside Community Health Center, arranged a meeting with Executive Director Michael Davis to discuss the initiative.

As the meeting began, Alicia noticed Michael's preoccupied demeanor, likely due to concerns about the program's financial implications. Demonstrating her skill in acknowledging multiple selves, Alicia opened the conversation by recognizing Michael's dedication to the center and the community, while also creating space for him to share his deeper concerns. She said, "Michael, I appreciate you taking the time to discuss this new outreach program. I know how dedicated you are to ensuring our center provides the best possible care to our community, and I can see that you have a lot on your mind."

Alicia's statement demonstrated her skill in acknowledging multiple selves. She recognized Michael's External Self by acknowledging his professional role and dedication to the center. By noting that he had "a lot on your mind," Alicia created an opportunity for Michael to reveal his Internal Self or potentially his Vulnerable Self, establishing a safe space for him to share deeper concerns or motivations. This approach allowed Alicia to potentially access his underlying beliefs and values about healthcare or any worries or insecurities he might have about the new program. By using this subtle yet effective acknowledgment, Alicia created the foundation for a more open and productive discussion, where Michael could feel comfortable sharing his true thoughts and concerns about the outreach program.

By skillfully navigating Michael's Multiple Selves and creating a safe space for dialogue, Alicia guided the conversation toward a balanced discussion that weighed the program's potential benefits against practical resource considerations. This approach successfully encouraged Michael to open up about his mixed feelings. He responded, "You're right, Alicia. I believe in the importance of this program, but I'm also concerned about how we'll manage the additional resources it will require."

Employing active listening techniques, Alicia reflected Michael's statement and encouraged further elaboration: "It sounds like you value the impact this program could have on our community's mental health and well-being, but you also have valid concerns about the financial implications. Can you share more about what aspects of the program resonate with you the most, and what specific resource concerns you have?"

Michael expanded on his thoughts, expressing excitement about reaching underserved populations and breaking down barriers to mental health services, while also voicing concerns about staff allocation and funding without straining existing services.

Alicia validated Michael's perspectives, acknowledging his commitment to the program's mission, strengthening the rapport between them. She also acknowledged Michael's vulnerability regarding resource concerns, creating an atmosphere of trust and openness that allowed her to steer the conversation toward problem-solving: "Thank you for sharing those insights. It's clear that you're committed to both the program's mission and the center's overall sustainability. Let's explore how we can address those concerns while still moving forward with this important initiative."

Alicia then demonstrated the appreciative inquiry approach by shifting the conversation to focus on strengths and opportunities, encouraging a more positive and solution-oriented mindset. She reminded Michael of their successful collaboration with the local school district on flu vaccinations, asking, "What lessons can we draw from that experience to help us make this outreach program a success?" This prompted Michael to reflect on their team's creativity and ability to form strong community partnerships, highlighting how these strengths could be applied to the new program. By identifying past successes, Alicia highlighted the team's creativity and ability to form effective community partnerships, guiding the conversation toward a more positive and solution-oriented direction and setting the stage for future-focused visioning. She also encouraged Michael to consider how these strengths could be applied to the new outreach program, fostering a sense of possibility and shared purpose.

Alicia's final technique was also her ultimate goal: developing a collaborative plan. Building on the positive momentum created by Acknowledgment, Alicia suggested brainstorming potential funding sources and partnerships to support the program. She proposed reaching out to local foundations, businesses, and other community organizations to explore collaboration opportunities. Michael responded enthusiastically, adding the idea of looking into grants and state or federal funds for mental health initiatives. Together, they began to develop a plan to leverage their combined expertise and networks to identify opportunities for support and create a timeline for implementation. Alicia concluded by expressing confidence in their ability to make the program a reality by working together and building on their strengths. Throughout the process, Alicia maintained a focus on the shared goal of improving community mental health and well-being, ensuring that the negotiation remained grounded in the center's core mission and values.

Conclusion: The Value of Acknowledgment

A fundamental insight of this chapter is how mastering the art of Acknowledgment can profoundly enhance negotiation effectiveness in the healthcare field. This approach requires an understanding of Active Listening, Multiple Selves Theory, Transformative Mediation Principles, and

Appreciative Inquiry. The integration of these concepts serves as a valuable tool for navigating the complexities of healthcare discussions with greater skill and empathy. By methodically applying these techniques, healthcare professionals can bridge gaps, foster true collaboration, and create an environment conducive to outcomes that benefit all parties involved, including patients.

As you progress through the practice of Acknowledgment and deepen your grasp of cross-disciplinary dynamics, your ability to navigate complex healthcare negotiations will increase. By offering Healthcare-Specific Acknowledgment strategies, this approach embraces a new mindset focused on empathy over indifference, understanding over assumption, and uniting diverse perspectives in the service of optimal patient care and organizational effectiveness.

Implementing this approach requires continuous refinement, but the potential benefits are far-reaching: enhanced patient experiences, improved communication between healthcare providers and administrators, fortified interprofessional partnerships, and a revitalized healthcare system equipped to address evolving challenges. By integrating Acknowledgment principles with Empowerment and a Relational Mindset as articulated in the HEAR Approach™, healthcare professionals can drive transformative change, fostering a more responsive, collaborative, and patient-centered healthcare environment. This not only enhances their negotiation skills but also aligns with the fundamental goal of healthcare: providing the best possible care for patients while navigating the complex landscape of modern healthcare delivery.

REFLECTION EXERCISE: APPLYING ACTIVE LISTENING AND MULTIPLE SELVES IN HEALTHCARE NEGOTIATIONS

Reflect on a recent healthcare negotiation you participated in or observed. Take 15 minutes to create a visual map of the various "selves" presented by the different stakeholders during the negotiation.

Now identify one specific active listening technique or acknowledgment strategy from this chapter that you could apply to enhance your approach in future negotiations. How might it change the dynamics and outcomes?

Finally, consider how applying the Multiple Selves framework might change your perspective:

- How could recognizing the External, Internal, and Vulnerability Selves of other stakeholders improve your understanding of their positions?
- In what ways could you use Appreciative Inquiry to reframe challenges as opportunities for collaboration?
- How might acknowledging and addressing the different "selves" lead to more innovative and mutually beneficial solutions?

This structured reflection will help you integrate these concepts into your negotiation practice, enhancing your ability to navigate the complex landscape of healthcare discussions with greater empathy and effectiveness.

Key Takeaways

1. Active Listening serves as a cornerstone of effective healthcare negotiations, enabling professionals to build trust, gain deeper insights, and create an environment where all stakeholders feel valued and understood, ultimately leading to more productive outcomes.
2. Understanding and addressing the External, Internal, and Vulnerable Selves of negotiation counterparts allow healthcare professionals to tailor their communication strategies, fostering stronger connections and more effectively addressing underlying concerns across various healthcare scenarios.
3. Incorporating Appreciative Inquiry techniques into healthcare negotiations shifts discussions from problem-centric to strength-based approaches, encouraging innovative thinking and collaborative problem-solving that can lead to improved patient care and organizational effectiveness.
4. While implementing Acknowledgment strategies in healthcare settings can be challenging due to time constraints and systemic issues, consistent application of these techniques can transform potentially adversarial situations into collaborative dialogues, enhancing negotiation outcomes and overall healthcare delivery.

Notes

1. William Ury, *Getting Past No: Negotiating in Difficult Situations* (New York: Bantam Books, 1991), 37.
2. Roger Fisher and William Ury, *Getting to Yes: Negotiating Agreement without Giving In* (New York: Penguin Books, 2011), 33–34.
3. Amy C. Edmondson, *The Fearless Organization: Creating Psychological Safety in the Workplace for Learning, Innovation, and Growth* (Hoboken, NJ: John Wiley & Sons, 2018), 156–158.
4. UMass Memorial Health, "UMass Memorial Health Recognized as a 'Best-in-State Employer' by Forbes," accessed September 28, 2024, https://www.ummhealth.org/umass-memorial-health/news/umass-memorial-health-recognized-best-state-employer-forbes.
5. Eric W. Dickson, Ziad Obermeyer, and Anupam B. Jena, "The Value of Thought Diversity in Medicine," *Harvard Business Review*, April 17, 2019, https://hbr.org/2019/04/the-value-of-thought-diversity-in-medicine.
6. Edgar H. Schein and Peter A. Schein, *Organizational Culture and Leadership* (Hoboken, NJ: John Wiley & Sons, 2016), 301–303.
7. John P. Kotter, *Leading Change* (Boston, MA: Harvard Business Review Press, 2012), 153–155.
8. Advisory Board Company, "The Impact of Organizational Culture on Hospital Performance," Research Brief, Washington, DC, 2019, https://www.advisory.com/research/health-care-advisory-board/studies/2019/the-impact-of-organizational-culture-on-hospital-performance.
9. Mohammadreza Hojat et al., "Physician Empathy and Diabetes Outcomes," *American Journal of Managed Care* 24, no. 10 (2018): 455–461.
10. John M. Kelley, Gordon Kraft-Todd, Lidia Schapira, Joe Kossowsky, and Helen Riess, "The Influence of the Patient-Clinician Relationship on Healthcare Outcomes: A Systematic Review and Meta-Analysis of Randomized Controlled Trials," *PLOS ONE* 9, no. 4 (2014): e94207, https://doi.org/10.1371/journal.pone.0094207.
11. Jeremy Howick, Charlene Bizzari, and Harald Duttke, "Empathic Healthcare: A Systematic Review and Meta-Analysis of the Association between Physician Empathy and Patient Outcomes," *Journal of the Royal Society of Medicine* 115, no. 10 (2022): 391–402, https://doi.org/10.1177/01410768221124403.
12. Kelley et al., "The Influence of the Patient-Clinician Relationship on Healthcare Outcomes."
13. Brigid M. Gillespie, Wendy Chaboyer, and Nicole Fairweather, "Interruptions and Miscommunications in Surgery: An Observational Study," *AORN Journal* 95, no. 5 (2012): 576–590.
14. Constantine Sedikides and Marilynn B. Brewer, eds., *Individual Self, Relational Self, Collective Self* (New York: Psychology Press, 2001), 1–4.
15. Stacey B. Lee, "Healthcare Negotiations for Faculty," in *The Academic Medicine Starter Kit: Timeless Tips & Guidance for Early-Career Faculty Members*, ed. K. A. Skarupski (Self-published, 2024).

16. Daniel L. Shapiro, "Identity Is More than Meets the 'I': The Power of Identity in Shaping Negotiation Behavior," *Marquette Law Review* 87 (2004), 809–816.
17. Chris Voss and Tahl Raz, *Never Split the Difference: Negotiating as If Your Life Depended on It* (New York: HarperBusiness, 2016), 15–17.
18. Robert A. Baruch Bush and Joseph P. Folger, *The Promise of Mediation: The Transformative Approach to Conflict*, rev. ed. (San Francisco, CA: Jossey-Bass, 2004), 41–44.
19. Bush and Folger, *The Promise of Mediation*, 75–77.
20. David L. Cooperrider and Diana Whitney, *Appreciative Inquiry: A Positive Revolution in Change* (San Francisco, CA: Berrett-Koehler Publishers, 2005), 8–10.
21. Gervase R. Bushe, "Appreciative Inquiry: Theory and Critique," in *The Routledge Companion to Organizational Change*, ed. David Boje, Bernard Burnes, and John Hassard (Oxford: Routledge, 2012), 87–103.

Chapter 6

Recasting

Navigating New Realities Together

Coming together is a beginning; keeping together is progress; working together is success.

– Henry Ford

DOI: 10.4324/9781003336013-7

Dr. Liam Novak took a deep, steadying breath as he entered the conference room at HealthTech Innovations.[1] Today's meeting had heavy implications for their flagship project – an Artificial Intelligence (AI) system designed to revolutionize early cancer detection. As Novak's eyes swept across the gathered stakeholders, he could feel the weight of their diverse perspectives. The brows of data scientists like Amir furrowed over concerns about the quality of clinical datasets. The clinical research team, led by Dr. Emily Larsson, was determined to maintain rigorous standards despite logistical challenges. And the business executives, epitomized by Vice President Lena Chait, lasered in on go-to-market pressures from investors and potential clients.

As the meeting kicked off, tensions quickly surfaced. "We can't build an accurate AI model without clean, comprehensive data," Amir argued. "The datasets we've received so far are fragmented and inconsistent." Dr. Larsson countered: "Collecting pristine data takes time. We're working with over 50 hospitals, each with their own protocols and systems. We're doing our best to standardize the data collection process." Meanwhile, the business development team grew impatient. "We need to move faster," urged Chait. "We have investors and potential clients waiting for a prototype. If we don't show progress soon, we risk losing their interest and funding."

Dr. Novak could see the frustration and conflicting priorities in the room. He knew that the project's success depended on finding a way to bridge these divides. "Let's take a step back," he said. "We all joined this company because we believe in the potential of AI to transform healthcare. Our goal is not just to build a product, but to create something that will genuinely help doctors detect cancer earlier and save lives."

He turned to Amir and Dr. Larsson. "I hear your concerns about data quality. What if we collaborate with a few key hospitals to pilot a standardized data collection protocol? We can use that experience to refine our processes and demonstrate the value of our approach to other partners." Dr. Novak then addressed Lena and the business development team. "I understand the pressure to show progress to our investors. What if we reframe our milestones to focus on the pilot phase? We can showcase our collaborative approach and the potential impact of our work, even if we don't have a full-scale prototype yet."

As the meeting progressed, the atmosphere shifted from one of tension to one of collaboration. The team began to see how their individual priorities could be aligned toward a common purpose. They started brainstorming ideas for the pilot study, discussing ways to streamline data collection, and exploring creative strategies to communicate their progress to stakeholders.

"What if we involve some of our potential clients in the pilot study?" suggested one of the software engineers. "It could give them early buy-in and valuable insights into the development process."

"And we could use the pilot to refine our AI algorithms incrementally," Amir added, his earlier frustration replaced by enthusiasm. "It would allow us to demonstrate progress while continually improving our model's accuracy."

Dr. Novak smiled, sensing the transformation in the room. By Recasting the challenge from conflicting individual priorities to a shared mission, they had begun the process of unlocking a wellspring of creativity and cooperation. The team was no longer working against each other but with each other toward a common goal.

As they delved into the details of the pilot study, discussing data collection strategies and communication plans, Dr. Novak reflected on the power of reframing. By shifting the conversation from an adversarial "my priorities versus yours" to a collaborative "our shared vision," they had not only found a way forward but had strengthened their team. However, he recognized that this was just the beginning of an iterative process. Each new idea or concern would likely require revisiting their shared goals, acknowledging new perspectives, and sometimes even stepping back to re-empathize with stakeholders. Dr. Novak knew that they would need to continually apply and refine this approach as they navigated the complex landscape of AI development in healthcare.

Introduction to Recasting: A Collaborative Path Forward

The HealthTech scenario illustrates the transformative potential of Recasting, the culminating stage of the HEAR Framework. Building upon the foundations of Empowerment and Acknowledgment, Recasting involves reframing the negotiation to focus on shared interests and collaborative problem-solving. It shifts mindsets from an adversarial, "me"-based approach to a cooperative, "us"-based one.

Recasting has its roots in the principles of interest-based negotiation as described in the seminal work *Getting to Yes* by Roger Fisher and William Ury.[2] They argue that focusing on interests rather than positions can unlock new possibilities for mutually beneficial outcomes. In recent years, thought leaders like Deepak Malhotra have expanded on this approach, emphasizing creative problem-solving techniques that keep possibilities open through an appreciative, opportunity-minded outlook.[3]

What is meant by an interest-based approach that keeps possibilities open? An all-too-common scenario in healthcare is a patient with a chronic condition being continually admitted to the hospital over a short span of time. Her physician believes a more aggressive treatment plan is necessary to manage the patient's symptoms and prevent future hospitalizations. However, the patient resists, expressing concerns about the potential side effects and its impact on her daily life.

In a traditional negotiation, this situation could quickly devolve into a battle of wills, with the physician insisting on their recommended course of action and the patient refusing to comply. However, with Recasting, the physician can take a step back and seek to understand the patient's underlying interests. Through empathetic questioning, he learns that the patient worries about the treatment's impact on her ability to care for her young children and maintain her job. The patient also fears the long-term implications of the more aggressive approach.

Armed with this understanding, the physician can reframe the conversation, acknowledging the patient's concerns and validating her desire to maintain her quality of life. Instead of forcefully recommending a course of action, the physician adopts a collaborative approach to develop a treatment plan that balances the need for symptom management with the patient's personal and professional obligations. Together, they consider the patient's support system, work environment, and personal preferences, ultimately creating a customized treatment plan that incorporates lifestyle modifications, targeted therapies, and a schedule that minimizes disruptions to the patient's daily routine.

This example demonstrates the power of Recasting in driving patient-centered care. By reframing the conversation around shared interests and engaging in collaborative problem-solving, the physician transforms a potentially adversarial situation into a productive partnership. The patient feels heard, respected, and empowered, leading to increased trust and buy-in. The resulting treatment plan is not only medically sound but also tailored to the patient's unique needs and circumstances, increasing the likelihood of adherence and improved outcomes.

The Importance of Recasting in Healthcare Negotiation

While the principles of Recasting are universally applicable, they are particularly significant within the intricate healthcare landscape, where their impact is felt across the three pillars of healthcare: Practice of Medicine (Operating Room), Delivery of Care (Exam Room), and Business of Health (Boardroom).

The complexity of aligning diverse stakeholders – patients, providers, administrators, and others – behind the shared mission of optimal care delivery can often lead to adversarial positioning. However, Recasting allows healthcare professionals to navigate these complex dynamics by reframing conflicts as opportunities to uncover innovative, mutually beneficial solutions centered on shared priorities. This approach proves valuable whether healthcare providers are negotiating to implement a new electronic health record system, resolving interprofessional collaboration challenges, or aligning organizational strategies with frontline realities.

Recasting serves as a crucial tool for healthcare professionals, enabling them to navigate the intricate dynamics and conflicting priorities inherent in medical negotiations. This approach proves invaluable across various healthcare scenarios:

1. **Development and Fundraising**: When a potential donor is passionate about cardiac care but a hospital's most pressing need is updating the pediatric ward, Recasting can help healthcare professionals frame the pediatric improvements in terms of overall hospital excellence, potentially benefiting cardiac patients as well.
2. **Community Health Initiatives**: In cases where local communities are resistant to new health programs, Recasting can help frame these initiatives in ways that preserve cultural values while improving health outcomes.
3. **Pharmaceutical Negotiations**: When discussing drug pricing with government agencies, pharmaceutical companies can use Recasting to shift the conversation from cost alone to a broader discussion of value, including factors like improved patient outcomes and reduced long-term healthcare expenses.

Whether healthcare professionals are development officers seeking to align donor interests with hospital needs, community health workers bridging cultural gaps in local health initiatives, or pharmaceutical company representatives negotiating drug pricing with government agencies, Recasting helps them find common ground. By fostering a collaborative mindset and aligning efforts toward shared objectives, healthcare professionals can drive meaningful change, overcome obstacles, and deliver better outcomes for their patients and organizations.

Recasting Defined: Transforming Healthcare Negotiations

Recasting is the practice of reframing a negotiation by shifting the focus from competing "External Selves" to a collaborative exploration of underlying "Internal Selves" and shared goals. Instead of adopting a "my way or the highway" mentality, Recasting fosters an open mindset where creative problem-solving can flourish.

This transformative shift is embodied in Recasting's core principles:

1. **Uncovering Internal Selves, Not Just External Selves**: External Selves represent the surface-level demands each party asserts ("I want X"), while Internal Selves represent the deeper motivations behind those stances ("I want X because..."). Consider a physical therapist negotiating for new equipment in their rehabilitation center. Their External Self might focus on acquiring the latest, most advanced machines. However, their Internal Self is driven by providing the best possible care to patients while optimizing treatment outcomes. By focusing on Internal Selves rather than External Selves, healthcare professionals open the door to innovative solutions that satisfy everyone's needs.
2. **Redefining Problems to Expand Solutions**: Assumptions about a problem's "nature" can limit the ability to find creative solutions. Take a healthcare IT specialist tasked with implementing a new patient data management system. If they view the problem solely through a technical lens, they may overlook the importance of engaging end-users to ensure the system meets their needs. Recasting encourages a holistic approach to problem definition, broadening the range of potential solutions.
3. **Emphasizing Shared Objectives**: In healthcare's interconnected ecosystem, all stakeholders ultimately share the same overarching goals: providing exceptional patient care and optimizing system-wide performance. Recasting shifts the focus from individual stances to these unifying objectives. Imagine a pharmacist and a physician debating the merits of a new medication. By reminding them of their shared purpose – ensuring the best possible patient outcomes – healthcare professionals can redirect their energy toward collaborative problem-solving.

4. **Cultivating an Appreciative Mindset**: Scarcity thinking, rooted in perceived limitations, stifles creativity. Recasting counters this by promoting an appreciative, opportunity-oriented outlook. When a healthcare administrator expresses frustration with budgetary constraints, an empowered Recasting mindset identifies this as an opportunity to brainstorm innovative, cost-effective solutions rather than accepting the status quo.

As healthcare professionals build mutual understanding and reduce defensive posturing, they unlock the transformative potential of Recasting. By letting go of their External Selves, they become more receptive to expressing underlying Internal Selves and motivations. A genuine dialogue emerges as they explore each other's perspectives in a non-adversarial manner. This mutual understanding unleashes the transformative power of Recasting. Bolstered by this mutual understanding, healthcare professionals reframe the entire negotiation through a new collaborative lens. Priorities realign, rigidity fades, and innovative, mutually beneficial solutions come into focus.

FROM RESISTANCE TO COLLABORATION: RECASTING IN ACTION

The following scenario demonstrates how the four core principles of Recasting can transform a negotiation in a healthcare setting, moving parties from potential conflict to collaborative problem-solving. A physical therapist is advocating for a new patient education program, believing it will empower patients to take a more active role in their recovery and lead to better outcomes and reduced readmission rates, but faces resistance from the operations manager.

Physical Therapist: "I understand your concerns about the time and resources needed for this patient education program. Can you tell me more about what worries you?" – Initiating the process of uncovering Internal Selves.

Operations Manager: "We're already stretched thin. I don't see how we can add another program without compromising our current services" – Expressing External Self's concerns, hinting at scarcity thinking.

Physical Therapist: "I appreciate your candor. It sounds like you're deeply committed to maintaining the quality of our current services. That's something we both care about deeply" – Acknowledging concerns while hinting at shared Internal Selves.

Operations Manager: "Absolutely. Our patients rely on us, and I can't justify anything that might jeopardize the care we provide" – Revealing Internal Self's commitment to patient care.

Physical Therapist: "I share that commitment. What if we look at this differently? Instead of adding a new program, could we explore how patient education might enhance our existing services?" – Redefining the problem to expand solutions.

Operations Manager: "I'm listening. How do you envision this working?" – Showing openness to new perspectives.

Physical Therapist: "By educating patients about managing their condition, we could potentially reduce the number of sessions some patients need, freeing up time for others. This aligns with our shared goal of serving our patients effectively and efficiently" – Emphasizing shared objectives.

Operations Manager: "That's interesting. I hadn't considered that education could actually save us time in the long run. But how do we handle the initial investment?" – Demonstrating a shift toward problem-solving.

Physical Therapist: "Great question. What if we start with a small pilot program? We could integrate education into existing sessions for a select group of patients and gather data on outcomes without significantly disrupting current operations" – Cultivating an appreciative mindset by focusing on possibilities.

This scenario illustrates the four core principles of Recasting in action:

1. **Uncovering Internal Selves**: The physical therapist probes beyond the operations manager's initial resistance to reveal their shared commitment to patient care.
2. **Redefining Problems to Expand Solutions**: By reframing the education program as an enhancement to existing services rather than an additional burden, new possibilities emerge.
3. **Emphasizing Shared Objectives**: Throughout the conversation, the focus remains on their mutual goal of providing effective and efficient patient care.
4. **Cultivating an Appreciative Mindset**: The physical therapist consistently looks for opportunities within constraints, shifting the conversation from limitations to possibilities.

The Science Behind Recasting: From Acknowledgment to Creative Problem-Solving

Research supports the effectiveness of Recasting in negotiations and problem-solving scenarios. While Acknowledgment (as discussed in Chapter 5) establishes the groundwork by lowering defensiveness through empathetic listening, Recasting takes this a step further by actively reframing the conversation.

Studies show that the open-minded state created by empathetic Acknowledgment enhances creative cognitive processing.[4] This heightened creativity is crucial for the success of Recasting techniques. Harvard negotiation expert Kathleen Valley explains that this receptive mental state allows parties to transcend their hardened External Selves and discover previously overlooked areas of shared Internal Selves.[5]

Here's how Recasting distinguishes itself from simple Acknowledgment:

1. **Active Reframing**: While Acknowledgment creates a safe space for open dialogue, Recasting actively reshapes the conversation's direction.
2. **Solution-Oriented**: Recasting moves beyond understanding to actively seek new perspectives and solutions.
3. **Shared Objectives Focus**: Recasting emphasizes finding and building upon shared goals, whereas Acknowledgment primarily focuses on individual experiences and emotions.
4. **Creative Problem-Solving**: The open mind state achieved through Acknowledgment becomes a launching pad for the creative problem-solving inherent in Recasting.

By building on Acknowledgment's foundation, Recasting leverages the lowered defenses and increased empathy to drive toward innovative, mutually beneficial solutions.

The Recasting process is often non-linear, requiring flexibility from healthcare professionals. When challenges arise or emotions intensify, revisiting earlier stages of the HEAR Approach™ may be necessary to maintain a Relational Mindset and keep negotiations on track. For instance, professionals might employ the RESET protocol (Chapter 4) when faced with negativity, or revisit Empowerment practices (Chapter 4) if they feel off-balance. Should their counterpart's Vulnerability Self surface, a return to Acknowledgment (Chapter 5) becomes crucial to re-establish a sense of safety. This adaptability ensures the continued progress of the negotiation, even in the face of unexpected hurdles.

Ultimately, healthcare professionals will sense that the Recasting phase has arrived when both parties begin to:

- Reframe the negotiation's purpose toward shared goals and values rather than individual External Self demands.
- Explore options collaboratively with a shared commitment to finding creative, ethical solutions.
- Display openness to adjusting initial objectives in the service of optimizing outcomes for all stakeholders.

Recasting transforms potential conflicts into collaborative partnerships in healthcare settings. By emphasizing active listening and openness, this process shifts dialogues from confrontational to cooperative, fostering an environment ripe for innovation. Healthcare professionals leveraging Recasting can unlock "aha" moments, leading to forward-thinking solutions that benefit all stakeholders. This approach not only resolves immediate issues but also lays the groundwork for sustained, positive relationships among diverse healthcare actors, ultimately enhancing patient care and systemic efficiency.

Tools for Successful Recasting

Healthcare professionals can use a variety of tools to successfully carry out Recasting. By employing these techniques, providers can transform their approach to complex healthcare issues, moving beyond surface-level solutions to address root causes and create more sustainable, patient-centered outcomes. These tools help reframe problems in ways that reveal new insights, uncover hidden opportunities, and foster collaborative solutions across diverse stakeholder groups.

The *360-Degree Stakeholder Analysis* is a powerful tool for Recasting complex healthcare issues by broadening the perspective beyond immediate stakeholders. To use this tool, healthcare professionals start by listing all parties potentially affected by or involved in the issue at hand, including patients, families, healthcare providers, administrators, insurance companies, community organizations, and even policymakers. For each stakeholder, they identify specific needs, concerns, and potential contributions related to the problem.

By systematically exploring the viewpoints of all stakeholders, this analysis often reveals hidden interconnections and opportunities for collaborative solutions. For example, when addressing the challenge of reducing hospital readmissions, a 360-Degree Stakeholder Analysis might uncover that local community organizations have resources and programs that could support patients post-discharge, leading to a Recasting of the problem from a purely clinical issue to a community-wide health initiative. This broader perspective can inspire innovative partnerships and interventions that address root causes and create more sustainable solutions.

Another tool providers can turn to for challenging assumptions and exploring alternative perspectives on healthcare issues is the *Problem Reframing Matrix*. To use this matrix, healthcare professionals start by clearly stating the current problem frame in the top-left quadrant. They then fill in the remaining quadrants by considering the opposite frame (what if we shifted our focus to the opposite perspective?), a broader frame (how does this fit into a larger context?), and a narrower frame (what's the core issue here?).

This exercise often leads to surprising insights and novel approaches to long-standing challenges. For instance, when addressing the issue of medication non-adherence, the matrix might prompt a reframing from "How do we get patients to take their medications as prescribed?" (current frame) to "How might we design treatment plans that fit seamlessly into patients' lives?" (opposite frame). The broader frame might consider societal factors affecting health behaviors ("How can we create a society that supports and promotes health-conscious behaviors across all aspects of life?") while the narrower frame could focus on specific barriers to adherence for individual patients ("What specific daily challenges prevent this patient from taking his medication consistently?"). By exploring these different perspectives, healthcare professionals can recast the problem in ways that open up new solution spaces and foster more patient-centered approaches to care.

The *Future-Back Thinking and Constraint Removal Exercise* is a third tool for Recasting healthcare challenges by encouraging healthcare professionals to think beyond current limitations and envision ideal outcomes. To begin, participants articulate a detailed vision of the ideal future state related to the issue at hand. This might involve describing a healthcare system with perfect patient outcomes, seamless care coordination, or 100% patient satisfaction. Once this vision is established, they work backward, identifying the necessary changes and listing all perceived constraints that currently prevent this ideal state from existing.

The next step involves systematically examining each constraint and asking two critical questions: "What if this constraint didn't exist?" and "How might we work around this constraint?" This process often leads to innovative solutions and helps recast seemingly insurmountable problems into actionable challenges. For example, when addressing the issue of long wait times in emergency departments, this exercise might prompt healthcare professionals to envision a future where patients receive immediate care upon arrival. Working backward, they might identify constraints such as limited staff, physical space restrictions, and inefficient triage processes. By imagining these constraints don't exist or exploring creative workarounds, they might recast the problem from "How do we reduce wait times?" to "How can we reimagine the entire emergency care delivery model to provide immediate, personalized care?"

This approach to Recasting often leads to transformative ideas that challenge the status quo and inspire systemic change. It encourages healthcare professionals to think beyond incremental improvements and consider radical innovations that could revolutionize healthcare delivery. The exercise also helps identify underlying assumptions and biases that may be limiting current problem-solving efforts. By temporarily removing perceived constraints, healthcare professionals can explore solutions that might have previously seemed impossible or impractical. This expanded perspective can lead to Recasting healthcare challenges in ways that inspire cross-sector collaborations, technological innovations, or entirely new care delivery models that address root causes rather than symptoms of systemic issues.

Practicing Effective Recasting

Recasting is a skill that can be developed and refined through practice. Two powerful strategies for effectively Recasting in healthcare negotiations are joint problem definition and reframing external selves as internal and vulnerable selves. These approaches help transform adversarial encounters into collaborative problem-solving sessions, fostering trust and mutual understanding.

Joint Problem Definition

Joint problem definition is a collaborative approach that encourages all parties to co-create a shared understanding of the challenge at hand.

This strategy helps break down silos, align perspectives, and uncover innovative solutions that address the core issues rather than surface-level symptoms.

To apply joint problem definition in healthcare negotiations, consider the following actionable steps:

1. Approach the negotiation with an open mind and a genuine willingness to collaborate.
2. Invite all parties to share their unique perspectives on the problem or challenge.
3. Practice active listening, asking clarifying questions to ensure a comprehensive understanding of each viewpoint.
4. Identify common ground and shared interests among all stakeholders.
5. Collaboratively craft a joint problem statement that accurately reflects everyone's concerns, goals, and priorities.
6. Use this shared definition as a foundation for brainstorming innovative solutions that address the needs of all parties involved.

Revisiting the opening vignette with Dr. Novak and his team at HealthTech Innovations can illustrate how joint problem definition works. Recall that Dr. Novak and his team at HealthTech Innovations were faced with tensions arising from team members' different priorities and concerns. Amir and Dr. Larsson expressed concerns about data quality and consistency, while Lena and the business development team pushed for faster progress.

Recognizing the need for a collaborative approach, Dr. Novak addressed the team:

> Let's take a step back and focus on our shared goal: developing an AI tool that will genuinely help doctors detect cancer earlier and save lives. We all bring different perspectives and expertise to the table, and by working together, we can find a way to address these challenges. I propose we start by clearly defining the problem we're trying to solve. Amir, can you share your thoughts on what an ideal dataset would look like to build a robust AI model?

Amir responded, "Ideally, we'd have consistent, high-quality data from a diverse range of patients and cancer types. The data should be properly labeled and formatted to ensure accurate analysis."

Dr. Novak then turned to Dr. Larsson, "Emily, given your experience working with multiple healthcare providers, what do you think are the key obstacles to obtaining such a dataset?"

Dr. Larsson explained, "The main challenges are the varying data collection practices and the time required to standardize the data. We also need to ensure patient privacy and obtain the necessary consent."

Lena chimed in, "From a business perspective, we need to balance the time and resources required for data collection with the need to demonstrate progress to our stakeholders."

Dr. Novak then offers this summary: "So, our joint problem statement could be 'How can we efficiently collect and standardize high-quality, diverse cancer data while respecting patient privacy and meeting our business objectives?'"

By creating a space for all stakeholders to voice their concerns and perspectives, the team was able to recast their challenge from a conflict of priorities into a shared mission. This process not only aligned the team's efforts but also uncovered a more comprehensive understanding of the problem at hand. The resulting joint problem statement – addressing data quality, privacy concerns, and business objectives simultaneously – provides a solid foundation for innovative solutions that balance technical rigor with practical implementation.

Reframing External Selves as Internal and Vulnerable Selves

This strategy involves looking beyond the surface-level positions or "External Selves" that people present in negotiations to understand the deeper, more vulnerable aspects of their identities and motivations. By acknowledging and addressing these "Internal selves," negotiators can create more empathetic and sustainable solutions.

To effectively reframe External Selves as Internal and Vulnerable Selves in healthcare negotiations, providers should:

1. Listen attentively to each party's expressed perspective, seeking to understand the underlying internal and vulnerable selves.
2. Ask thoughtful, probing questions to uncover the deeper values, beliefs, fears, and motivations behind their external self.
3. Reframe the external self as an internal or vulnerable self, using empathetic, non-judgmental language that resonates with the individual.

4. Validate the legitimacy of each party's internal and vulnerable selves, expressing a sincere willingness to find solutions that honor these core aspects of their identity.
5. Explore creative options that address the underlying internal and vulnerable selves of all parties involved, fostering a sense of psychological safety and mutual respect.
6. Regularly check in throughout the negotiation process to ensure that proposed solutions continue to align with the identified internal and vulnerable selves.

Revisiting the opening vignette can also illustrate how reframing external selves as internal and vulnerable selves can advance the conversation:

Dr. Novak then shifted the focus: "I appreciate everyone's candor in sharing their concerns. Let's explore the underlying motivations and values driving each of our perspectives." He turned to Amir, "Amir, your dedication to building an accurate AI model is clear. Can you share what drives your commitment to this project?"

Amir reflected,

> I've seen firsthand how cancer can devastate families. My uncle passed away from colon cancer that was detected too late. I believe that if we can create a reliable early detection tool, we can save countless lives and spare families the pain of losing loved ones.

Dr. Novak acknowledged, "Thank you for sharing that, Amir. Your personal connection to our mission is powerful." He then addressed Dr. Larsson: "Emily, your tireless efforts to coordinate with multiple healthcare providers are commendable. What motivates you to take on such a challenging task?"

"As a physician, I've witnessed the impact of early cancer detection on patient outcomes," Dr. Larsson shared. "I want to help create a tool my colleagues can trust and use to make a real difference in patient lives."

Lena then added,

> I understand the importance of meeting our business objectives, but at the end of the day, our success is measured by the lives we improve. We need to find a way to balance our business needs with our ultimate goal of revolutionizing cancer care.

Dr. Novak expressed his appreciation,

> Thank you all for sharing your deeper motivations. It's clear that we're all driven by a shared desire to make a meaningful impact in the fight against cancer. By keeping this greater purpose at the forefront, I believe we can find innovative solutions to the challenges we face.

By delving deeper into each stakeholder's underlying motivations and personal connections to the project, the team transformed surface-level positions into more nuanced, empathetic understandings. This approach revealed shared values and a common purpose in improving cancer care, fostering a sense of psychological safety and mutual respect. The resulting dialogue laid the groundwork for creative solutions that honor each individual's core values and address their deeper concerns.

Exploring Possibilities

With a newfound understanding of each other's internal selves, the team began exploring potential approaches to address their joint problem statement.

Dr. Larsson suggested, "Perhaps we could explore collaborating with a subset of healthcare providers who already have robust data collection practices in place. This could help us refine our data standards and build a high-quality initial dataset."

Amir considered,

> That's an interesting idea. We could potentially use that initial dataset to train our AI model and demonstrate its potential. As we iterate and improve the model, we might be able to gradually expand our data collection efforts to include more providers.

Lena added,

> From a business perspective, a phased approach could allow us to show our investors and potential clients tangible progress. We could showcase the value of our AI tool in a real-world setting and use that to secure further support and funding.

Dr. Novak nodded,

> These are great starting points for us to explore. By considering a focused, high-quality dataset and iteratively expanding, we might be able to balance our data needs with our resource constraints. And by demonstrating the real-world impact of our AI tool, we could build trust and momentum with our stakeholders.

Through the HEAR Approach™, the team successfully transformed their initial conflicts into a collaborative exploration of innovative solutions. By uncovering and addressing each member's internal motivations and vulnerabilities, they cultivated a shared vision that balanced technical excellence, clinical trust, and business viability. This newfound alignment not only resolved immediate tensions but also established a robust foundation for tackling future challenges. The team's journey from surface-level disagreements to deep, mutual understanding exemplified the power of joint problem definition and reframing External Selves as Internal and Vulnerable Selves in complex healthcare negotiations.

Measuring the Success of Recasting in Healthcare Negotiations

To evaluate the effectiveness of Recasting efforts, healthcare professionals could utilize one or more of the following key performance indicators and metrics:

1. **Collaboration Index**: Measure the ratio of collaborative solutions proposed to adversarial positions taken. A higher ratio indicates more successful Recasting and improved team dynamics.
2. **Stakeholder Satisfaction**: Use post-negotiation surveys to gauge satisfaction levels among all parties involved. Higher satisfaction scores often correlate with effective Recasting and long-term buy-in.
3. **Implementation Success Rate**: Track the percentage of negotiated agreements that are successfully implemented within agreed timelines. Effective Recasting should lead to more feasible, mutually beneficial solutions with higher implementation rates.

4. **Time to Resolution**: Monitor the time taken to reach agreements, including any follow-up negotiations. Successful Recasting often leads to faster resolutions as parties align around shared goals more quickly.
5. **Innovation Metric**: Count the number and quality of novel solutions or approaches generated during negotiations. Increased innovation often indicates successful reframing of problems and enhanced collaboration.
6. **Relationship Quality Index**: Assess the quality of relationships before and after negotiations using standardized relationship assessment tools. Improved relationships suggest effective Recasting and better long-term outcomes.
7. **Patient Outcome Measures**: For clinical negotiations, track relevant patient outcome measures (e.g., treatment adherence, patient satisfaction, health outcomes) that may be influenced by the negotiated solutions, both short-term and long-term.
8. **Cost-Effectiveness Ratio**: Calculate the ratio of value created (e.g., improved outcomes, increased efficiency) to resources invested in the negotiation process, considering both immediate and long-term impacts.
9. **Conflict Recurrence Rate**: Monitor how often similar conflicts or negotiations recur and the time between recurrences. Lower recurrence rates may indicate more sustainable solutions achieved through effective Recasting.
10. **Learning and Growth Metric**: Assess team members' perceived growth in negotiation skills, their ability to apply Recasting techniques over time, and the transfer of these skills to other areas of their work.

By regularly tracking these metrics and analyzing trends over time, providers can gauge the effectiveness of their Recasting efforts, identify areas for improvement, and demonstrate the value of this approach in their healthcare setting.

Overcoming Challenges in Recasting

Recasting offers a powerful approach to healthcare negotiations, but it faces several challenges. One of the most common obstacles is resistance to change. Healthcare professionals often feel comfortable with familiar methods and hesitate to try new approaches. This resistance can manifest as skepticism about Recasting's value or reluctance to engage in collaborative problem-solving.

To address these challenges, healthcare professionals should approach conversations with empathy and understanding. They should acknowledge the validity of their counterpart's concerns and listen to their perspective. Using the RESET framework from Chapter 4 can guide their response:

1. *Recognize* the counterpart's skepticism and the reasons behind it.
2. *Evaluate* their perspective and validate their concerns.
3. *Step Back* to pause and consider the broader context of their views.
4. *Empathize* with all parties involved.
5. *Transform* the conversation by reframing it in terms of shared goals and values.

For example, when introducing a new interprofessional collaboration initiative, some team members may doubt its effectiveness, citing past failed attempts or concerns about increased workload. They may fall back into familiar patterns of siloed work and be reluctant to engage in the joint problem definition and creative brainstorming that Recasting entails.

When faced with resistance to a new patient engagement initiative, providers might use the RESET framework like this:

1. **Recognize:** "I understand you're hesitant about this initiative. Is it because you're concerned about the time it might take or how it could affect your existing workflow?"
2. **Evaluate:** "It makes sense to feel cautious about implementing something new, especially when the current processes feel manageable and familiar. Your concerns about workload and patient relationships are valid."
3. **Step Back:** "Looking at the bigger picture, this initiative aims to improve patient outcomes over time, but I see how the immediate changes might feel disruptive. Let's take a moment to consider the context of these adjustments."
4. **Empathize:** "I know these kinds of changes can be challenging, especially when you're already balancing a heavy workload. I can appreciate how this might feel like just one more thing to juggle."
5. **Transform:** "What if we explored a way to phase this in gradually, perhaps starting with a smaller group of patients? That could help us refine the process while ensuring it fits seamlessly into your practice."

This approach demonstrates how Recasting builds upon Acknowledgment. It begins by recognizing and empathizing with concerns, then progresses to sharing experiences and exploring new perspectives. The final step transforms the conversation into collaborative problem-solving, a key aspect of effective Recasting.

Another challenge is the tendency to revert to positional bargaining, even when attempting to use collaborative approaches. This can happen when healthcare providers or their counterparts feel strongly about their stances or when emotions run high. Power imbalances and hierarchical structures within healthcare organizations can make it even more difficult to create an environment of genuine collaboration and trust. In such cases, it's tempting to focus on defending one's position rather than exploring underlying interests and seeking mutually beneficial solutions.

Maintaining a Relational Mindset is crucial for overcoming such challenges and ensuring successful Recasting. Healthcare professionals should prioritize relationships, trust, and collaboration over individual positions or short-term gains. When faced with someone who is "dug in" and resistant to constructive negotiation, providers should lead by example in maintaining a Relational Mindset. They should model active listening, empathy, and respect in their interactions, creating a safe and respectful environment for all parties to share their perspectives. By encouraging open dialogue and actively seeking out the input of those with less power or authority, they emphasize the value of diverse perspectives and the importance of creating solutions that work for everyone.

Demonstrating a willingness to explore creative solutions and a commitment to finding mutually beneficial outcomes is crucial. Healthcare professionals should remind themselves and others of the shared goals and values that unite them. By embodying the principles of Recasting in their own behavior, healthcare providers inspire others to do the same and create a culture of collaboration and trust.

To maintain a Relational Mindset, healthcare professionals should regularly check in with themselves and others throughout the negotiation process. They can ask questions like, "How are we doing in terms of working together toward our shared purpose?" or "What can we do to strengthen our partnership and trust in one another?" These check-ins help identify issues early on and ensure everyone stays focused on the relational aspects of the negotiation.

Additionally, it's important to proactively address challenges by remembering to celebrate successes and milestones along the way. Healthcare professionals should acknowledge the collective progress they've made together and the positive outcomes resulting from their collaborative efforts. This reinforces the value of Recasting and sustains motivation and commitment to the process.

Overcoming challenges in Recasting requires empathy, persuasion, and a steadfast commitment to the relational mindset. By using frameworks like RESET and regularly engaging in self-reflection, healthcare professionals can navigate obstacles and resistance with skill and grace. By prioritizing relationships and collaboration over individual positions, they unlock the full potential of Recasting to drive positive change and create value in their healthcare negotiations.

Preparing for Successful Negotiations Across Healthcare Pillars

The HEAR Approach™ is a versatile framework that healthcare professionals can apply across the three pillars of healthcare: Practice of Medicine Operating Room Delivery of Care (Exam Room), and Business of Health (Boardroom). By mastering the skills of Empowerment, Acknowledgment, and Recasting, healthcare providers can navigate the unique challenges and opportunities within each pillar with confidence and effectiveness.

Throughout Part I of this book, we've explored how the HEAR Approach™ helps healthcare professionals create the mental clarity and emotional readiness needed for effective negotiation. By empowering themselves and acknowledging others, they set the stage for the Recasting process, ensuring that all parties are in the optimal state to begin collaborative problem-solving. And this readiness is not limited to one healthcare area but spans all three pillars.

In the Practice of Medicine pillar, Recasting facilitates interprofessional collaboration and resource allocation by focusing on the shared goal of providing high-quality patient care. When negotiating the implementation of a new telehealth program, healthcare professionals can use the HEAR Approach™ to bring together diverse healthcare professionals, understand their perspectives, and recast the conversation to develop a strategy that enhances patient care while addressing the needs of all stakeholders.

Similarly, in the Delivery of Care pillar, Recasting enables healthcare providers to negotiate treatment plans with patients and families by reframing the conversation around shared goals of health and well-being. For example, when a patient expresses concerns about the financial burden of a recommended treatment, healthcare professionals can use the HEAR Approach™ to empathize with their situation, acknowledge their concerns, and recast the discussion to explore affordable and effective care options that align with their needs and values.

In the Business of Health pillar, Recasting enables healthcare professionals to negotiate contracts, partnerships, and strategic initiatives by reframing the conversation around the shared goal of creating value and improving population health. When negotiating a partnership between a hospital and a community health organization, healthcare providers can use the HEAR Approach™ to acknowledge the complex interplay of financial, operational, and clinical factors, and recast the discussion to explore innovative collaboration models that align resources and expertise to improve health outcomes for underserved populations.

As healthcare professionals prepare to delve into Part II of this book, which focuses on specific negotiation strategies and tactics needed to navigate within and across the three pillars of healthcare, they should remember that the HEAR Approach™ forms the foundation for these skills. By consistently applying the principles of Empowerment, Acknowledgment, and Recasting, they will create the Relational Mindset and collaborative environment necessary for successful negotiations. In the chapters that follow, healthcare professionals will take a deeper look at specific negotiation strategies and tactics, building upon the HEAR Framework and the Recasting techniques presented in Part I. Armed with these tools, healthcare professionals are well-equipped to become transformative forces in their organizations, driving positive change and fostering trust, creativity, and mutual understanding in every negotiation.

Conclusion: The Importance of Recasting

As the culminating stage of the HEAR Approach™, Recasting represents a powerful tool for transforming healthcare negotiations. By building upon the foundations of Empowerment and Acknowledgment, Recasting elevates discussions from potentially adversarial encounters to collaborative problem-solving sessions. This chapter has demonstrated how Recasting techniques, such as joint problem definition and reframing external selves as internal and vulnerable selves, can help navigate the complex, often emotionally charged landscape of healthcare negotiations. Whether in the Practice of

Medicine, Delivery of Care, or Business of Health pillars, Recasting enables healthcare professionals to navigate complex dynamics and drive positive change.

Mastering Recasting requires a deep understanding of collaborative problem-solving, reframing techniques, and the principles of the HEAR Approach™. The integration of these concepts serves as a valuable tool for navigating the complexities of healthcare discussions with greater skill and empathy. By methodically applying these techniques, healthcare professionals can bridge gaps, foster true collaboration, and create an environment conducive to outcomes that benefit all parties involved, including patients. As practitioners deepen their grasp of Recasting and its cross-disciplinary dynamics, their ability to navigate complex healthcare negotiations will increase.

Implementing this approach requires continuous refinement, but the potential benefits are far-reaching: enhanced interprofessional relationships, improved communication across healthcare pillars, innovative solutions to complex challenges, and a revitalized healthcare system equipped to address evolving needs. By integrating Recasting principles with Empowerment and Acknowledgment, healthcare professionals can drive transformative change, fostering a more responsive, collaborative, and patient-centered healthcare environment. This not only enhances their negotiation skills but also aligns with the fundamental goal of healthcare: providing the best possible care for patients while navigating the complex landscape of modern healthcare delivery.

REFLECTION EXERCISE: RECASTING IN ACTION

Reflect on a recent challenging healthcare negotiation you participated in or observed. Create a visual map of the initial positions (External Selves) and underlying motivations (Internal Selves) of the different stakeholders involved in the negotiation. Identify one specific Recasting technique from this chapter (e.g., 360-Degree Stakeholder Analysis, joint problem definition) that you could apply to enhance your approach in future negotiations. How might applying the Recasting framework transform your perspective and change the dynamics and outcomes?

- How could redefining the problem collaboratively improve your understanding of stakeholders' positions and create new possibilities for solutions?

- In what ways could you use joint problem definition to foster a more collaborative atmosphere and emphasize shared objectives?
- How might acknowledging and addressing both External and Internal Selves lead to more innovative and mutually beneficial solutions?
- What specific strategies could you employ to overcome potential resistance or skepticism from various stakeholders when introducing Recasting techniques?

This structured reflection will help you integrate Recasting concepts into your negotiation practice, enhancing your ability to transform potentially adversarial healthcare discussions into collaborative problem-solving sessions with greater empathy and effectiveness.

Key Takeaways

1. Recasting serves as the culminating stage of the HEAR Approach™, transforming potentially adversarial healthcare negotiations into collaborative problem-solving sessions by reframing issues and aligning stakeholders around shared goals and values.
2. Joint problem definition enables healthcare professionals to foster a collective understanding of challenges, encouraging innovative thinking, and creating a foundation for more comprehensive, mutually beneficial solutions across various healthcare scenarios.
3. Reframing External Selves as Internal and Vulnerable Selves allows negotiators to address underlying motivations and concerns, leading to more empathetic, sustainable agreements that honor the core values of all stakeholders involved in healthcare negotiations.
4. While implementing Recasting techniques in complex healthcare settings can be challenging, consistent application of these strategies can significantly enhance negotiation outcomes, improve interprofessional relationships, and ultimately contribute to better patient care and organizational effectiveness.

Notes

1. The following scenario is based on the real-life consequences of the recent emergence of AI in healthcare research. Google's AlphaFold breakthrough in 2020 with respect to protein folding has set off a wellspring of interest in AI applications to healthcare issues. At the same time, it has also heightened already fraught negotiations within companies about resource allocation and strategy for product development.
2. Roger Fisher and William Ury, *Getting to Yes: Negotiating Agreement without Giving In* (New York: Penguin Books, 2011).
3. Deepak Malhotra, *Negotiation Genius: How to Overcome Obstacles and Achieve Brilliant Results at the Bargaining Table and Beyond* (New York: Bantam Dell, 2008).
4. Alice M. Isen, Kimberly A. Daubman, and Gary P. Nowicki, "Positive Affect Facilitates Creative Problem Solving," *Journal of Personality and Social Psychology* 52, no. 6 (1987): 1122–1131, https://doi.org/10.1037/0022-3514.52.6.1122.
5. Kathleen L. Valley, Joseph Morone, and Max H. Bazerman, "The Foundations of Cooperative Strategy," in *Negotiation Theory and Research*, ed. Leigh L. Thompson (New York: Psychology Press, 2006), 3–24.

References

1. Michael E. Porter and Elizabeth O. Teisberg, *Redefining Health Care: Creating Value-Based Competition on Results* (Boston, MA: Harvard Business School Press, 2006).
2. John P. Kotter, "Leading Change: Why Transformation Efforts Fail," *Harvard Business Review*, May–June 1995.
3. Moira Stewart et al., "The Impact of Patient-Centered Care on Outcomes," *Journal of Family Practice* 49, no. 9 (2000): 796–804.
4. Victor R. Fuchs, *Who Shall Live? Health, Economics, And Social Choice*, 2nd Expanded ed. (Boston, MA: World Scientific, 2011).
5. Mirjam Körner, Sarah Bütof, Christian Müller, Linda Zimmermann, Sonja Becker and Jürgen Bengel, "Interprofessional Teamwork and Team Interventions in Chronic Care: A Systematic Review," *Journal of Interprofessional Care* 30, no. 1 (2015): 1–14. https://doi.org/10.3109/13561820.2015.1051616.
6. Douglas Stone, Bruce Patton, and Sheila Heen, *Difficult Conversations: How to Discuss What Matters Most* (New York: Penguin Books, 2010).

7. David L. Cooperrider and Diana Whitney, *Appreciative Inquiry: A Positive Revolution in Change* (San Francisco, CA: Berrett-Koehler Publishers, 2005).
8. Jody H. Gittell, *Transforming Relationships for High Performance: The Power of Relational Coordination* (Stanford, CA: Stanford University Press, 2016).
9. Richard M. Bohmer, "The Hard Work of Health Care Transformation," *New England Journal of Medicine* 375, no. 8 (2016): 709–711.

II

ADVANCED NEGOTIATION STRATEGIES, TACTICS, AND PLANNING TOOLS

Strategy without tactics is the slowest route to victory. Tactics without strategy is the noise before defeat.

– **Sun Tzu**

Mastering strategy and in-the-moment adaptability is essential for delivering patient-centered outcomes and building collaborative solutions. Part II of this book equips you with the skills needed for high-stakes healthcare negotiations, advancing from strategic foundations to real-time tactics and comprehensive planning. Each chapter and tool is designed to meet the unique challenges of healthcare negotiation across the Practice of Medicine, Delivery of Care, and Business of Health.

Navigating Part II: Your Roadmap to Strategic Mastery and Tactical Precision

The chapters in Part II builds on the relational skills introduced in Part I, advancing toward an adaptable, Healthcare-Specific toolkit.

DOI: 10.4324/9781003336013-8

Understanding Advanced Healthcare Negotiation Strategies and Tactics

Chapter 7: Advanced Negotiation Strategies for Complex Challenges

These techniques equip you to balance competing interests across healthcare pillars and sustain long-term collaboration. Designed for complex scenarios, these strategies prepare you to address healthcare's unique balance of patient-centered goals and institutional priorities.

Chapter 8: Mastering Real-Time Negotiation Tactics

These skills allow you to respond flexibly in high-pressure situations, fostering trust, and collaborative problem-solving. This chapter enhances your ability to remain agile and empathetic, a critical factor in emotionally charged healthcare negotiations.

Planning Guides: Practical Tools for Implementation

Two planning guides anchor Part II, helping you apply advanced strategies and tactics in real-world settings: the *Negotiation Planner* (NP) for single-pillar negotiations within one area of healthcare and the *Trilingual Planner* (TP) for cross-pillar negotiations that demand coordination across multiple domains.

As you prepare to apply these planning tools, selecting the right planner for your specific negotiation context is crucial. Just as healthcare providers carefully choose diagnostic tools based on presenting symptoms, negotiators must select the appropriate planner based on their negotiation's characteristics and scope. The following decision framework will guide your selection process, helping you determine whether your scenario calls for the focused approach of the NP or the comprehensive scope of the TP.

This framework serves as your initial diagnostic tool, guiding you through the key factors that differentiate single-pillar from cross-pillar negotiations. As you progress through the case studies in Chapters 9 and 10, you'll see how these deciding factors manifest in real-world scenarios. The framework will become an increasingly valuable reference point as you encounter your own negotiation challenges.

Applying Your Skills: Real-World Case Studies

Each planner is paired with a case study, illustrating how to apply these skills in authentic healthcare scenarios.

Chapter 9: Applying the Negotiation Planner

This single-pillar negotiation case study in biopharmaceuticals for a pediatric cancer drug shows the NP in action, offering a practical guide to focused negotiation within a specific healthcare pillar.

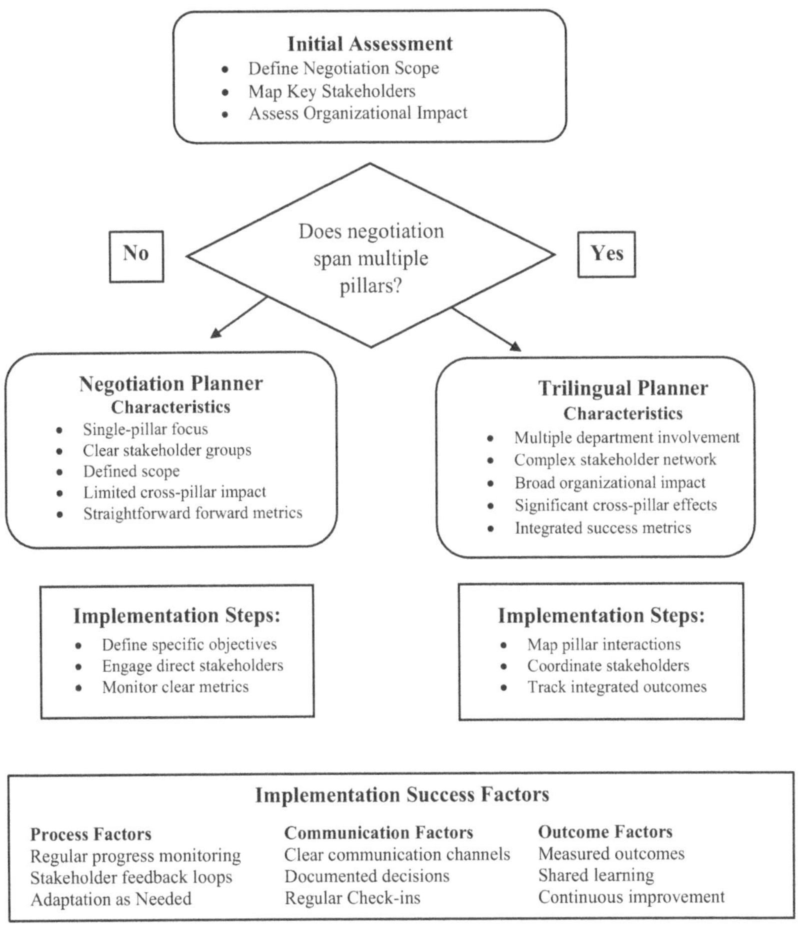

Figure P.II.1 Healthcare negotiation decision framework.

The figure shows the "Healthcare negotiation decision framework" that helps readers choose between the Negotiation Planner (for single-pillar negotiations) and the Trilingual Planner (for cross-pillar negotiations). It serves as an introductory diagnostic tool for Part II before readers proceed to the specific case studies in Chapters 9 and 10.

Chapter 10: Applying the Trilateral Planner

The cross-pillar negotiation case study for the Health Education Alliance demonstrates how the Trilateral Planner balances stakeholder interests across healthcare's pillars, fostering collaboration and unified goals.

Making Part II Work for You

Each chapter and planner in Part II is part of an adaptable toolkit that grows with your negotiation experience. Whether addressing a single-pillar issue or a multi-pillar challenge, these resources offer structured approaches for planning, real-time adaptability, and reflection. Revisit these tools to refine your skills and build confidence in healthcare negotiation.

Chapter 7

Advanced Negotiation Strategies for Complex Challenges

However beautiful the strategy, you should occasionally look at the results.

– Winston Churchill

DOI: 10.4324/9781003336013-9

Dr. Sarah Bianchi took a deep breath outside the hospital boardroom. As Chief of Emergency Medicine, she had ten minutes to convince the executive team to support her proposal for expanding the Emergency Department (ED). The challenges were clear – overcrowding, staff burnout, declining patient satisfaction scores – but listing problems alone wouldn't secure the necessary resources. With every department competing for the same limited budget, she needed a different approach.

Earlier that morning, Marcus, her senior nurse manager, had laid out the data. "We've got solid statistics supporting the expansion. The numbers speak for themselves," he insisted. But Dr. Bianchi knew that data alone wouldn't be enough. "I wish it were that simple," she replied. "We need to help them see why this matters – not just to us, but to their priorities too."

As she organized her thoughts, Dr. Bianchi reflected on how traditional negotiation strategies often fall short in healthcare's uniquely complex environment. Approaching the discussion as a win-lose battle could damage the relationships she needed to maintain and might even compromise patient care. She needed to clearly articulate the ED's value to the hospital's broader mission while demonstrating a genuine understanding of other departments' constraints.

With her presentation materials in hand, Dr. Bianchi squared her shoulders and opened the boardroom door. It was time to put theory into practice…

This scenario captures the reality of complex negotiations that healthcare professionals face across all three pillars – Practice of Medicine (Operating room), Delivery of Care (Exam room), and Business of Health (Boardroom). Whether advocating for resources, implementing protocols, or coordinating care, healthcare negotiators need more than just a basic strategic orientation. They need an advanced strategic toolkit to navigate these situations effectively.

In previous chapters, the HEAR Approach™ laid the groundwork for effective healthcare negotiations, emphasizing Empowerment, Acknowledgment, and Recasting. As negotiations become more complex, advanced strategies are needed to achieve optimal outcomes.

Advanced Strategies: Building Blocks for Complex Healthcare Negotiations

Successful healthcare negotiations require carefully chosen strategies that drive positive outcomes. Through extensive research and practitioner interviews, seven foundational strategies have emerged as consistently effective in healthcare settings. These strategies form a comprehensive toolkit that addresses the unique challenges of healthcare negotiation while expanding upon established communication and conflict resolution principles. Each builds upon the HEAR Approach™ introduced earlier, and they work together systematically to achieve negotiation success:

1. Understanding and Setting Your Value helps organizations articulate their contributions in meaningful ways across different healthcare contexts.
2. Strategic Questioning enables deep exploration of stakeholder interests and priorities, building on trust, and understanding.
3. Logrolling for Mutual Benefit leverages opportunities for value creation by leveraging different priorities, interests, or preferences of parties to find mutually advantageous trade-offs and agreements.
4. Multiple Equivalent Simultaneous Offers (MESOs) provide structured choice while maintaining value, combining Empowerment with Acknowledgment.
5. Concession Management ensures that necessary compromises build rather than erode value, strengthening the Relational Mindset.
6. Contingency Agreements address uncertainty through flexible frameworks, creating sustainable partnerships.
7. Post-Settlement Agreements enable ongoing refinement and value creation, maintaining long-term collaboration.

These strategies prove particularly effective in healthcare settings for several key reasons. First, they specifically address the unique challenges of healthcare negotiations, where professionals must bridge significant communication gaps across clinical, operational, and financial domains. The strategies help balance competing priorities while maintaining an unwavering focus on patient care, and they effectively navigate the complex power dynamics inherent in healthcare settings.

Second, these advanced negotiation approaches build directly on fundamental HEAR principles, creating a comprehensive framework for healthcare negotiations. Contingency Agreements and Post-Settlement Agreements amplify the Relational Mindset by establishing frameworks for shared risks and rewards. Understanding and Setting Your Value enhances Empowerment by strengthening the negotiating position. Strategic Questioning amplifies Acknowledgment by demonstrating genuine curiosity about others' perspectives, and Logrolling for Mutual Benefit exemplifies Recasting by transforming zero-sum negotiations into opportunities for mutual gain. Multiple Equivalent Simultaneous Offers build upon both Empowerment and Acknowledgment by combining choice with value maintenance, while Concession Management enables negotiators to shape exchanges strategically while building trust and flexibility.

Third, research demonstrates that advanced negotiation skills are critical for success across healthcare's three pillars: the Operating room (Practice of Medicine), the Exam room (Delivery of Care), and the Boardroom (Business of Health). Whether navigating complex treatment discussions, coordinating interdisciplinary care, or securing vital resources, healthcare professionals who excel in advanced negotiation strategies achieve significantly better outcomes.[1] Surgeons who effectively employ techniques like logrolling and contingency agreements consistently demonstrate improved resource allocation and build stronger professional relationships across specialties and departments.[2] The influence goes far beyond individual interactions: Healthcare organizations implementing comprehensive negotiation training programs show measurable improvements in patient care coordination, staff retention rates, and overall operational efficiency.[3] The evidence is clear: developing advanced negotiation capabilities is not just beneficial but essential for healthcare professionals seeking to drive positive change in today's increasingly complex healthcare landscape.

Preparing and Using Advanced Healthcare Negotiation Strategies

Thorough preparation is the cornerstone of successful healthcare negotiations, particularly when employing advanced strategies in high-stakes scenarios. While experienced negotiators may lean on intuition, researchers have shown that structured preparation leads to superior outcomes.[4] Healthcare professionals should systematically prepare for complex negotiations across all three pillars of healthcare.

The process begins with comprehensive stakeholder analysis and mapping, utilizing the Healthcare Negotiation Mapping Tool introduced in Chapter 3. This critical first step involves more than simply identifying direct participants – it requires a nuanced understanding of all stakeholders affected by negotiation outcomes, both directly and indirectly. Healthcare professionals must carefully analyze stakeholder interests and priorities across pillars, examine power dynamics and historical relationships, identify potential areas of alignment and conflict, and understand cross-pillar impacts and connections that could influence negotiation dynamics.

The second step centers on rigorous data collection and analysis, recognizing that successful healthcare negotiations must be grounded in evidence-based arguments. This involves gathering and synthesizing relevant clinical metrics and outcomes data, operational efficiency measures, financial projections, cost analyses, and comparative industry benchmarks. Healthcare professionals must transform this data into compelling visual representations and prepare evidence-based responses to anticipate potential counterarguments, ensuring they can effectively support their positions with concrete evidence.

Scenario planning and strategy selection form the third crucial step of preparation. Negotiators must develop comprehensive "what-if" scenarios and decision trees that anticipate different negotiation paths and potential outcomes. Strategy selection must carefully consider multiple factors, including context and setting, stakeholder dynamics, time constraints, available resources, and organizational culture. This systematic approach enables negotiators to prepare for various contingencies while maintaining flexibility in their strategic approach.

Finally, practice and refinement are essential for developing effective negotiation capabilities. Healthcare professionals must engage in regular role-play exercises with colleagues, record and analyze mock negotiations, and actively incorporate feedback to refine their approach. The RESET method, introduced in Chapter 4, provides a structured framework for emotional preparation, ensuring negotiators can maintain composure and effectiveness even in challenging situations. Through this deliberate practice, negotiators develop the muscle memory and confidence needed to execute advanced negotiation strategies in real-world healthcare settings.

Advanced healthcare strategies manifest distinctly across healthcare's three foundational pillars – Operating Rroom (Practice of Medicine), Exam Room (Delivery of Care), and Boardroom (Business of Health). Each pillar presents unique opportunities for strategic implementation, with different approaches yielding optimal results based on the specific context and stakeholder dynamics involved:

- **Operating Room (Practice of Medicine)**: Strategies like Contingency Agreements help address complex resource utilization challenges while keeping patient care at the center of the conversation.
- **Exam Room (Delivery of Care)**: Logrolling for Mutual Benefit excels in improving care coordination and workflow efficiency, while Strategic Questioning reveals opportunities to enhance staff satisfaction and patient experience.
- **Boardroom (Business of Health)**: Concession Management helps navigate complex financial trade-offs while maintaining strategic priorities, while MESOs create flexibility in addressing regulatory requirements while preserving business objectives.

To successfully implement these strategies across healthcare settings, providers must follow a structured yet flexible approach. This begins with identifying the primary pillar(s) involved in the negotiation and selecting appropriate strategies based on the specific context and challenges. As negotiations progress, healthcare professionals must continually adapt their strategic approach for specific stakeholders while maintaining the flexibility to adjust as dynamics evolve. Throughout this process, all decisions must remain firmly grounded in their potential impact on patient care. This systematic approach ensures that healthcare professionals can effectively prepare for and execute complex negotiations while never losing sight of their fundamental mission: achieving optimal clinical outcomes.

To illustrate the advanced negotiation strategies at work, each is first introduced and analyzed through the HEAR lens, then unpacked through a case study involving a Business of Health context that showcases its practical implementation. Each is then followed by insights on adapting the strategy across the other healthcare pillars, highlighting their versatility and broad applicability.

Advanced Strategies in Action in a Boardroom Scenario

At AIDS Care Group (ACG), co-founder Eric Strauss faces a critical negotiation with pharmaceutical executives and insurance representatives to secure affordable HIV medications for his organization's growing patient base while ensuring financial sustainability. After twenty years of partnering with underserved communities, ACG was facing a pivotal moment that would impact every aspect of its healthcare delivery.

Earlier that morning, ACG's Chief Medical Officer had presented compelling clinical data. "Our outcomes speak for themselves," she emphasized, showcasing their reduced hospitalization rates and industry-leading medication adherence programs. However, Strauss knew that even the most impressive data wouldn't be enough to secure the critical partnerships they needed. "The numbers are important," he acknowledged, "but we must convey our comprehensive value across every dimension of healthcare delivery. This negotiation will shape everything – from prescription protocols and patient care workflows to our financial sustainability."

The obstacles spanned all three healthcare pillars: physicians needed flexibility to prescribe optimal drug regimens, clinic staff required reliable medication access to maintain consistent treatment protocols, and sustainable pricing models were essential for organizational survival. The stakeholder landscape was equally complex:

- Pharmaceutical executives, focusing on profit margins and market position.
- Insurance representatives, analyzing cost-effectiveness data.
- Clinic physicians, fearing loss of prescribing autonomy.
- Nurses and care coordinators worrying about treatment continuity.
- Patient advocates, demanding affordable medication access.
- Community leaders, seeking sustainable healthcare solutions.

As he gathered his materials, Strauss considered his approach. Success would require more than just a basic strategic orientation – it demanded a comprehensive framework that could align diverse interests while maintaining focus on ACG's core mission. His first task was establishing ACG's value proposition in terms that would resonate from the boardroom to the exam room.

Strategy One: Understanding and Setting Your Value

Understanding and Setting Your Value represents a foundational negotiation strategy that transforms organizational capabilities into compelling value propositions across healthcare's three pillars. Most effective when established early in complex negotiations, this strategy proves crucial when multiple stakeholders must understand your contributions from different perspectives.

At its core, this strategy involves quantifying your value proposition and translating it into terms that resonate with negotiation partners in healthcare's complex landscape. As David Lax and James Sebenius highlight in their work on 3-D negotiation, success in healthcare negotiations often hinges on a clear understanding of one's distinct worth and the ability to communicate it effectively.[5]

In healthcare settings, "value" extends beyond traditional financial metrics. It includes clinical outcomes, patient satisfaction, operational efficiency, and broader impacts like community health. The ability to articulate this multifaceted value is what transforms a simple transaction into an opportunity for collaborative innovation and sustained partnership.

Boardroom Case Study: AIDS Care Group Partnership Development

In the first meeting with pharmaceutical executives and insurance representatives, Strauss began demonstrating ACG's comprehensive value proposition:

Strauss: "Before we discuss pricing structures, I'd like to share ACG's impact across the healthcare spectrum. Our integrated care model has cut long-term healthcare costs by 30% over five years while maintaining 92% medication adherence rates – significantly above industry standards."

Pharmaceutical Executive: "Impressive numbers, but how sustainable are these outcomes?"

Strauss: "Our success comes from integration across all healthcare domains. Our clinical protocols have reduced emergency visits by 45%. Our care delivery model achieves these results through coordinated patient support, reducing the total cost of care. This creates value for insurers through lower claims and for pharmaceutical partners through consistent, predictable medication utilization."

Insurance Representative: "We've seen similar claims before. What makes ACG different?"

Strauss: "Let me be specific. We're not just asking for lower prices – we're offering a partnership that transforms care delivery. Our model has grown prescription volumes by 40% while reducing per-patient costs. We've created a reproducible system that benefits every stakeholder: better patient outcomes, lower insurance costs, and sustainable pharmaceutical revenue streams."

This exchange demonstrates several key value-setting elements in healthcare negotiations. It quantifies impact across all three healthcare pillars while linking clinical excellence to concrete business outcomes. Through careful presentation, it demonstrates sustainable value creation and effectively positions partnership benefits for each stakeholder involved. This approach establishes a comprehensive framework for developing collaborative solutions that serve all parties' interests.

Key Implementation Steps

1. Prepare: To lay the groundwork for effective value setting, begin with a comprehensive value analysis spanning all three pillars. Develop clear metrics that demonstrate clinical, operational, and financial impact while creating stakeholder-specific value frameworks. Map out critical value connections between pillars and identify key sustainability indicators. Support your value claims with robust evidence, and design effective visual tools to communicate your value proposition clearly and convincingly.
2. Execute: During negotiations, present value propositions carefully tailored to each stakeholder group, ensuring you link value metrics across healthcare pillars while demonstrating sustainable impact potential. Build a progressive value narrative that connects directly to your organizational mission. Support all claims with concrete evidence while maintaining focus on developing long-term partnerships rather than short-term gains.
3. Follow Through: Monitor progress by tracking value recognition across stakeholder groups and documenting value-creation patterns. Strengthen value frameworks based on implementation experience and adjust messaging in response to stakeholder feedback. Maintain focus on value enhancement while preparing for the next strategic phase of engagement.

Common Challenges and Solutions

Challenge: Value metrics seem disconnected across pillars
Solution: Create integrated value frameworks showing cross-pillar impacts

Challenge: Stakeholders focus solely on financial metrics
Solution: Develop comprehensive value narratives linking outcomes to costs

Challenge: Difficulty quantifying intangible benefits
Solution: Establish proxy measures and comparative benchmarks

Things to Avoid

In healthcare negotiations, several pitfalls must be actively avoided. Never present siloed value propositions that fail to account for cross-pillar impacts. Guard against overlooking opportunities for cross-pillar value creation or focusing solely on short-term metrics. Take care not to ignore stakeholder-specific value drivers that could enhance your negotiating position.

Cross-Pillar Applications

Practice of Medicine: Quantifying clinical excellence through outcome metrics while demonstrating operational efficiency and cost-effectiveness

Delivery of Care: Creating value frameworks that connect service quality improvements to resource optimization and financial sustainability

Business of Health: Developing comprehensive value propositions that align financial performance with clinical outcomes and operational excellence

Measuring Success

In healthcare negotiations, value setting works best when it creates integrated frameworks with measurable outcomes demonstrating sustainable impact across all three pillars while maintaining clear connections to stakeholder priorities. Success depends on quantifiable benchmarks that monitor value proposition effectiveness and achievement of established metrics while assessing cross-pillar integration. Effective implementation requires ongoing measurement of operational indicators alongside stakeholder satisfaction levels. The long-term sustainability of negotiated value creation emerges through systematic performance tracking and outcome assessment.

As Strauss established ACG's value proposition, he recognized the need to understand stakeholders' deeper priorities and concerns. Success would require moving beyond surface-level positions to uncover underlying interests through Strategic Questioning.

Strategy Two: Strategic Questioning

Strategic Questioning is an essential negotiation approach that transforms surface-level discussions into deeper explorations of underlying interests by employing carefully structured inquiries. It establishes frameworks for ongoing dialogue and relationship building. Most effective after establishing initial value propositions but before detailed solution development, this strategy enables healthcare professionals to uncover unstated needs, concerns, and opportunities that span multiple stakeholders and pillars.

Grounded in cognitive interview techniques developed by psychologists Ronald Fisher and Edward Geiselman[6] and refined by negotiation scholars like Leigh Thompson,[7] Strategic Questioning changes standard discussions into opportunities for deeper understanding and mutual value creation through the artful use of focused questions. This approach is best employed throughout negotiations to uncover underlying interests, guide discussions, and build rapport.[8] By using systematic inquiry, negotiators can uncover hidden interests and generate new opportunities for collaboration.

Through the lens of HEAR, strategic questioning primarily amplifies Acknowledgment by demonstrating genuine curiosity about stakeholders' perspectives while laying the groundwork for effective Recasting. This approach helps negotiators go beyond initial positions to identify shared goals, making it an essential tool for generating mutual value.

Boardroom Case Study: AIDS Care Group Partnership Development [Continued]

Building on ACG's value proposition, Strauss recognized the need to understand stakeholders' deeper interests:

Insurance Representative: "Your outcomes data is compelling, but implementation across our network would be complex."

Strauss: "Help me understand what specific implementation challenges you foresee?"

Insurance Rep: "Well, coordinating care across multiple providers, tracking outcomes..."

Strauss: "If we could demonstrate a scalable coordination model, what metrics would you need to see?"

Pharmaceutical Executive: "Even with strong outcomes, changing our pricing structure affects our entire business model."

Strauss: "Could you walk me through how pricing flexibility in one market segment impacts your broader strategy? Understanding these constraints will help us design a more sustainable partnership."

This exchange illustrates the essential elements of effective strategic questioning in healthcare negotiations. Through systematic inquiry, it reveals underlying concerns while exploring implications across healthcare pillars. The approach creates a solid foundation for solution development and maintains consistent focus on building a long-term partnership. Most importantly, it builds a shared understanding of both constraints and opportunities, enabling more productive dialogue moving forward.

Key Implementation Steps

1. Prepare: Begin by thoroughly reviewing value frameworks established in earlier stages while developing strategic lines of questioning aligned with key value metrics. Design pillar-specific inquiry pathways and carefully map stakeholder interconnections. Develop comprehensive probing sequences for each value domain, prepare follow-up frameworks, and create a clear plan for question progression that maintains strategic focus throughout the negotiation process.
2. Execute: Start with broad value-based inquiries before progressing to more specific pillar-specific exploration. Work to link questions across healthcare domains while building on revealed connections. Maintain strategic focus throughout the process and draw out deeper implications from each response. Create adequate space for discovery and new insights to emerge organically through dialogue.
3. Follow Through: Document all revealed insights carefully and map emerging patterns in stakeholder responses. Connect new discoveries to your existing value framework while tracking relationship development.

Plan the next inquiry phases strategically and prepare for potential strategic trades. Build toward comprehensive option development based on accumulated insights.

Common Challenges and Solutions

Challenge: Questions remain surface-level.
Solution: Develop deeper probing frameworks linked to value metrics.

Challenge: Stakeholders provide vague responses.
Solution: Create structured follow-up sequences tied to specific value domains.

Challenge: Missing cross-pillar connections.
Solution: Design integrated questioning pathways spanning all healthcare domains.

Things to Avoid

When implementing strategic questioning, several critical pitfalls must be avoided. Guard against asking disconnected questions that fail to build toward strategic objectives. Be careful not to miss value-creation opportunities that emerge through dialogue or fail to probe the deeper implications of responses. Avoid overlooking stakeholder interconnections or ignoring emotional undercurrents in the conversation. Never rush through responses or lose sight of your strategic direction.

Cross-Pillar Applications

Practice of Medicine: Exploring clinical value creation through structured inquiry that reveals quality improvement opportunities while maintaining operational feasibility.

Delivery of Care: Investigating service enhancement potential through questions that connect workflow optimization with resource utilization and patient outcomes.

Business of Health: Examining value alignment through strategic inquiry that links financial performance with clinical excellence and operational efficiency.

Measuring Success

In healthcare negotiations, Strategic Questioning works best when it systematically explores value-creation opportunities across all three pillars while building toward integrated solutions. Systematic measurement validates the quality of information gathered and confirms the generation of valuable insights across stakeholders. Regular assessment of cross-pillar integration effectiveness and implementation progress provides critical performance data. Continuous monitoring of stakeholder satisfaction levels throughout the process reinforces the long-term sustainability of established relationships and agreements.

As Strauss' Strategic Questioning revealed potential areas for collaboration, he began identifying opportunities for value-creating trades. The situation called for the careful application of Logrolling for Mutual Benefit to transform different priorities into shared gains.

Strategy Three: Logrolling for Mutual Benefit

Logrolling is an advanced negotiation strategy rooted in integrative bargaining theory, developed by Mary Parker Follett and refined by researchers like Dean Pruitt. With the purpose of changing seemingly competitive situations into opportunities for mutual gain, this strategy is best employed when multiple issues are on the table, allowing for trade-offs that align with varying priorities. It leverages the fact that different stakeholders often have varying priorities, making it possible to create mutually beneficial exchanges by trading across issues.[9] In healthcare negotiations, where needs span clinical outcomes, cost efficiencies, and patient satisfaction, Logrolling is a powerful tool for generating shared value. Logrolling primarily amplifies HEAR's Recasting step by transforming what might appear as zero-sum negotiations into opportunities for mutual gain.

Boardroom Case Study: AIDS Care Group Partnership Development [Continued]

With a deeper understanding gained through strategic questioning, Strauss began constructing potential trade packages:

Pharma Executive: "Our biggest concern remains maintaining pricing integrity across market segments."

Strauss: "What if we structured this as a performance-based partnership? You maintain list prices, while we create value-based metrics tied to prescription volumes and outcomes."

Insurance Rep: "Volume commitments would interest us, but we need predictable costs."

Strauss: "Consider this framework: ACG commits to specific prescription volume targets and adherence rates. In exchange, we implement a tiered pricing model based on outcomes achievement."

Pharma Executive: "That structure could work. What specific metrics would you propose?"

Strauss: "If we achieve a 25% reduction in hospitalization rates and maintain 90% medication adherence, pricing drops to tier one. Lower performance maintains standard rates. Additionally, we could share our care coordination protocols to help scale this model across your network."

This exchange demonstrates the key elements of successful Logrolling in healthcare negotiations. Through careful planning, it creates systematic trade packages that span across pillars while effectively linking different stakeholders' priorities. The approach builds progressive value through strategic trades and maintains a consistent focus on developing a long-term partnership. Importantly, it enables structured scaling of solutions, allowing for sustainable growth and adaptation over time.

Key Implementation Steps

1. Prepare: Begin by reviewing value metrics to identify promising trade opportunities while analyzing insights from Strategic Questioning to map stakeholder priorities effectively. Create comprehensive trade packages that span all pillars and carefully quantify the value of potential exchanges. Develop clear sequencing frameworks and design implementation pathways that account for organizational complexities. Plan value-enhancement combinations that can maximize benefits for all parties involved.
2. Execute: Present trades firmly grounded in established value metrics, referencing Strategic Questioning insights when proposing exchanges. Demonstrate clear cross-pillar benefits while building progressive value through carefully constructed combinations. Maintain active stakeholder engagement throughout the process and consistently link trades to

shared goals. Create positive momentum through strategic sequencing of proposals and agreements.
3. Follow Through: Document all trade agreements thoroughly and track value creation throughout implementation. Monitor implementation progress carefully while assessing ongoing stakeholder satisfaction. Plan future exchanges strategically and work to strengthen the collaborative framework established through successful trades. Prepare comprehensively for future option development based on established patterns of success.

Common Challenges and Solutions

Challenge: Trades appear disconnected from value framework.
Solution: Create integrated packages showing clear value alignment.

Challenge: Stakeholders resist complex exchanges.
Solution: Build progressive trade sequences starting with clear wins.

Challenge: Cross-pillar implementation difficulties.
Solution: Develop coordinated implementation pathways across domains.

Things to Avoid

When implementing Logrolling strategies, several critical pitfalls must be avoided. Never create unbalanced trade packages that could damagc trust or lose connection to your fundamental value framework. Avoid overlooking stakeholder priorities or missing cross-pillar implications of proposed trades. Guard against forcing premature trades or neglecting implementation feasibility. Most importantly, never compromise long-term value for short-term gains.

Cross-Pillar Applications

Practice of Medicine: Structuring clinical protocol trades that enhance quality while optimizing resource utilization and maintaining financial sustainability.

Delivery of Care: Creating service delivery exchanges that improve patient outcomes while balancing operational efficiency and cost-effectiveness.

Business of Health: Developing financial trade packages that align economic incentives with clinical excellence and operational optimization.

Measuring Success

In healthcare business settings, Logrolling succeeds when trades create demonstrable value across pillars while addressing each stakeholder's core interests. Measurement against defined performance indicators provides clear validation of effectiveness and value creation while monitoring cross-pillar integration success. Continuous assessment of implementation metrics alongside quantified stakeholder satisfaction levels reveals ongoing progress. Data-driven evaluation ensures the long-term sustainability of established agreements and relationships through systematic performance tracking.

As Strauss developed trading possibilities with the pharmaceutical and insurance executives, he recognized that different stakeholders valued different aspects of potential agreements. Success would require presenting options that addressed varying priorities while maintaining equivalent value.

Strategy Four: Multiple Equivalent Simultaneous Offers

Multiple Equivalent Simultaneous Offers (MESOs) are an advanced negotiation strategy that enhances flexibility and satisfaction by presenting several carefully calibrated options at once. This approach focuses on providing three options of equal value to create flexibility and increase the likelihood of a mutually beneficial outcome and proves most effective when negotiations are at a standstill or when seeking to understand counterpart priorities through choice. Developed by negotiation scholars Victoria Medvec and Adam Galinsky,[10] it leverages decision theory's insights into the psychology of choice. By offering multiple options of similar value, MESOs empower counterparts to select the option that aligns most with their needs while allowing the proposer to maintain their desired outcomes.

Research consistently demonstrates that MESOs not only improve negotiation outcomes but also increase satisfaction levels, as they combine the psychological benefit of choice with the practical advantage of maintaining value parameters.

Boardroom Case Study: AIDS Care Group Partnership Development [Continued]

Building on the trust established through strategic questioning and initial trade discussions, Strauss prepared to present three carefully structured partnership approaches:

> Strauss: "Based on our discussions about pricing flexibility and performance metrics," Strauss began, "I'd like to propose three partnership models. Each creates equivalent value but through different mechanisms that address our shared concerns about accessibility and sustainability. Our first option," Strauss explained, referencing the outcome metrics they'd discussed earlier, "builds directly on our proven performance track record. We commit to specific volume targets and adherence rates, with pricing tied to achievement."
>
> The insurance representative leaned forward, recognizing how this addressed her earlier concerns about predictable costs. "That would help us forecast more accurately"
>
> "The second approach," Strauss continued, acknowledging the pharmaceutical executive's market concerns, "focuses on progressive implementation. We start with standard pricing but implement incremental reductions as we hit coordinated care milestones."
>
> "That could help us manage market impact more effectively," the pharmaceutical executive noted, building on their earlier discussion about pricing integrity.
>
> "Finally," Strauss offered, "our Value Integration model maintains current pricing but creates a three-way partnership where we share cost savings from reduced hospitalizations. This aligns everyone's interests – sustainable pharmaceutical revenue, lower insurance costs, and enhanced patient care."

This dialogue demonstrates the essential elements of successful MESO implementation in healthcare settings. Through careful preparation, it builds on understanding developed through earlier strategies while addressing concerns revealed through strategic questioning. The approach creates comprehensive frameworks for value-creating trades and enables meaningful stakeholder choice while maintaining consistent value. Most importantly, it supports cross-pillar solution development, fostering sustainable agreements that serve all parties' interests.

Key Implementation Steps

1. Prepare: Begin by reviewing your value analysis thoroughly and incorporating key insights gained from strategic questioning. Develop multiple options that effectively integrate potential trades while creating clear evaluation frameworks for stakeholders to assess proposals. Design comprehensive implementation pathways for each option presented, ensuring feasibility and value preservation throughout the process.
2. Execute: Present options in a way that clearly demonstrates progressive value creation, linking each option explicitly to previously identified stakeholder interests. Show how each option builds upon established trust and remains open to option combination as discussions progress. Support informed decision-making across pillars by providing clear information about the implications and benefits of each choice.
3. Follow Through: Document chosen approaches and their underlying rationale carefully. Develop detailed implementation plans that account for all affected pillars while monitoring progress against established metrics. Track outcomes and stakeholder satisfaction consistently, making adjustments to the framework as needed based on real-world experience and feedback.

Things to Avoid

When implementing MESOs, several critical pitfalls must be avoided. Never create options without clear value equivalence, and never lose connection to your organizational mission. Guard against overlooking implementation feasibility or failing to maintain stakeholder engagement throughout the process. Take care not to ignore cross-pillar impacts or sacrifice long-term value for short-term gains. Keep the focus on creating sustainable solutions that serve all parties' interests.

Common Challenges and Solutions

Challenge: Options appear disconnected from organizational goals.
Solution: Ground each option in an established value proposition.

Challenge: Stakeholders resist comparing options.
Solution: Create clear evaluation frameworks linked to shared interests.

Challenge: Cross-pillar implementation concerns.
Solution: Develop integrated implementation pathways.

Cross-Pillar Applications

Practice of Medicine: Structuring clinical protocol options that maintain quality while offering implementation flexibility.

Delivery of Care: Developing care coordination models that balance resource utilization with service enhancement.

Business of Health: Creating financial frameworks that align incentives while maintaining organizational sustainability.

Measuring Success

In healthcare business negotiations, MESOs work best when options maintain equivalent value while offering meaningful choices in the implementation approach. Comparative analysis of option outcomes through defined metrics validates equivalent value creation and tracks implementation pathway effectiveness. Regular assessment of concession impacts and integration success across pillars generates actionable performance data. Systematic evaluation of stakeholder satisfaction trends and agreement durability demonstrates the sustained benefits achieved through structured MESO deployment.

As the discussion of partnership options progressed, Strauss recognized that moving from possibilities to agreement would require careful coordination of compromises.

Strategy Five: Concession Management

Concession management strategically transforms sacrifices into opportunities for building trust and advancing discussions. This approach aims to transform the give-and-take of bargaining into a strategic tool for building momentum and fostering reciprocity throughout negotiations, and proves most effective when discussions reach a stalemate, goodwill needs to be created, or agreements must be locked in during complex negotiations. Anchored in game theory and strategic bargaining models developed by

John Nash and refined by negotiation scholars Richard Walton and Robert McKersie, it uses the psychology of reciprocity to create structured pathways toward agreement in healthcare's high-stakes environment.[11]

Concession management amplifies both Empowerment and Recasting by enabling negotiators to shape the rhythm of exchanges while demonstrating flexibility. Through strategic concessions, negotiators can diffuse rising tensions during emotionally charged discussions, seal deals, or secure interim agreements, and show genuine intent to foster trust and create a more collaborative atmosphere. However, for concessions to be effective, they must be communicated clearly. Concessions hold value only when the other side understands the difficulty of making them. Therefore, when making a concession, explicitly state its significance and articulate what is expected in return.

Boardroom Case Study: AIDS Care Group Partnership Development [Continued]

Building on the momentum from presenting multiple partnership options, Strauss began guiding the give-and-take process:

> "I hear your concerns about our proposed timeline," [Strauss acknowledged, addressing the pharmaceutical executive's earlier hesitation]. "While we believe rapid implementation offers significant benefits, we could adjust our evaluation periods to align better with your standard processes."
>
> [The pharmaceutical executive nodded]. "Semi-annual evaluations would fit our existing review cycles."
>
> "In that case," [Strauss continued, connecting this concession to value creation], "we could enhance our metrics package to include detailed prescription adherence data and total cost of care analysis. This would give everyone more robust performance data, even with longer evaluation periods."
>
> [The insurance representative leaned forward]. "More comprehensive metrics would help, but we'd need to adjust initial performance thresholds."
>
> "What if we started at 15% hospitalization reduction and 85% adherence for the first six months?" Strauss proposed, carefully balancing accommodation with ambition. "This gives everyone time

to optimize while maintaining meaningful goals. In exchange, we'd accelerate full implementation once we hit these targets, potentially tripling volume within the first year."

This exchange demonstrates the key elements of effective Concession Management in healthcare negotiations. The approach strategically times concessions to maintain negotiating momentum while carefully linking concessions to specific gains. Through thoughtful implementation, it maintains value balance throughout the negotiation process and builds positive momentum toward agreement. Importantly, it creates effective reciprocity cycles that strengthen relationships and foster long-term collaboration.

Key Implementation Steps

1. Prepare: Begin by reviewing your value framework to establish clear concession boundaries while using Strategic Questioning insights to anticipate stakeholder needs. Analyze Logrolling patterns to inform concession packages and consider MESO frameworks when structuring potential concessions. Map out potential concession sequences carefully and create comprehensive value-preservation guidelines. Design effective reciprocity triggers that can maintain momentum throughout the negotiation process.
2. Execute: Ground all concessions firmly in established value metrics and reference insights from Strategic Questioning when making offers. Link concessions to successful trade patterns while presenting options that maintain MESO principles. Build progressive value through carefully staged concessions and maintain strategic momentum throughout the process. Monitor value preservation consistently to ensure sustainable outcomes.
3. Follow Through: Document concession patterns thoroughly and track value maintenance throughout implementation. Assess reciprocity effectiveness and monitor implementation progress carefully. Plan future exchanges strategically and work consistently to strengthen relationship frameworks established through successful concessions. Prepare comprehensively for contingency planning based on established patterns and outcomes.

Common Challenges and Solutions

Challenge: Value erosion through concessions.
Solution: Create integrated frameworks linking concessions to value creation.

Challenge: Lack of reciprocity from stakeholders.
Solution: Develop structured exchange protocols tied to value metrics.

Challenge: Cross-pillar implementation conflicts.
Solution: Design coordinated concession pathways across domains.

Things to Avoid

When managing concessions, several critical pitfalls must be avoided. Never make disconnected concessions that fail to align with your value framework or lose sight of your strategic objectives. Guard against overlooking stakeholder relationships or missing cross-pillar impacts of proposed concessions. Take care not to rush concession sequences or fail to secure appropriate reciprocity. Most importantly, avoid compromising long-term sustainability for short-term gains.

Cross-Pillar Applications

Practice of Medicine: Managing clinical protocol adjustments that maintain quality standards while accommodating operational constraints and financial parameters.

Delivery of Care: Structuring service delivery concessions that optimize patient care while balancing resource utilization and cost considerations.

Business of Health: Creating financial concession frameworks that preserve economic value while supporting clinical excellence and operational efficiency.

Measuring Success

In healthcare business negotiations, Concession Management succeeds when it maintains value while building momentum toward agreement through strategic trades. Success in Concession Management can be evaluated through several key indicators. Monitor concession effectiveness and value preservation while assessing cross-pillar integration success. Track implementation effectiveness alongside stakeholder satisfaction levels. And most of all, maintain a consistent focus on ensuring the long-term sustainability of agreements and relationships established through the concession process.

The emerging partnership framework showed promise, but Strauss knew that long-term success would require addressing uncertainties about future performance, market conditions, and implementation challenges. Rather than letting these unknowns create barriers, they could become the foundation for deeper collaboration.

Strategy Six: Contingency Agreements

Contingency Agreements transform uncertainty from a barrier into an opportunity by creating flexible deals that protect both parties' interests and adapt to future circumstances. They are particularly effective when facing uncertain future outcomes, differing forecasts, or when seeking to build long-term strategic partnerships.

Rooted in decision analysis and risk management theory developed by Howard Raiffa and refined through ongoing negotiation research, this approach utilizes structured uncertainty to align incentives and foster sustainable partnerships in healthcare's dynamic environment.[12] Contingency Agreements primarily amplify HEAR's Relational Mindset, establishing frameworks for ongoing collaboration where parties share both risks and rewards, building enduring partnerships rather than one-time transactions.

Boardroom Case Study: AIDS Care Group Partnership Development [Continued]

With basic agreement parameters taking shape, Strauss moved to transform the remaining uncertainties into opportunities for aligned incentives:

> "Let's build in specific performance tiers that share both risk and reward," Strauss suggested, connecting back to earlier value discussions. "For example, if we achieve both 90% adherence and 25% cost reduction, pricing would drop an additional 10%."

The insurance representative shifted forward. "And if results fall short?"

"Fair question," Strauss acknowledged. "If we don't hit base targets, we maintain standard pricing and implement rapid improvement protocols within 30 days. However," he added, building on their earlier discussions about shared value creation, "if we exceed targets, we'd share the additional savings three ways."

The pharmaceutical executive tapped his pen thoughtfully. "We'd need very clear measurement protocols."

"Absolutely," Strauss agreed. "We propose monthly dashboard reviews with all parties. Success in two consecutive quarters could trigger accelerated expansion, while missing targets would pause growth until we demonstrate improvement."

"What about market changes?" the insurance representative asked. "New drug approvals could shift the landscape significantly."

"That's exactly why we should include market adjustment provisions," Strauss replied. "We could establish specific triggers for reviewing and adjusting our framework while maintaining our core partnership principles."

This dialogue demonstrates the essential elements of successful Contingency Agreement development in healthcare negotiations. The approach effectively transforms uncertainties into opportunities for collaboration while creating balanced risk-reward frameworks that serve all parties' interests. Through careful structuring, it establishes clear performance metrics and enables structured adaptation over time. Most importantly, it maintains strong stakeholder alignment throughout the agreement's implementation, fostering sustainable partnerships that can evolve with changing circumstances.

Key Implementation Steps

1. Prepare: Begin by reviewing value metrics to identify key uncertainties while using Strategic Questioning insights to map risk perceptions comprehensively. Incorporate successful Logrolling patterns in contingency design and consider MESO frameworks when developing contingency options. Build on established concession patterns to identify effective trigger points and create robust measurement protocols. Design adaptation frameworks that can accommodate evolving needs while maintaining value preservation.

2. Execute: Ground all contingencies firmly in established value metrics and reference stakeholder insights when proposing triggers. Link contingencies to successful trade patterns while presenting flexible implementation options that maintain strategic alignment. Build progressive adaptation pathways that can evolve with changing circumstances and maintain a consistent focus on core objectives. Monitor performance metrics carefully throughout implementation.
3. Follow Through: Document contingency implementation thoroughly and track adaptation effectiveness over time. Monitor value preservation carefully while assessing ongoing stakeholder engagement levels. Plan future adjustments strategically and work consistently to strengthen collaborative frameworks established through successful contingency agreements. Prepare comprehensively for the post-settlement phase of implementation.

Common Challenges and Solutions

Challenge: Contingencies appear disconnected from value framework.
Solution: Create integrated triggers linked to value metrics.

Challenge: Stakeholders resist complex frameworks.
Solution: Develop staged implementation tied to clear value drivers.

Challenge: Cross-pillar coordination difficulties.
Solution: Design coordinated adaptation pathways across domains.

Things to Avoid

When developing Contingency Agreements, several critical pitfalls must be avoided. Never create overly complex frameworks that could hinder implementation or lose connection to your core value proposition. Guard against overlooking stakeholder concerns or missing cross-pillar impacts of proposed contingencies. Take care not to rush implementation or neglect measurement protocols. Most importantly, avoid compromising long-term sustainability for short-term convenience.

Cross-Pillar Applications

Practice of Medicine: Developing clinical adaptation frameworks that maintain quality while enabling evidence-based evolution.

Delivery of Care: Creating service delivery contingencies that optimize care while managing resource utilization.

Business of Health: Structuring financial adaptation mechanisms that preserve value while supporting operational flexibility.

Measuring Success

In healthcare negotiations, Contingency Agreements work best when they enable structured adaptation while maintaining value across all three pillars. Performance indicators built into trigger points and milestone reviews validate framework effectiveness and confirm value preservation across integrated pillars. Systematic assessment of adaptation mechanisms through predefined metrics reveals implementation success rates and stakeholder satisfaction trends. Regular evaluation of established thresholds and outcomes data demonstrates the sustained effectiveness of contingency-based frameworks in preserving long-term agreement stability.

As the contingency framework took shape, Strauss recognized the opportunity to create additional value through ongoing collaboration. The situation called for the careful development of post-settlement agreements.

Strategy Seven: Post-Settlement Agreements

As the partnership framework neared completion, Strauss understood that their initial agreement, however comprehensive, would need to evolve with healthcare's changing landscape. Building in structured opportunities for review and refinement would transform their agreement from a static document into a living framework for ongoing collaboration.

Post-Settlement Agreements represent an advanced negotiation strategy that transforms initial agreements into opportunities for ongoing refinement by scheduling structured follow-up reviews after the deal is finalized. This approach proves most effective when implemented at the moment of agreement by scheduling specific future check-in dates to proactively address implementation challenges before they escalate into major issues.

Grounded in negotiation theory developed by Howard Raiffa and refined through real-world healthcare applications, Post-Settlement Agreements leverage predetermined review points to maintain accountability and ensure long-term success.[13] Through the HEAR lens, Post-Settlement agreements primarily amplify both Acknowledgment and Recasting by creating structured opportunities to validate implementation experiences and adapt approaches based on real-world feedback.

Boardroom Case Study: AIDS Care Group Partnership Development [Continued]

Three months after establishing their core partnership agreement, Strauss convened the first quarterly review meeting with the pharmaceutical and insurance representatives:

> "Before we dive into performance metrics," Strauss began, "I'd like to acknowledge something remarkable. In just three months, we're seeing medication adherence rates exceed our initial targets in several patient populations."
>
> The pharmaceutical executive nodded. "We've noticed interesting patterns in the adherence data. Some demographics are showing particularly strong results."
>
> "That's exactly why these review sessions are crucial," Strauss replied. "Our base agreement gives us the flexibility to optimize our approach based on real-world data. What if we developed targeted support programs for these high-performing demographics while studying their success factors?"
>
> The insurance representative leaned forward. "Our care management teams have identified some promising practices in those populations."
>
> "This is the kind of insight we hoped to generate," Strauss noted. "We could pilot enhanced support programs in these communities while maintaining our core protocols elsewhere. The framework we established supports this kind of innovation."

This dialogue demonstrates the key elements of effective Post-Settlement Agreement implementation in healthcare negotiations. Through careful planning, it enables the identification of opportunities to exceed initial targets while developing plans for targeted program enhancement. The approach maintains a consistent focus on continuous improvement and strengthens collaborative relationships over time. Importantly, it creates clear pathways for broader impact, allowing successful initiatives to scale effectively across the organization.

Key Implementation Steps

1. Prepare: Begin by building on established value metrics and incorporating relationship insights gained through strategic questioning. Integrate successful trades identified through Logrolling and design review frameworks that maintain MESO flexibility throughout implementation. Align with existing concession patterns and contingency triggers while creating comprehensive evaluation criteria that span all pillars. Develop structured modification protocols that can accommodate evolving needs while preserving core value.
2. Execute: Launch the review process with clear connections to the original agreement value and link ongoing assessments to previously identified stakeholder priorities. Demonstrate how modifications build on established collaboration while maintaining flexibility for continuous improvement. Support evidence-based adaptation across pillars and document progress against initial benchmarks carefully. Foster ongoing stakeholder engagement throughout the implementation process.
3. Follow Through: Track agreement evolution and value creation consistently while monitoring cross-pillar impacts of modifications. Document lessons learned and best practices thoroughly, and work to strengthen collaborative relationships established through the process. Scale successful elements to other areas strategically and adjust review frequency based on emerging needs. Maintain focus on planning for long-term sustainability.

Common Challenges and Solutions

Challenge: Losing momentum between reviews.
Solution: Create clear value-tracking mechanisms linked to the original agreement.

Challenge: Stakeholder turnover affecting continuity.
Solution: Develop robust documentation and onboarding processes.

Challenge: Modification requests threatening agreement integrity.
Solution: Establish clear criteria for evaluating changes against original value proposition.

Things to Avoid

When implementing Post-Settlement Agreements, several critical pitfalls must be avoided. Never disconnect reviews from the original agreement's purpose or lose sight of cross-pillar impacts. Guard against allowing modifications without clear value assessment or failing to document the evolution of agreements properly. Take care not to neglect stakeholder relationship maintenance or miss opportunities for value creation. Most importantly, avoid compromising long-term sustainability for short-term adjustments.

Cross-Pillar Applications

Practice of Medicine: Creating structured clinical protocol review processes that maintain quality while enabling evidence-based adaptation.

Delivery of Care: Establishing regular operational assessment frameworks that optimize resource utilization while enhancing service delivery.

Business of Health: Developing systematic partnership review mechanisms that align stakeholder interests while driving continuous value creation.

Measuring Success

In healthcare business negotiations, Post-Settlement Agreements work best when they create structured opportunities for value enhancement while maintaining focus on original agreement principles and cross-pillar impacts. Evaluation criteria measure review effectiveness and validate incremental value creation through systematic assessment of integration milestones. Continuous monitoring of operational indicators and satisfaction metrics reveals implementation success rates against established baselines. Performance tracking using longitudinal data analysis helps demonstrate how structured enhancements contribute to sustained benefits—preserving both agreement integrity and long-term relationship stability.

COMMON PITFALLS IN ADVANCED HEALTHCARE NEGOTIATIONS

Strategic excellence in healthcare negotiations demands more than just knowledge of core strategic approaches – it requires awareness of potential missteps that can compromise outcomes. This section examines eight fundamental strategic pitfalls in healthcare negotiation, offering guidance on maintaining strategic integrity while achieving meaningful results.

One common challenge is *overreliance* on a single strategy. When negotiators use the same strategy repeatedly, it may lose impact and appear predictable. Effective negotiation in healthcare requires flexibility and the willingness to adapt methods to suit the unique context of each situation, whether it's a high-stakes boardroom discussion or a fast-paced clinical negotiation.

Lack of preparation is another potential pitfall, as unprepared negotiators may miss critical information or fail to address key issues. In high-stakes healthcare environments, thorough preparation is indispensable for confident and informed decision-making.

The *risk of balancing competing priorities* is a significant challenge in complex healthcare negotiations. While clinicians naturally focus on optimizing patient outcomes, negotiations often involve multiple considerations including workflow efficiency, resource allocation, and system-wide impacts. Effective negotiators help create frameworks where clinical excellence and operational sustainability can coexist, ensuring that agreements advance patient care within practical constraints. This balanced approach respects both clinical expertise and organizational realities without suggesting that either perspective alone represents the complete picture.

There are also specific pitfalls related to particular strategies. *Premature concession-making* represents a significant pitfall in healthcare negotiations. When negotiators offer concessions too quickly or without clear justification, they risk undermining their position and creating expectations for further compromises. Effective negotiation requires a deliberate approach to concession management, starting with smaller compromises and advancing to larger ones only when there is clear reciprocity and mutual understanding of value.

The *misalignment of MESOs* with stakeholder priorities can derail otherwise promising negotiations. Without proper research and understanding of counterpart interests, these offers may appear superficial or manipulative rather than genuine attempts at resolution. Success with MESOs depends on thorough preparation and careful tailoring of proposals to address authentic stakeholder concerns while maintaining clear value propositions.

In healthcare's dynamic environment, an overreliance on *Contingency Agreements* poses unique challenges. While these agreements can effectively manage uncertainty, excessive use can create unwieldy arrangements that prove difficult to implement or monitor in fast-paced healthcare settings. The key lies in judicious application, focusing on critical uncertainties while maintaining clarity and practicality in agreement terms.

Neglecting Post-Settlement Agreement reviews represents an often-overlooked weakness in negotiation practice. After reaching agreement, parties may move forward without establishing clear follow-up mechanisms, allowing potential issues to develop unchecked. Building regular review points into agreements ensures ongoing accountability and provides opportunities to address emerging challenges before they escalate into larger problems.

Finally, *avoiding ethical blindspots* is paramount in healthcare negotiations. In the pursuit of favorable terms, professionals must remain vigilant about the ethical implications of their strategies, upholding healthcare's guiding principles and ensuring that patient welfare and organizational integrity are never compromised.

Countering Advanced Negotiation Strategies in Healthcare

Negotiating effectively requires anticipating and responding to common responses. This section examines specific countermoves to each foundational strategy, with several techniques drawing from the advanced tactics explored in Chapter 8, providing practical guidance for maintaining negotiation momentum while preserving relationships.

Countering Strategy One: Value Positioning

The art of Value Positioning reveals itself most dramatically when experienced negotiators attempt to reshape the metrics of success. You might encounter a vendor who dismissively waves away your quality metrics in favor of their preferred cost-savings calculations, or a partner organization that strategically minimizes your unique capabilities to strengthen their bargaining position. These subtle devaluations often precede aggressive pricing discussions or resource allocation debates, particularly when counterparts attempt to shift focus to metrics that favor their position while downplaying your demonstrated value.

Success in defending your value requires more than mere data – it demands strategic reframing and Emotional Intelligence. Consider responding: "While cost savings are certainly important, let's examine how our quality metrics translate directly into reduced readmission rates and improved patient outcomes. These factors significantly impact your bottom line through value-based care incentives." This approach transcends immediate financial concerns by connecting your value to broader organizational success metrics.

Skilled negotiators often enhance this position through Chapter 8's Tactical Empathy: "I understand your focus on immediate cost reduction – it's a critical priority in today's healthcare environment. Let me show you how our approach actually serves this goal through improved quality metrics and reduced complications." They might further strengthen their position by reframing short-term costs against long-term value: "When we examine three-year outcome data, our approach demonstrates substantial returns through reduced readmissions and improved patient satisfaction scores, directly impacting your value-based care payments."

Countering Strategy Two: Logrolling

Logrolling represents one of healthcare negotiation's most nuanced skills – the delicate trading of differing priorities for mutual gain. Yet watch carefully as negotiators attempt to mask imbalanced trades behind complex proposals. Like a chess player thinking several moves ahead, they might offer immediate small concessions while securing far more valuable long-term advantages, particularly in complex healthcare systems where the true value of trades may not be immediately apparent.

Mastering this exchange requires both precision and patience, grounded in clear prioritization of interests. Rather than rushing to accept seemingly attractive trades, experienced negotiators might respond: "Your proposal to adjust our staffing schedules in exchange for equipment upgrades is interesting. Let's break down the long-term implications of both elements to ensure we're creating balanced value for both departments." This methodical approach prevents hasty trades while building toward truly mutual benefits.

Skilled practitioners often employ strategic questions to clarify terms: "When you mention "flexible scheduling," could you specify exactly what adjustments you're envisioning? This helps us assess the true value exchange." They might also recast proposals to better align with prioritized interests: "What if we modified the trade to include immediate schedule adjustments for specific high-demand periods, paired with a phased equipment upgrade plan? This could better serve both our immediate operational needs and long-term strategic goals." This structured approach ensures that trades serve core interests while maintaining negotiating leverage.

Countering Strategy Three: Concession Management

The subtle dynamics of Concession Management often determine negotiation success long before final agreements are reached. In healthcare's complex environment, each concession carries multiple ripple effects – consider how a simple scheduling adjustment might impact care coordination, staff satisfaction, and patient outcomes. Yet many negotiators misread these carefully calibrated moves as mere opening positions rather than the valuable trades they represent, particularly when concessions are offered without clear communication of their significance. Protecting the value of your concessions requires clear communication of their true costs and implications, coupled with strategic incremental deployment.

A skilled administrator might note: "By adjusting our clinic hours, we're fundamentally restructuring our care delivery model. This represents a significant operational shift that will require corresponding adjustments in other areas. We'll need to see reciprocal flexibility in resource allocation to make this work." This framing ensures concessions receive appropriate weight in the broader negotiation. Experienced negotiators often enhance this approach by making smaller, calculated concessions: "Let's start with a pilot program in one department to demonstrate the impact of these changes before expanding further." They consistently pair concessions with requests for reciprocity: "Given the substantial operational changes we're considering, what specific commitments can you offer to ensure balanced implementation?" This measured approach maintains leverage while encouraging mutual commitment to successful outcomes.

Countering Strategy Four: Strategic Questioning

In healthcare negotiations, strategic questioning can uncover more insight than direct answers alone. Like a diagnostic process, skilled questioning peels back layers of stated positions to reveal underlying interests and concerns. Yet many negotiators face deliberately vague or evasive responses that obscure critical insights, particularly when discussing complex healthcare systems where details matter immensely and ambiguity can hide significant implications.

Breaking through this fog requires a precisely calibrated approach to inquiry. Consider this progression: "When you mention 'improved efficiency,' what specific metrics would demonstrate success? How do these align with your department's current performance indicators?" Such focused questioning illuminates hidden constraints and opportunities while maintaining collaborative dialogue.

Experienced negotiators often start with broad exploratory questions before narrowing focus: "Could you help me understand your overall vision for departmental efficiency? Now, specifically regarding staff utilization, what benchmarks are you currently using?" They might then deploy "window" questions to clarify ambiguous terms: "You've mentioned 'optimal staffing' several times – could you define exactly what that means in your context? What specific staff-to-patient ratios are you envisioning?" This systematic approach transforms vague discussions into concrete understanding.

Countering Strategy Five: Multiple Equivalent Simultaneous Offers

Multiple Equivalent Simultaneous Offers provide negotiators with powerful tools for exploring solution spaces, yet their effectiveness can be undermined by counterparts who perceive them as overwhelming or manipulative. In healthcare settings, where decisions often impact multiple stakeholders, this resistance can manifest as wholesale rejection rather than constructive engagement, particularly when options appear too numerous or complex.

Successful deployment of MESOs requires careful framing, collaborative exploration, and strategic simplification when needed. A skilled negotiator might position multiple options this way: "I've outlined three approaches to our staffing challenge – each addresses our core needs differently while offering distinct advantages for your team. Which elements from these options resonate most strongly with your priorities?" This approach transforms the potential to overwhelm negotiators into productive solution-building.

When faced with resistance, experienced practitioners often clarify their intent: "These options aren't meant to complicate our discussion, but rather to explore different ways we might meet both our needs. Let's focus on which elements feel most promising." They actively seek feedback: "Which aspects of these proposals align best with your operational constraints?" If complexity remains a barrier, they might suggest: "Let's focus on the two approaches that seemed to generate the most interest and explore how we might combine their strongest elements."

Countering Strategy Six: Contingency Agreements

The architecture of effective Contingency Agreements builds bridges across uncertainty, yet many healthcare negotiations stumble when these structures appear too complex or risky. Watch for the subtle signs of resistance – the quick dismissal of performance metrics or the push for simpler, less nuanced arrangements that might leave both parties vulnerable to future challenges, particularly in healthcare settings where outcomes can be difficult to measure precisely.

Crafting acceptable contingencies requires balancing sophistication with simplicity, clear incentive alignment, and regular review opportunities. Consider this approach: "Let's start with tracking just two key quality indicators that directly impact both our goals. We can schedule quarterly reviews to assess their effectiveness and adjust as needed." This framework provides necessary protections while maintaining manageable complexity.

Experienced negotiators often strengthen this foundation by clearly aligning incentives via Chapter 8's Double Magnet Approach: "These metrics directly connect to our shared goal of improving patient outcomes while managing costs effectively. When we succeed, both organizations benefit measurably." They might also build in structured review points: "Let's establish monthly check-ins for the first quarter to ensure our tracking methods work for both teams, then adjust the frequency based on our experiences." This approach creates a robust yet flexible framework that can evolve with changing circumstances while maintaining clear accountability measures.

Countering Strategy Seven: Post-Settlement Enhancements

Finally, one particularly challenging negotiation tactic to watch for is known as "the Nibble" – a deceptively simple yet potentially costly post-settlement enhancement maneuver that emerges just as an agreement appears to be finalized. This last-minute request for additional concessions can be especially frustrating in healthcare settings, where contracts often involve complex systems and long-term commitments. Consider a scenario where, moments before signing a contract for a new electronic health record system, a vendor suddenly introduces an unexpected maintenance fee.

The most effective counter to this tactic is known as "the Boomerang" approach, which turns the late-stage request back on the party attempting the Nibble. Respond by flipping the dynamic: "If we're reopening negotiations, we'd like to discuss adding the advanced analytics module at no extra cost. Otherwise, let's stick to our original agreement." This approach effectively communicates that any attempt to modify the agreement at the eleventh hour opens the door for both parties to revisit terms, often encouraging the original party to withdraw their last-minute request.

Conclusion: The Importance of Negotiating Strategically

Mastering advanced negotiation strategies is essential for healthcare professionals navigating complex, high-stakes environments. The foundational strategies outlined in this chapter offer a comprehensive practical toolkit for achieving better outcomes across healthcare's three pillars. By tailoring each strategy to fit the unique dynamics of clinical, operational, and financial contexts, healthcare professionals can create mutually beneficial agreements while maintaining a focus on patient-centered outcomes. As healthcare providers apply these strategies, they should remain adaptable, culturally aware, and ethically grounded, ensuring that negotiations foster collaboration and drive positive change throughout the healthcare system.

REFLECTION EXERCISE: MASTERING ADVANCED HEALTHCARE NEGOTIATION STRATEGIES

Consider a complex negotiation you're currently facing or anticipate in your healthcare role. Take 30 minutes to work through the following structured reflection:

1. **Strategic Analysis:** Begin by considering the following:
   - Map out the stakeholders across all three healthcare pillars (Operating Room, Exam Room, Boardroom).
   - For each stakeholder, identify their likely priorities, concerns, and constraints.
   - Consider which advanced strategies (e.g., MESOs, Logrolling, Contingency Agreements) might be most effective with each stakeholder.

2. **Strategic Planning:** For each strategy, formulate a plan to use it during negotiations. For example:
   - Draft three different MESOs you could present, ensuring they're of equivalent value.
   - Identify potential areas for Logrolling – what could you trade to create mutual value?
   - Design a Contingency Agreement that could help bridge key uncertainties.
3. **Integration and Application:** Finally, consider:
   - How could combining multiple strategies strengthen your approach?
   - What metrics or contingencies could help align stakeholder interests?
   - What potential pitfalls should you watch for?
   - How will you maintain focus on patient care while pursuing organizational goals?

Document your insights and create an action plan for implementing these strategies in your upcoming negotiation. Review and refine your approach after the negotiation, noting what worked well and what you might adjust for future situations.

Key Takeaways

1. Thorough preparation represents the foundation of successful healthcare negotiations, requiring systematic stakeholder analysis, rigorous data collection, scenario planning, and strategic selection. Effective preparation must span healthcare's three pillars (Operating Room, Exam Room, Boardroom) while maintaining flexibility to adapt as negotiations evolve. This cross-pillar application ensures strategies remain effective whether negotiating clinical protocols, resource allocation, or organizational changes, enabling healthcare professionals to enter complex negotiations with both the evidence and strategic framework needed to achieve optimal outcomes.
2. The seven advanced negotiation strategies provide healthcare professionals with a comprehensive toolkit for complex negotiations. Each strategy builds upon fundamental HEAR principles while addressing distinct negotiation challenges across healthcares three pillars. This

systematic framework enables healthcare professionals to change challenging negotiations into opportunities for sustainable value creation while maintaining strong stakeholder relationships and an unwavering focus on patient care.

3. Understanding and avoiding common pitfalls is essential for healthcare negotiators, particularly regarding overreliance on single strategies, inadequate preparation, and losing sight of patient-centered care. Success requires vigilance against premature concessions, misaligned offers, and ethical blind spots while maintaining clear accountability through post-settlement reviews. This awareness of potential challenges helps healthcare professionals navigate complex negotiations while upholding both organizational and patient care objectives.
4. Healthcare professionals must develop adept responses to advanced negotiation strategies, particularly when counterparts attempt to reshape value metrics, mask imbalanced trades, or introduce last-minute changes. Effective countering requires a combination of tactical empathy, strategic questioning, and structured approaches to maintaining leverage while building collaborative relationships. This defensive capability ensures healthcare professionals can protect core interests while maintaining focus on positive outcomes across all three pillars.

Notes

1. Dimitri J. Anastakis, "Negotiation Skills for Physicians," *The American Journal of Surgery* 185, no. 1 (2003): 74–78, https://doi.org/10.1016/S0002-9610(02)01108-2.
2. Jeffrey W. Berlin and Frank J. Lexa, "Negotiation Techniques for Health Care Professionals," *Journal of the American College of Radiology* 4, no. 7 (July 2007): 487–491, https://doi.org/10.1016/j.jacr.2006.12.015.
3. Anastakis, "Negotiation Skills for Physicians."
4. Roy J. Lewicki, David M. Saunders, and Bruce Barry, *Negotiation: Readings, Exercises, and Cases* (New York: McGraw-Hill Education, 2014); Randall S. Peterson and Kristin J. Behfar, "The Dynamic Relationship between Performance Feedback, Trust, and Conflict in Groups: A Longitudinal Study," *Organizational Behavior and Human Decision Processes* 102, no. 2 (2007): 226–238; Anastakis, "Negotiation Skills for Physicians."
5. David A. Lax and James K. Sebenius, *3-D Negotiation: Powerful Tools to Change the Game in Your Most Important Deals* (Boston, MA: Harvard Business Press, 2006).

6. R. P. Fisher and R. E. Geiselman, *Memory-Enhancing Techniques for Investigative Interviewing: The Cognitive Interview* (Springfield, IL: Charles C. Thomas Publisher, 1992); R. E. Geiselman and R. P. Fisher, "Interviewing Witnesses and Victims," in *Investigative Interviewing: The Essentials*, ed. M. St-Yves (Toronto: Carswell, 2014), 29–62.
7. Leigh L. Thompson, *The Mind and Heart of the Negotiator*, 7th ed. (Boston, MA: Pearson, 2020).
8. Leonard L. Marcus, Barry C. Dorn, and Eric J. McNulty, *Renegotiating Health Care: Resolving Conflict to Build Collaboration* (New York: Jossey-Bass, 2011).
9. Dean G. Pruitt, *Negotiation Behavior* (New York: Academic Press, 1981); Mary Parker Follett, *Dynamic Administration: The Collected Papers of Mary Parker Follett*, ed. Henry C. Metcalf and L. Urwick (New York: Harper & Brothers, 1940).
10. Medvec, Victoria H., and Adam D. Galinsky, "Putting More on the Table: How Making Multiple Offers Can Increase the Final Value of the Deal," *HBS Negotiation Newsletter* 8 (2005): 4–6; Adam D. Galinsky and Thomas Mussweiler, "First Offers as Anchors: The Role of Perspective-Taking and Negotiator Focus," *Journal of Personality and Social Psychology* 81, no. 4 (2001): 657–669.
11. John F. Nash, "The Bargaining Problem," *Econometrica* 18, no. 2 (1950): 155–162; Richard E. Walton and Robert B. McKersie, *A Behavioral Theory of Labor Negotiations: An Analysis of a Social Interaction System* (Ithaca, NY: Cornell University Press, 1965); Deepak Malhotra and Max H. Bazerman, *Negotiation Genius: How to Overcome Obstacles and Achieve Brilliant Results at the Bargaining Table and Beyond* (New York: Bantam, 2007).
12. Howard Raiffa, *The Art and Science of Negotiation* (Cambridge, MA: Harvard University Press, 1982); Max H. Bazerman and James J. Gillespie, "Betting on the Future: The Virtues of Contingent Contracts," *Harvard Business Review* 77, no. 5 (1999): 155–160.
13. Raiffa, *The Art and Science of Negotiation*.

Chapter 8

Mastering Real-Time Negotiation Tactics

Tactics are like quicksilver. They adapt, shift, and flow in response to the pressure of the moment, creating pathways to unexpected solutions.

– **Howard Raiff**

DOI: 10.4324/9781003336013-10

Dr. Kiran Sharma paused in the hospital cafeteria, using these final moments before his presentation to mentally rehearse his approach. As Director of Neurology Services, he had orchestrated countless complex negotiations, but today's stakes felt different. The new stroke treatment protocol he was proposing wasn't just about improving outcomes – it required a fundamental shift in how departments worked together.

The morning's impromptu conversation with Mark, the hospital's chief financial officer, still echoed in his mind. "Your data on improved patient outcomes is compelling," Mark had noted, studying the charts spread across his desk. "But you'll need more than numbers to win them over. Every department head in that room will be thinking about how this affects their territory."

Dr. Sharma understood the subtext. While the treatment could significantly improve patient outcomes and reduce long-term costs, it demanded immediate cross-departmental collaboration and resource reallocation. The financial team was already wary of exceeding this year's budget, and other department heads were protective of their existing protocols.

Gathering his materials, Dr. Sharma considered his tactical arsenal. Traditional negotiation approaches wouldn't suffice – he needed a range of precise maneuvers to address concerns about risk that would emerge and need to be immediately addressed lest they fester. Success would depend not just on what he proposed, but on how he managed the moment-to-moment dynamics of the discussion.

As he headed toward the boardroom, Dr. Sharma felt prepared for the complex meeting ahead. He knew that advanced negotiation tactics in the moment were just as critical as the advanced negotiation strategies that got him to this point. Each response, each pause, and each reframe could prove crucial to navigating the high-stakes negotiations ahead.

This scenario exemplifies the need for tactical versatility in healthcare negotiations, whether in the Practice of Medicine (Operating Room), Delivery of Care (Exam Room), or Business of Health (Boardroom). This chapter shifts from advanced strategies to specific tactics that enable negotiators to adapt quickly, counter resistance, and maintain control under pressure.

Preparing and Using Advanced Healthcare Negotiation Tactics

The distinction between strategies and tactics is crucial in healthcare negotiations. Strategies serve as broad, guiding principles to achieve overarching negotiation goals, establish the foundation, and shape the long-term direction. Tactics, in contrast, are precise, situational tools used to gain short-term advantages, manage momentum, or respond to sudden shifts in the negotiation. While strategies set the overall plan, tactics are the specific moves negotiators use to advance their position in real-time.

The timing of strategies versus tactics plays a vital role in successful negotiations. Strategies are typically employed during the early phases to establish positions, set the tone, and create a framework for discussion. For instance, strategies like Understanding and Setting Your Value help build a strong foundation for the entire negotiation process. Tactics, however, prove most effective during mid-negotiation phases or critical turning points, where adaptability and quick responses are crucial. Using Tactical Empathy helps negotiators maintain rapport and gather information, while Anchoring and Framing create an immediate reference point in discussions, shaping subsequent decisions.

Effective tactical implementation requires careful preparation through several key steps. Just as with strategies, tactical preparation begins with thorough stakeholder analysis. This involves considering the specific dynamics of each negotiation – whether it's a boardroom discussion about resource allocation, a clinical conversation about treatment protocols, or an interdisciplinary meeting focused on care delivery. Second, negotiators must clarify objectives and leverage points, identifying specific goals that can be achieved with tactical maneuvers, such as gaining concessions, managing power dynamics, or redirecting discussions. They must remain aware of leverage points, such as urgent timelines, resource constraints, or shifting priorities, and use tactics to capitalize on them. Healthcare professionals must also identify specific negotiation phases where tactics can be most effective and use them to complement their broader strategy, adapting quickly to changes in the negotiation environment. Throughout this process, it's crucial to balance assertiveness with empathy, ensuring that tactical maneuvers enhance rather than undermine trust and collaboration while grounding all tactical applications in ethical considerations and patient-centered outcomes.

The third step involves developing the ability to adapt to real-time dynamics. Negotiators must be prepared to switch between different tactics as negotiations evolve. For example, they might use Tactical Flinches to create pressure when resistance emerges but then employ Tactical Silence to regain control of the negotiation. Finally, practicing tactical maneuvers is essential. Advanced tactics, such as Pivots and Turns or Yes, And... require practice to execute effectively. Role-playing with colleagues, simulating real-time scenarios, and receiving feedback can enhance tactical precision and timing.

Like strategies, tactics can be applied across healthcare's three pillars: the Operating Room (Practice of Medicine), the Exam Room (Delivery of Care), and the Boardroom (Business of Health). However, tactics offer distinct advantages in rapidly changing or contentious situations, making them particularly valuable for managing immediate challenges in healthcare negotiations:

- **Operating Room (Practice of Medicine):**
  - Tactics like Tactical Empathy can de-escalate tension in high-stress environments, ensuring patient safety remains the focus.
- **Exam Room (Delivery of Care):**
  - In discussions about patient care, tactics like Yes, And... foster collaborative dialogue among interdisciplinary teams, while Pivots and Turns allow for quick adaptations when treatment plans require adjustments.
- **Boardroom (Business of Health):**
  - Techniques like Tactical Silence or Tactical Flinches can apply pressure during financial negotiations, while the Double Magnet Approach can align competing interests through reciprocal benefits.

This chapter explores several key tactics essential for healthcare negotiations. Tactical Empathy is a fundamental approach that enhances rapport by understanding and acknowledging patients' emotions. Anchoring techniques help set and frame strong discussion reference points, effectively shaping subsequent decisions. More dynamic tactics include Tactical Flinches, which involve demonstrating visible reactions to prompt reconsideration or adjustments from counterparts, and the use of Tactical Silence to create pressure, gather information, or shift momentum. The chapter also covers Pivots and Turns, which enable quick shifts in approach to respond to changing dynamics and keep negotiations moving forward, as well as the Yes, And... technique, which encourages collaboration by building on ideas even when disagreement is present. Finally, the Double Magnet Approach rounds out the tactical toolkit by offering methods to align competing interests through reciprocal benefits.

To illustrate the advanced negotiation tactics at work, each is first introduced and analyzed through the HEAR lens, then unpacked through a case study involving a Practice of Medicine context that showcases its practical implementation. Each is followed by insights on adapting the tactic across the other healthcare pillars, highlighting their versatility and broad applicability.

Advanced Tactics in Action in an Operating Room Scenario

Dr. Maya Wilmer walked the quiet corridors of Western Memorial Hospital's surgical wing, using the early morning calm to mentally organize her approach. After fifteen years as a surgical oncologist and three years as Director of Surgical Services, she understood that clinical evidence alone rarely drove change. The data on Enhanced Recovery After Surgery (ERAS) was compelling – a 40% reduction in length of stay, a 30% decrease in complications, significant improvements in patient satisfaction, and substantial cost savings. Yet, implementing such a comprehensive protocol would require careful tactical maneuvering to align multiple stakeholders.

Passing the currently empty pre-op area, she paused to review her tablet one final time. Each space she passed represented a different aspect of the challenge ahead – the pre-op bay where anesthesiologists would need to modify their protocols, the Post-Anesthesia Care Unit (PACU) where nurses would implement early mobilization, and the staff lounge where skeptical surgeons discussed their concerns about "cookbook medicine."

The current state of perioperative care at Western Memorial reflected the fragmented nature of surgical care delivery nationwide. Each surgical specialty had its own pre-operative preparation routines. Anesthesiologists followed individual preferences for pain management. Post-operative care varied widely between units. While outcomes were good, the variation created inefficiencies, increased costs, and sometimes led to longer recoveries than necessary.

Dr. Wilmer had assembled a diverse implementation team:

- Dr. James Ozonoff, Chief of Anesthesiology – Known for his evidence-based approach but protective of his department's autonomy.
- Sarah Rodriguez, RN, PACU Manager – A skilled nurse leader concerned about staffing for early mobilization.
- Dr. Thomas Williams, Head of Surgical Oncology – Respected surgeon, skeptical of "cookbook medicine."

- Maria Gonzalez, PT, Rehabilitation Director – Enthusiastic about early mobility but worried about resources.
- Dr. Rachel Kim, Pain Management Specialist – Advocate for multimodal pain management but facing resistance from traditionalists.
- Mark Thompson, Care Coordination Director – Sees ERAS' potential but is concerned about the documentation burden.

As she reviewed her notes from preliminary discussions, the challenges were clear. Dr. Ozonoff had insisted they couldn't standardize anesthesia protocols, arguing that every patient was different. Sarah Rodriguez had raised concerns about early mobilization, pointing out that while it was great in theory, they were already stretched too thin to help patients walk. Dr. Williams had contended that while these protocols might work at academic centers, their patient population was different.

Dr. Wilmer knew that tomorrow's initial team meeting would be crucial. Success would require more than just presenting data – she needed to change potential resistance into collaborative problem-solving. She would need every negotiation tactic at her disposal: empathy to acknowledge each specialty's expertise, tactical silence to create space for concerns to emerge, careful anchoring to frame the discussion, and the flexibility to pivot as needed.

As she gathered her materials, her phone buzzed with a message from Dr. Williams: "Just reviewed the proposed protocol. We need to talk before tomorrow's meeting. This is going to completely disrupt our workflow".

Dr. Wilmer took a deep breath. This was exactly the kind of challenge that would require skilled tactical navigation. Her response now would set the tone for the entire implementation process.

Tactic One: Employing Tactical Empathy

Tactical Empathy represents an advanced negotiation approach that transforms challenging interactions into opportunities for deeper understanding by consciously demonstrating genuine comprehension of others' perspectives and emotional states. This tactic is most effective in emotionally charged discussions or when encountering resistance, as it fosters psychological safety and trust. This methodology, grounded in Emotional Intelligence theory developed by Daniel Goleman and refined through Chris Voss's work in high-stakes negotiations, harnesses the power of cognitive empathy to build authentic connections and uncover underlying interests in healthcare's emotionally charged environment.[1] Through the lens of HEAR, tactical empathy primarily amplifies Acknowledgment by creating psychological safety and demonstrating genuine curiosity about others' viewpoints, even in situations of disagreement or conflict.

Operating Room Case Study: Enhanced Recovery After Surgery Implementation

Dr. Wilmer met with Dr. Williams before the team meeting to address his concerns about workflow disruption:

Dr. Williams (Surgical Oncology): "Maya, I've reviewed the protocol. These pre-op requirements will completely disrupt our clinic flow. And the standardized post-op orders? Every cancer case is unique. We can't cookie-cutter this".

Dr. Wilmer (Director of Surgical Services): "Tom, when you talk about disruption and standardization, I hear someone deeply committed to maintaining the surgical excellence you've built in this department. Your concerns about preserving clinical judgment are exactly what we need to consider".

Dr. Williams: "Exactly. We've spent years fine-tuning our processes. Our outcomes are already strong. Why risk changing what works?"

Dr. Wilmer: "Your point about our current outcomes is crucial. You've developed highly effective protocols that other departments look to as models. That's precisely why your input on adapting ERAS to our specific patient population is so valuable".

Dr. Williams: "Well, I do see some potential in the prehabilitation components. But coordinating all these pre-op elements – nutrition, PT assessments, patient education – that's going to be challenging".

Dr. Wilmer: "You've identified a key implementation challenge. Would you be willing to help us design a pre-op workflow that maintains your clinic's efficiency while incorporating these new elements? Your experience with complex care coordination would be invaluable".

This exchange demonstrates the key elements of tactical empathy. Through specific Acknowledgment of clinical expertise and investment, it effectively addresses legitimate operational concerns while transforming resistance into opportunities for input. The approach creates a foundation for collaborative problem-solving and maintains focus on shared patient care goals throughout the interaction. This careful balance of validation and forward momentum enables meaningful progress while preserving professional relationships.

Key Implementation Steps

1. Prepare: Begin by researching stakeholder backgrounds and identifying potential emotional triggers and concerns. Prepare specific Acknowledgment statements and review relevant clinical data and metrics. Plan empathetic responses to likely objections while developing follow-up questions for deeper exploration. Create psychological safety protocols to ensure productive dialogue. This comprehensive preparation enables authentic and effective empathetic engagement.
2. Execute: Listen actively for underlying emotions and demonstrate understanding through both verbal and non-verbal cues. Validate expertise using concrete examples while bridging to collaborative problem-solving. Monitor the emotional temperature of discussions and adjust the approach based on real-time feedback. Maintain a consistent focus on shared patient care goals throughout the interaction. Support authentic engagement through careful attention to both spoken and unspoken communications.
3. Follow Through: Document effective, empathetic responses and track relationship development carefully. Monitor implementation progress while planning future engagement strategies. Strengthen collaborative frameworks established throughout the process and prepare for the next tactical phases. Build on established trust through consistent follow-up and attention to relationship maintenance. This thorough follow-through ensures sustainable progress and strengthens professional bonds.

Common Challenges and Solutions

Challenge: Maintaining professional composure with emotional content.
Solution: Practice measured responses that balance empathy with clinical objectivity.

Challenge: Multiple stakeholder perspectives requiring Acknowledgment.
Solution: Create structured frameworks for recognizing diverse viewpoints systematically.

Challenge: Building trust while maintaining boundaries.
Solution: Develop clear protocols for empathetic engagement that preserve professional relationships.

Things to Avoid

Tactical Empathy in healthcare settings can falter through several key missteps. Generic acknowledgments that lack clinical specificity undermine credibility. Using empathy as a manipulative tool rather than a path to understanding breeds distrust. Rushing through emotional moments or dismissing legitimate concerns similarly defeats the technique's purpose, as does any departure from authentic, Healthcare-Specific interactions.

Cross-Pillar Applications

Practice of Medicine: Using empathetic responses to acknowledge clinical expertise while validating concerns and measuring impact on protocol adoption

Delivery of Care: Demonstrating an understanding of workflow challenges while tracking staff engagement and evaluating implementation effectiveness

Business of Health: Acknowledging resource constraints while monitoring stakeholder satisfaction and measuring operational improvements

Measuring Success

In surgical settings, tactical empathy proves most effective when it authentically acknowledges specialty-specific clinical concerns while keeping shared patient care objectives at the forefront. By tracking stakeholder engagement throughout protocol development, negotiators can gauge how effectively empathy bridges interdisciplinary perspectives. The depth of discipline-specific protocol modifications often reveals the success of empathetic approaches, while tracking implementation milestone achievements highlight growing cross-disciplinary trust. Furthermore, consistent monitoring of staff satisfaction measures and long-term protocol adherence demonstrates how Tactical Empathy strengthens sustainable collaborative relationships and enhances overall surgical outcomes.

As Dr. Wilmer's empathetic acknowledgments created psychological safety in the room, she noticed a subtle shift in Dr. Williams. Initially defensive, he was now leaning forward slightly. In subsequent conversations with Sarah Rodriguez and Dr. Ozonoff, Wilmer used the same tactic with similar positive results.

It was time to deepen the dialogue. Instead of immediately offering solutions to the concerns raised, Dr. Wilmer recognized an opportunity to employ a more nuanced approach. She knew that in complex clinical discussions, the most crucial information often emerges in the spaces between words.

Tactic Two: Tactical Silence

Tactical Silence is an advanced negotiation technique that turns purposeful pauses into opportunities for deeper insight and strategic advantage. By creating deliberate moments of quiet, negotiators can invite reflection, signal thoughtful consideration, and encourage others to share more openly—often revealing concerns that might otherwise remain unspoken.

Rooted in communication theory and validated by Alison Wood Brooks' research on negotiation dynamics, This technique leverages the psychological power of well-timed silence to foster clarity and connection. It is especially effective in situations where emotions run high, stakes are significant, or mutual understanding feels just out of reach.[2]

Tactical Silence primarily amplifies Acknowledgment by demonstrating deep listening and creating psychological space for others to expand their thoughts, often leading to spontaneous revelations of underlying interests and concerns. In healthcare negotiations, where emotions run high, and stakes are significant, silence can encourage self-reflection, draw out additional information, and ultimately foster more collaborative solutions.

Operating Room Case Study: Enhanced Recovery After Surgery Implementation [Continued]

After her initial empathetic acknowledgments, Dr. Wilmer noticed the shift in team dynamics and deliberately chose to create space for deeper concerns to emerge during the next team meeting:

Maria Gonzalez (PT Director): "Even if we coordinate early mobilization with PACU, we still need to consider patient safety. Post-operative pain management impacts mobility success". [shifts uncomfortably]

Dr. Wilmer (Director of Surgical Services): [maintains engaged eye contact, nods slightly but remains silent]

Maria: [after several seconds] "And honestly, I'm worried about our weekend coverage. If we're promising early mobility seven days a week, we need to ensure consistent staffing".

Dr. Wilmer: [continues attentive silence while maintaining open body language]

Dr. Rachel Kim (Pain Management): [leaning forward] "Maria raises a critical point. Our current post-op pain protocols might not support early mobility. We'd need to completely revise our approach".

Dr. Wilmer: [allows silence to draw out more thoughts]

Dr. Kim: "Though if we implemented multimodal pain management preemptively..". [trails off]

Dr. Ozonoff (Anesthesiology): "That could work if we aligned our intraoperative medication choices with the post-op plan".

Mark Thompson (Care Coordination): "And if we're revising pain protocols, we should consider how this affects discharge planning…".

This exchange illustrates how Tactical Silence can transform group dynamics in healthcare negotiations. By creating deliberate space for interconnected concerns to emerge naturally, Tactical Silence enables stakeholders to build organically on each other's insights. This approach reveals critical operational dependencies while facilitating natural problem-solving processes. Perhaps most importantly, it encourages genuine cross-disciplinary dialogue that might otherwise remain unexpressed, creating a richer understanding of complex healthcare challenges.

Key Implementation Steps

1. Prepare: Successful deployment of Tactical Silence begins with a thorough identification of key discussion points likely to benefit from reflection. Healthcare professionals must practice maintaining comfort with extended silence while planning appropriate non-verbal engagement cues. Understanding interdepartmental dependencies helps anticipate where silence might yield the most insight. By mapping potential silence opportunities and creating response frameworks, negotiators

can design follow-up sequences that maximize the value of information revealed during these purposeful pauses.

2. Execute: During negotiations, create intentional pauses after significant statements while maintaining engaged body language that demonstrates active listening. The discipline of counting to 5–7 seconds before responding allows time for deeper reflection and the emergence of underlying concerns. Watch carefully for non-verbal cues indicating more thoughts are forming, using supportive gestures like nodding and eye contact to maintain psychological safety. By monitoring stakeholder comfort levels and guiding discussion rhythm through strategic silence, negotiators can foster an environment where meaningful insights surface naturally.
3. Follow-through: Effective follow-through requires careful documentation of concerns that emerge during silent periods and noting interdisciplinary connections revealed through this process. Schedule focused discussions on newly identified issues while tracking the effectiveness of silence patterns over time. Planning future silence points strategically helps build on revealed insights and strengthens trust through consistent engagement, ensuring the value gained through tactical silence translates into concrete outcomes.

Common Challenges and Solutions

Challenge: Multiple stakeholders trying to speak simultaneously.
Solution: Use hand gestures to maintain the current speaker's space.

Challenge: Time constraints in clinical settings.
Solution: Use shorter but still effective silence intervals (3–5 seconds).

Challenge: Stakeholder discomfort with silence.
Solution: Maintain engaged body language to create psychological safety.

Things to Avoid

The misuse of tactical silence in healthcare negotiations can quickly derail its effectiveness. Breaking eye contact, displaying impatience, or wielding silence as a power play creates unnecessary tension rather than space for reflection. Failing to account for cultural differences in silence tolerance or allowing extended silences during crisis situations similarly undermines the technique. Above all, tactical silence must serve to enhance collaborative dialogue rather than create barriers to communication.

Cross-Pillar Applications

Practice of Medicine: Creating space for surgical team members to voice safety concerns during protocol development while tracking feedback participation and measuring protocol refinement effectiveness.

Delivery of Care: Allowing staff time to fully articulate the workflow impact of new procedures while documenting implementation insights and measuring process improvement outcomes.

Business of Health: Giving stakeholders time to process resource allocation implications while monitoring engagement levels and evaluating strategic alignment effectiveness.

Measuring Success

In surgical settings, strategic silence proves most effective when it fosters psychological safety, encouraging open discussion of patient safety and clinical workflow concerns while keeping the focus on implementation goals. By analyzing patterns and complexities of concerns raised during these silent moments, measurable metrics of technique effectiveness can be generated. Additionally, mapping interdisciplinary connections that emerge during these discussions highlights the broader systemic impact. Key success indicators, such as the sophistication of proposed solutions and cross-functional participation rates, validate Tactical Silence as a tool for deeper collaborative analysis. Furthermore, systematic evaluations of implementation frameworks and satisfaction survey data confirm the measurable contributions of strategic silence to achieving negotiated outcomes based on established performance criteria.

As the silence allowed interconnections between pain management, mobility, and staffing to emerge naturally, Dr. Wilmer recognized an opportunity to introduce data from other successful ERAS implementations. The team was now ready for the careful Anchoring of expectations.

Tactic Three: Anchoring and Framing

Anchoring represents an advanced negotiation tactic that transforms initial interactions into powerful framing opportunities by establishing reference points that shape the psychological landscape of the entire discussion. When setting effective reference points and guiding perceptions, this tactic is best deployed early and mid-negotiation to influence expectations and shift discussions toward shared outcomes. Rooted in behavioral economics research by Amos Tversky and Daniel Kahneman[3] and further developed by Adam Galinsky's work[4] in negotiation dynamics, anchoring leverages cognitive biases to influence how options are perceived. It aligns with the Recasting aspect of the HEAR Approach™, as it intentionally shapes the framework of discussions, guiding conversations toward more ambitious and mutually beneficial outcomes.

Framing, closely related to Anchoring, is the art of presenting information in a way that influences perceptions.[5] Effective framing aligns the negotiation with stakeholder priorities, helping negotiators steer conversations toward shared goals and collaborative solutions. When combined, Anchoring and Framing help negotiators establish control over the dialogue, shifting the focus to more advantageous terms.

Operating Room Case Study: Enhanced Recovery After Surgery Implementation [Continued]

After allowing concerns about interdepartmental coordination to emerge through silence, Dr. Wilmer carefully introduced comparative data:

Dr. Wilmer (Director of Surgical Services): "The concerns you've raised about coordination are crucial. Looking at hospitals similar to ours that have implemented ERAS, we see some compelling patterns. Centers achieving full protocol compliance have reduced length of stay by 40% and decreased complications by 35%. Even those reaching 75% compliance saw significant improvements".

Dr. Williams (Surgical Oncology: "Forty percent? That seems extraordinarily optimistic".

Dr. Wilmer: "It's worth examining the components of that number. Sites with the strongest outcomes focused first on their highest-volume procedures, achieving a 20-25% reduction in the first six months. They then expanded and optimized, reaching 40% by eighteen months. What if we took a similar graduated approach?"

Sarah Rodriguez (PACU): "Starting with specific procedures could help us develop our workflows. But what about staffing requirements?"

Dr. Wilmer: "Looking at staffing data, successful programs actually redistributed rather than added resources. With shorter patient stays, PACU nurses reported more manageable workloads despite the early mobility requirements. Some units saw a 30% reduction in overtime hours".

Dr. Ozonoff (Anesthesiology): "And the anesthesia protocols?"

Dr. Wilmer: "Centers maintaining surgeon and anesthesiologist autonomy while following ERAS principles saw a 45% reduction in post-operative opioid use and a 50% decrease in post-operative nausea. Dr. Ozonoff, your expertise would be invaluable in adapting these protocols to our specific patient population".

By setting ambitious but well-documented initial anchors, such as the 40% reduction target, this exchange establishes a framework for meaningful discussion while providing realistic staged implementation targets. The careful framing of changes as optimization rather than disruption helps maintain stakeholder engagement while linking outcomes directly to stakeholder-specific concerns and creates personal investment in success. Throughout the process, maintaining flexibility while keeping high aspirations proves crucial for building momentum toward meaningful change.

Key Implementation Steps

1. Prepare: Effective Anchoring and Framing begin with comprehensive research into relevant benchmarks from similar institutions. Healthcare professionals must identify stakeholder-specific outcome measures that resonate with different audiences while preparing clear data visualization tools that support their positions. Developing implementation staging options provides flexibility in negotiations, while creating value-based anchors for each pillar ensures alignment across clinical, operational, and financial domains. Planning framing sequences and designing reframing tactics in advance enable smooth adaptation to stakeholder responses during negotiations.
2. Execute: During negotiations, present ambitious but achievable targets that inspire while remaining within the bounds of credibility. Frame changes as enhancements to existing excellence rather than criticisms of

current practice, connecting outcomes directly to departmental priorities. Allow for staged goal-setting that builds confidence through early wins while maintaining focus on shared quality objectives. Link anchors to established metrics that provide concrete validation, adjusting frames based on real-time feedback and stakeholder responses.

3. Follow Through: Success requires careful documentation of agreed-upon targets coupled with the establishment of robust monitoring mechanisms. Plan regular review points that maintain accountability while preparing adjustment strategies for when circumstances change. Track frame effectiveness consistently and monitor anchor impacts to ensure continued alignment with objectives. Build on successful frames by extending their application to related areas, creating a comprehensive framework for sustained improvement.

Common Challenges and Solutions

Challenge: Resistance to ambitious benchmarks.
Solution: Present staged implementation data with clear supporting evidence.

Challenge: Stakeholder skepticism about comparisons.
Solution: Use multiple validated reference points from similar institutions.

Challenge: Maintaining anchor credibility over time.
Solution: Create robust tracking systems for progress against established benchmarks.

Things to Avoid

The effective use of Anchoring and Framing in healthcare settings can be compromised by several critical missteps. Unsubstantiated benchmarks damage credibility, while rigid adherence to initial targets reveals negotiation inexperience. Failing to adjust anchors based on feedback or setting unrealistic targets erodes trust, particularly when proposed goals conflict with operational realities and implementation constraints.

Cross-Pillar Applications

Practice of Medicine: Setting clinical quality benchmarks while tracking outcome improvements and measuring protocol compliance.

Delivery of Care: Establishing operational efficiency targets while monitoring workflow improvements and evaluating staff adaptation.

Business of Health: Creating financial performance anchors while tracking cost reduction and measuring sustainable improvements.

Measuring Success

In surgical settings, Anchoring is most effective when leveraging peer institution data directly tied to quality metrics, while remaining adaptable to local contexts and focused on patient outcomes. Early acceptance of the initial target serves as an indicator of strategy effectiveness, while successful completion of the implementation phase signals sustained buy-in. Concrete progress can be measured through milestone achievement rates and staff engagement levels, while trends in protocol compliance and improvements in patient outcomes provide objective validation of success.

The ambitious benchmarks had created a palpable tension in the room. Dr. Wilmer noticed Dr. Williams's furrowed brow and slight head shake at the complication rate data. Other team members were exchanging glances, their body language suggesting unspoken concerns about the proposed targets. Rather than pushing forward with more data, Dr. Wilmer recognized an opportunity to acknowledge these concerns through her own careful reaction. Sometimes, she knew, the most effective way to address skepticism is to visibly share it.

Tactic Four: Tactical Flinching

The Tactical Flinch represents a nuanced negotiation tactic that transforms non-verbal communication into a powerful tool for signaling concerns and prompting reconsideration without direct confrontation. This approach, based on non-verbal communication theory developed by Albert Mehrabian and refined through negotiation research, uses body language to subtly influence dialogue dynamics in healthcare's sensitive negotiation environment.[6] Through the lens of HEAR, the Tactical Flinching primarily amplifies Acknowledgment by providing an authentic, visceral way to demonstrate recognition of challenging proposals that leverages non-verbal communication to signal unease or disagreement.

This technique maintains psychological safety while signaling the need for reconsideration or further clarification of a proposal. It is particularly useful in healthcare settings, where direct confrontation may compromise collaboration or impede patient-centered decision-making.

Operating Room Case Study: Enhanced Recovery After Surgery Implementation [Continued]

Following the presentation of ambitious ERAS benchmarks:

Mark Thompson (Care Coordination): "If other centers are achieving these outcomes so quickly, we should aim to fully implement across all surgical services within six months".

Dr. Wilmer (Director of Surgical Services): [leans back slightly, eyebrows raised] "Six months for full implementation? That's... quite ambitious". [maintains concerned expression]

Dr. Williams (Surgical Oncology): "Exactly. We can't rush this kind of systematic change".

Dr. Wilmer: [tilts head thoughtfully] "Could you walk me through how you envision managing the training and protocol development timeline?"

Mark: [noting her reaction] "Well, maybe I'm being too aggressive with the timeline. What are you thinking?"

Dr. Wilmer: "Your enthusiasm for improving outcomes is crucial. What if we looked at how those successful centers staged their implementations? Most found success with a more graduated approach".

Dr. Kim (Pain Management): "A phased rollout would give us time to refine our multimodal pain protocols".

Sarah Rodriguez (PACU): "And help us identify staffing needs realistically".

This exchange demonstrates the nuanced power of Tactical Flinching. Through calibrated non-verbal cues signaling legitimate concerns, the approach creates space for others to voice their own hesitations without direct confrontation. This technique maintains collaborative dialogue while encouraging voluntary reconsideration of potentially problematic proposals. Most significantly, it guides the group toward realistic planning without damaging professional relationships or undermining team cohesion. The result is a natural evolution toward more feasible implementation approaches driven by collective insight rather than direct opposition.

Key Implementation Steps

1. Prepare: Effective Tactical Flinching begins with practicing appropriate response calibration that maintains a professional demeanor while conveying genuine concern. Healthcare professionals must identify quality and safety trigger points that warrant a response while developing follow-up questions that probe deeper into concerning proposals. Planning redirection strategies and mapping potential flinch moments enable thoughtful rather than reactive responses. Creating recovery protocols and designing response frameworks ensure that flinches serve as bridges to constructive dialogue rather than conversation stoppers.
2. Execute: During negotiations, display measured concern through carefully calibrated body language that maintains professional credibility. Follow flinches with specific questions that guide discussion toward realistic solutions while maintaining composure appropriate to the healthcare setting. Monitor the impact of each flinch carefully, adjusting intensity based on stakeholder responses and the situation's gravity. This measured approach ensures that concerns are registered effectively without creating unnecessary alarm or undermining collaborative relationships.
3. Follow Through: Success requires documenting concerns raised through Tactical Flinching while establishing realistic timelines for addressing them. Create clear safety checkpoints that maintain focus on patient care quality while monitoring implementation progress. Track flinch effectiveness to refine future applications while building on revealed concerns to strengthen protocols. This comprehensive follow-through transforms momentary signals into sustained improvement, strengthening trust through demonstrated commitment to addressing legitimate issues.

Common Challenges and Solutions

Challenge: Maintaining professional demeanor during flinching.
Solution: Practice calibrated responses that convey concern while preserving dignity.

Challenge: Timing flinches in group settings.
Solution: Develop clear triggers for when reactions serve strategic purposes.

Challenge: Avoiding overuse of the technique.
Solution: Create structured frameworks for determining genuine need for response.

Things to Avoid

Tactical flinching in healthcare negotiations can backfire through several key missteps. Using flinch responses manipulatively rather than expressing genuine concern undermines credibility while dismissing suggestions wholesale damages collaborative potential. Rushing past legitimate concerns or failing to maintain professional standards erodes trust, transforming what should be a tool for constructive dialogue into a barrier that creates unnecessary adversarial dynamics.

Cross-Pillar Applications

Practice of Medicine: Using measured reactions to question safety concerns while tracking protocol modifications and measuring outcome improvements.

Delivery of Care: Demonstrating appropriate concern about workflow disruptions while monitoring staff responses and evaluating process adjustments.

Business of Health: Showing thoughtful hesitation about resource allocations while tracking decision adjustments and measuring implementation success.

Measuring Success

In surgical settings, Tactical Flinching is most effective when it conveys genuine concern for patient safety and quality outcomes while preserving professional composure and showing respect for colleagues' input. Successful influence on planning processes is reflected in appropriate timeline adjustments and the incorporation of enhanced safety measures. Metrics such as team engagement levels and problem identification rates highlight the technique's contribution to collaborative improvement efforts. Additionally, the quality of developed solutions and implementation success rates offer concrete validation of its effectiveness in driving meaningful change. Together, these indicators provide a comprehensive view of tactical flinching's role in advancing healthcare negotiations and fostering professional relationships.

As the team began developing a more realistic implementation timeline, Dr. Wilmer recognized the need to redirect the conversation from potential barriers toward constructive planning. The situation called for careful pivoting to maintain momentum.

Tactic Five: Pivots and Turns

Pivots and Turns transform potential obstacles into strategic opportunities by skillfully redirecting conversations and reframing challenges into new possibilities. When redirecting conversations and reframing challenges into new opportunities to maintain forward momentum, this tactic is best deployed when negotiations hit a roadblock, when flexibility is needed to explore alternative pathways, or when faced with contentious remarks that could derail the discussion. This approach, rooted in framing theory developed by Erving Goffman[7] and refined by William Ury,[8] leverages redirection to maintain momentum and uncover alternative pathways in healthcare's complex negotiation landscape. Pivots and Turns primarily amplify Recasting by transforming apparent deadlocks into opportunities for creative problem-solving, enabling negotiators to navigate around obstacles while maintaining focus on core objectives.

Pivots and Turns is also an extension of the RESET technique, emphasizing emotional regulation during negotiations. When a counterpart makes a triggering or contentious remark – something likely to provoke an emotional response – pivoting and turning allows negotiators to maintain control and stay focused. Rather than getting derailed by the comment, pivoting and turning helps redirect the conversation back to the central issues.

Operating Room Case Study: Enhanced Recovery After Surgery Implementation [Continued]

With the team now more realistic about implementation timelines, new concerns emerged:

Dr. Williams (Surgical Oncology: "Even with a phased approach, we're looking at significant documentation requirements. Our surgeons already spend too much time on paperwork instead of patient care".

Dr. Wilmer (Director of Surgical Services): "You raise an important point about administrative burden. Let's look at how this could actually streamline our documentation. What if we used ERAS implementation to optimize our clinical documentation process?"

Sarah Rodriguez (PACU): "But that means retraining all our staff on new protocols".

Dr. Wilmer: "Think of it as an opportunity to enhance our skills. While we're updating protocols, we could incorporate those evidence-based practices your team has been wanting to implement".

Dr. Ozonoff:(Anesthesiology) "The learning curve will still impact OR efficiency".

Dr. Wilmer: "This gives us a perfect opportunity to redesign our OR workflow. Dr. Ozonoff, your expertise would be invaluable in creating an efficient pre-op process that coordinates anesthesia and surgical protocols".

Maria Gonzalez (PT Director): "Resources are still a major concern for PT coverage".

Dr. Wilmer: "Let's transform this into a chance to develop our interdisciplinary care model. Could we explore how early mobility might actually reduce overall resource needs through faster recovery?"

This exchange illustrates the power of skillful Pivots and Turns in healthcare negotiations. Through thoughtful redirection, documentation concerns evolve into opportunities for process improvement, while training challenges become pathways for skill enhancement. The approach successfully converts efficiency concerns into optimization opportunities, demonstrating how apparent obstacles can become catalysts for positive change. Perhaps most importantly, the technique transforms perceived resource limitations into chances for innovative redesign, showing how tactical Pivots and Turns can maintain momentum while addressing legitimate stakeholder concerns in healthcare settings.

Key Implementation Steps

1. Prepare: Effective pivoting and turning begins with a thorough identification of potential sticking points that could derail progress toward

healthcare objectives. Professionals must develop positive reframing options grounded in clinical evidence while planning tactical redirections that maintain focus on patient care. Preparing evidence-based alternatives creates a foundation for credible Pivots and Turns, while mapping potential pathways enables smooth transitions. Creating well-crafted transition phrases and designing recovery routes ensures that negotiators can maintain momentum even when encountering significant resistance.

2. Execute: Implementation requires active listening for Pivots and Turn opportunities while acknowledging original concerns in ways that validate stakeholders' perspectives. Redirect toward solutions that demonstrate an understanding of operational realities while maintaining forward momentum through carefully structured transitions. Engage stakeholders in new directions by connecting Pivots and Turns to their expressed interests and priorities. Monitor Pivots and Turn effectiveness continuously, adjusting approaches based on real-time feedback to ensure redirections serve rather than derail productive dialogue.
3. Follow Through: Successful pivoting and turning requires careful documentation of new approaches coupled with consistent tracking of progress on redirected initiatives. Monitor stakeholder engagement to ensure pivots strengthen rather than strain professional relationships. Adjust course as needed based on implementation feedback while strengthening new directions through demonstrated commitment to agreed-upon changes. Build on successful pivots by extending their application thoughtfully, planning future turning points that advance organizational objectives while maintaining trust.

Common Challenges and Solutions

Challenge: Maintaining momentum during direction changes.
Solution: Develop smooth transition phrases that preserve engagement.

Challenge: Keeping focus on core objectives.
Solution: Create clear frameworks linking new directions to original goals.

Challenge: Managing stakeholder resistance to redirection.
Solution: Build structured approaches for demonstrating value in new directions.

Things to Avoid

Pivots and Turns in healthcare negotiations can falter through several key missteps. Dismissing original concerns during redirection or forcing changes without a clear purpose damages credibility and breeds resistance. Losing sight of core objectives while pivoting or needlessly complicating straightforward solutions undermines progress. Above all, manipulative Pivots and Turns that break trust threaten the professional relationships essential to healthcare delivery and sustainable collaboration.

Cross-Pillar Applications

Practice of Medicine: Redirecting clinical concerns toward protocol improvements while tracking adoption rates and measuring outcome enhancements.

Delivery of Care: Pivoting workflow challenges into optimization opportunities while monitoring staff engagement and evaluating efficiency gains.

Business of Health: Transforming resource constraints into innovation catalysts while tracking cost savings and measuring sustainable improvements.

Measuring Success

Pivoting within surgical environments excels when it reframes operational challenges into opportunities for systemic improvement, all while prioritizing surgical excellence and patient outcomes. Analyzing stakeholder response patterns and the speed of implementation offers quantifiable evidence of its effectiveness, while tracking team engagement metrics highlights the depth of organizational adoption. Performance indicators such as outcome achievement rates and the flexibility of process adaptations underscore the strategic value of these directional changes. Additionally, longitudinal assessments of sustainability metrics and improvement trajectories validate Pivots and Turns' measurable impact on institutional progress, aligned with established success criteria.

As team members began offering their own ideas for transforming challenges into opportunities, Dr. Wilmer recognized the perfect moment to build on this collaborative energy.

Tactic Six: The "Yes, And..." Technique

The "Yes, and..." can turn potential points of disagreement into launching pads for collaborative innovation by building upon rather than blocking others' ideas. This tactic is best deployed when fostering a positive, constructive tone to generate novel solutions or when expanding on existing ideas to create momentum in discussions.

This approach, adapted from improvisational theater principles and aligned with collaborative negotiation theory by Roger Fisher and William Ury, emphasizes building on others' ideas instead of rejecting them.[9] It leverages the power of "Yes, and..." to maintain momentum and uncover creative solutions in healthcare's complex negotiation environment. The "Yes, and..." technique primarily amplifies Recasting by transforming what might be seen as obstacles into opportunities for creative problem-solving, while fostering an atmosphere of psychological safety that encourages bold thinking and genuine collaboration.

Operating Room Case Study: Enhanced Recovery After Surgery Implementation [Continued]

As team members began proposing solutions:

Maria Gonzalez (PT Director): "We could start mobility assessments in pre-op to identify high-risk patients".

Dr. Wilmer (Director of Surgical Services): "Yes, and we could use that information to customize post-op mobility plans. Dr. Kim, how might this inform pain management strategies?"

Dr. Kim (Pain Management): "Early mobility assessment would help us plan multimodal pain protocols..."

Dr. Wilmer: "Yes, and we could integrate these protocols with anesthesia planning. Dr. Ozonoff, thoughts on aligning pre-op pain planning with intraoperative management?"

Dr. Ozonoff (Anesthesiology): "Pre-emptive pain management could reduce post-op opioid requirements..".

Dr. Wilmer: "Yes, and reduced opioid use could facilitate earlier mobility. Sarah, how would this impact PACU workflow?"

Sarah Rodriguez (PACU): "Earlier mobility might actually reduce our staffing pressure during peak hours..".

Dr. Wilmer: "Yes, and more efficient PACU flow could improve OR turnover. Dr. Williams, could this help maintain surgical scheduling efficiency?"

Dr. Williams (Surgical Oncology: "If PACU flow improves, we could better predict case timing…"

Dr. Wilmer: "Yes, and better predictability could help us optimize clinic schedules for pre-op assessments".

Through systematic building on each team member's contributions, this exchange creates meaningful connections between departments while maintaining consistent forward momentum. By encouraging broad participation from diverse stakeholders, the technique develops comprehensive solutions that address complex healthcare challenges. Most significantly, this collaborative approach transforms individual insights into integrated implementation plans that span clinical, operational, and administrative domains, demonstrating how "Yes, And…" thinking can elevate healthcare negotiations beyond simple agreement to true innovation.

Key Implementation Steps

1. Prepare: Successful implementation begins with active listening for building opportunities that can advance patient care objectives. Healthcare professionals must identify cross-departmental connections that create value while planning linking questions that bridge different stakeholder perspectives. Anticipating integration points enables smooth transitions between ideas, while mapping potential additions helps maintain strategic focus. Creating effective bridging phrases and designing building sequences ensures that each "Yes, And…" contribution advances organizational goals while strengthening professional relationships.

2. Execute: During negotiations, acknowledge each contribution authentically while adding meaningful value that extends ideas in productive directions. Connect insights across disciplines to create comprehensive solutions while maintaining a clear focus on achievable outcomes. Encourage further input through supportive responses that demonstrate appreciation for diverse perspectives. Build progressive momentum by linking contributions to broader organizational objectives while supporting collaborative thinking that spans departmental boundaries.
3. Follow Through: Success requires careful documentation of integrated solutions and mapping of interdependencies across healthcare domains. Plan coordinated implementation that respects operational realities while monitoring collaboration effectiveness. Track solution evolution to ensure continued alignment with organizational objectives while strengthening partnerships forged through the process. Prepare thoughtfully for the next building phases that maintain momentum while advancing patient care goals.

Common Challenges and Solutions

Challenge: Maintaining strategic focus during building.
Solution: Create clear frameworks for evaluating additions against objectives.

Challenge: Managing scope expansion effectively.
Solution: Develop structured criteria for assessing new contributions.

Challenge: Ensuring meaningful rather than superficial additions.
Solution: Establish concrete standards for value-adding contributions.

Things to Avoid

The "Yes, And..." technique in healthcare settings can stumble through several critical missteps. Overlooking practical constraints while building on ideas or dominating the collaborative process undermines its core purpose, while excessive elaboration creates unnecessary complexity that derails progress. Rushing through responses risks missing valuable contributions, and losing sight of achievable outcomes transforms a tool for collaboration into an obstacle to meaningful healthcare solutions.

Cross-Pillar Applications

Practice of Medicine: Building on clinical insights to enhance protocols while tracking implementation success and measuring quality improvements.

Delivery of Care: Expanding workflow suggestions into comprehensive solutions while monitoring staff satisfaction and evaluating efficiency gains.

Business of Health: Developing resource proposals into sustainable programs while tracking cost-effectiveness and measuring long-term value.

Measuring Success

The "Yes, And..." approach thrives in surgical environments when it leverages clinical expertise to drive meaningful change, fostering solutions that enhance both surgical excellence and program development. Statistical analysis of collaborative solution patterns and interdepartmental integration rates offers measurable validation of its effectiveness. Metrics such as implementation success rates and team participation trends further demonstrate its impact on organizational dynamics. Additionally, systematic evaluations of innovation quality indicators and outcome improvement trajectories validate the technique's role in advancing healthcare objectives, supported by established evaluation criteria.

As the team developed an increasingly integrated implementation plan, Dr. Wilmer prepared to present two distinct but equally attractive approaches to rolling out their enhanced protocols.

Tactic Seven: The Double Magnet Approach

The Double Magnet Approach draws on behavioral psychology and negotiation theory, emphasizing that people are more likely to commit when offered two compelling choices rather than a single directive.[10] This technique is especially effective when implementing complex changes or when stakeholders need to retain a sense of control, as it creates psychological safety through meaningful options.

Grounded in decision theory research, the approach maintains forward momentum by honoring individuals' preference for autonomy.[11] Through the lens of HEAR, the Double Magnet Approach amplifies both Empowerment and Recasting by providing authentic options while ensuring all paths lead toward desired outcomes.

Operating Room Case Study: Enhanced Recovery After Surgery Implementation [Continued]

As the team's integrated solutions took shape, Dr. Wilmer presented two implementation approaches:

Dr. Wilmer (Director of Surgical Services): "Based on our discussion, I'd like to propose two ways we could roll out these enhanced protocols. Both paths lead to full ERAS implementation, but they offer different advantages. I'd value everyone's thoughts on which might work better for our teams".

Dr. Williams (Surgical Oncology): "What are you thinking?"

Dr. Wilmer: "Our first option is the 'Service Line Focus.' We'd start with colorectal surgery, implementing all ERAS components within that service. This allows us to perfect our approach within one specialty before expanding. Mayo Clinic took this route, achieving significant improvements within four months".

Sarah Rodriguez (PACU): "That would help us concentrate our training efforts…".

Dr. Wilmer: "Yes. The alternative is our 'Component Focus.' We'd implement specific ERAS elements – say, pre-op optimization and early mobility – across all surgical services, then gradually add components. Hopkins used this approach, seeing broader but more gradual improvements".

Dr. Ozonoff (Anesthesiology): "The component approach might be easier for anesthesia protocols…".

Dr. Kim (Pain Management): "But the service line focus could help us refine pain management more quickly".

Dr. Wilmer: "Both approaches have succeeded at similar institutions. We could also consider a hybrid that combines elements of both. What aspects of each appeal to your departments?"

This strategic exchange illustrates the Double Magnet Approach in healthcare negotiations. By presenting two viable implementation paths, each grounded in proven success at respected institutions, the technique creates meaningful choices while maintaining forward momentum. The approach highlights the distinct advantages of each option while preserving flexibility for hybrid solutions that combine the best elements from both paths. Perhaps most significantly, the technique supports both quick wins and gradual change, allowing teams to own their transformation process while ensuring quality outcomes. This balanced approach demonstrates how carefully structured choices can advance complex healthcare initiatives while maintaining stakeholder engagement.

Key Implementation Steps

1. Prepare: Effective implementation starts with crafting equally viable options, each supported by rigorous evidence drawn from healthcare settings. Begin by conducting thorough research to identify specific advantages tailored to the priorities of different stakeholder groups. Anticipate stakeholder preferences by considering their operational realities and create evaluation matrixes to enable objective comparisons. Incorporate hybrid solutions that offer flexibility while clearly outlining detailed implementation pathways for each option. This comprehensive preparation ensures that the proposed choices align with organizational objectives while respecting the professional autonomy of all parties involved.
2. Execute: Present options with clarity and precision, highlighting specific benefits relevant to different stakeholder groups. Allow genuine choice throughout the process while remaining open to hybridization that could better serve organizational needs. Support team decision-making through careful facilitation that maintains focus on patient care objectives. Monitor option reception continuously, guiding collaborative exploration of possibilities while maintaining professional standards and clinical excellence.
3. Follow Through: Document chosen approaches carefully while planning detailed implementation that respects operational constraints. Monitor progress consistently, adjusting course as needed based on real-world feedback. Track option effectiveness to inform future decision-making while building on selected elements that demonstrate particular value. Prepare thoughtfully for the next phases that maintain momentum while advancing organizational objectives. This thorough follow

through ensures selected approaches deliver promised benefits while strengthening professional relationships.

Common Challenges and Solutions

Challenge: Creating genuinely equivalent options.
Solution: Develop structured frameworks for assessing option parity.

Challenge: Preventing decision paralysis.
Solution: Establish clear evaluation criteria for option comparison.

Challenge: Managing hybrid solution complexity.
Solution: Create systematic approaches for combining option elements.

Things to Avoid

The Double Magnet Approach in healthcare settings can falter through several critical missteps. Presenting obviously inferior options or rushing stakeholders to decisions damages credibility, while arbitrarily limiting hybrid solutions prevents the discovery of optimal outcomes. Neglecting feasibility considerations risks operational disruption, and losing focus on patient care transforms what should be a tool for collaboration into an obstacle to meaningful healthcare improvement.

Cross-Pillar Applications

Practice of Medicine: Presenting equivalent clinical implementation paths while tracking protocol adoption and measuring outcome improvements.

Delivery of Care: Offering balanced workflow modification options while monitoring staff engagement and evaluating efficiency gains.

Business of Health: Providing comparable resource allocation approaches while tracking cost-effectiveness and measuring sustainable value.

Measuring Success

The Double Magnet Approach proves most effective when both options uphold high clinical standards and offer teams meaningful choices in the implementation process. This empowers teams to take ownership of change while ensuring quality outcomes. Analyzing stakeholder preferences and implementation speed provides measurable evidence of option equivalency, while tracking team engagement metrics highlights the depth of organizational commitment. Key performance indicators, such as outcome achievement rates and process adaptation flexibility, underscore the strategic value of this structured choice framework. Long-term evaluations of sustainability metrics and improvement trajectories further validate the Double Magnet technique's significant contribution to institutional progress, aligned with established success criteria.

As the team began evaluating the implementation options, Dr. Wilmer reflected on how far they'd come from the initial resistance to ERAS implementation. Through the careful application of negotiation tactics, potential obstacles had transformed into opportunities for collaborative innovation. The path ahead would require continued tactical flexibility, but the foundation for success was firmly established.

COMMON PITFALLS IN ADVANCED HEALTHCARE TACTICS

Healthcare negotiations require not just mastery of fundamental techniques but also awareness of common pitfalls that can derail even experienced professionals. This section explores critical missteps in healthcare negotiation, providing insights on how to recognize and avoid these challenges while maintaining authentic, productive dialogue.

Ignoring power dynamics can disrupt negotiations, especially in hierarchically structured healthcare settings. By recognizing and adapting to the varying levels of authority among participants, healthcare professionals can better manage the negotiation and ensure that the voices of less empowered stakeholders are considered.

Another pitfall is *neglecting Emotional Intelligence*. Building trust and rapport is essential in healthcare negotiations, as they often involve long-term relationships and collaborative care goals. Focusing too narrowly on tactical maneuvers without fostering empathy and trust can alienate partners, reducing the likelihood of productive, sustainable outcomes.

Pushing too hard can be detrimental in healthcare settings, where aggressive tactics such as excessive anchoring can strain or damage relationships. Balancing assertive tactical approaches with empathy and flexibility ensures that the negotiation remains collaborative and that the needs of all parties are acknowledged.

Misreading cultural cues can also derail negotiations. With diverse teams and stakeholder backgrounds, healthcare professionals must remain mindful of cultural differences, adapting their approach to respect and align with cultural norms. This can significantly affect how tactics like directness or assertiveness are perceived.

There are also specific pitfalls related to particular tactics. Inappropriate use of *Tactical Finching* can undermine trust in healthcare negotiations. When this technique is overused or poorly executed, it may be perceived as manipulative rather than a genuine expression of concern, particularly in sensitive healthcare discussions where authenticity is paramount. Success in healthcare negotiations requires judicious use of such tactics, reserving them for moments when they can genuinely advance the dialogue while maintaining psychological safety and trust.

Excessive Pivots and Turns during negotiations can create confusion and erode credibility in healthcare discussions. When negotiators frequently shift direction without a clear purpose, they risk appearing unfocused or lacking in strategic vision, potentially undermining their position and relationships. Effective negotiation requires purposeful and well-timed pivots that advance the conversation while maintaining clear communication and momentum.

Poor management of *Tactical Silence* represents another significant pitfall in healthcare negotiations. While silence can be a powerful tool for encouraging reflection and information sharing, its misuse or overextension can create discomfort and resistance among participants. Successful negotiators carefully balance Tactical Silence with active engagement, maintaining an attentive presence while creating space for meaningful dialogue and reflection.

Finally, while valuable for fostering collaboration, the *"Yes, And..."* technique can become problematic when applied indiscriminately. Overuse of this approach, particularly when addressing clearly unviable proposals, can appear disingenuous and undermine the negotiator's credibility. Effective use of this technique requires discernment – reserving it for ideas with real potential to ensure that collaboration feels authentic and drives meaningful outcomes.

Countering Advanced Negotiation Tactics in Healthcare

As healthcare professionals become more advanced in their use of negotiation tactics, it's crucial they recognize and effectively counter advanced tactics. This section provides in-depth approaches for identifying, responding to, and ethically navigating complex negotiation scenarios within the healthcare environment.

Foundational Tactic: "Good Cop/Bad Cop"

Perhaps the most common overarching tactic seen in complex negotiations is the "Good Cop/Bad Cop" routine, where negotiating partners deliberately adopt contrasting personas to manipulate outcomes. In this approach, one team member takes an aggressive stance while their colleague maintains a more conciliatory demeanor, creating a psychological dynamic designed to extract concessions. This tactic frequently surfaces in healthcare settings, particularly during sensitive negotiations like hospital mergers. For instance, one executive might adopt a hardline position about necessary staff reductions, while their colleague expresses empathy and understanding about job security concerns.

The most effective counter-tactic, known as "unite and conquer," involves addressing both parties simultaneously, compelling them to align their positions: "I appreciate both of your perspectives. Let's all agree on our shared goal of creating a strong, efficient merged entity. Can we collectively brainstorm staffing solutions that maintain quality care while addressing budget concerns?" This unified response effectively neutralizes the Good Cop/Bad Cop dynamic by creating a collaborative framework that requires both parties to work together rather than maintain their contrasting roles.

Tactic One: Tactical Empathy

Tactical Empathy is a subtle psychological tactic in which negotiators exploit Emotional Intelligence to gain a strategic advantage in discussions. This approach is frequently encountered in healthcare settings, particularly during resource allocation negotiations. Consider a department head who deliberately emphasizes their team's emotional exhaustion and personal sacrifices, painting vivid pictures of burnout and dedication. This calculated display of vulnerability attempts to create an emotional obligation, making it psychologically harder for administrators to maintain objective criteria in decision-making.

To effectively counter Tactical Empathy, healthcare professionals must maintain emotional awareness while establishing objective frameworks. The most effective approach involves acknowledging emotional elements while immediately redirecting to measurable criteria: "Your team's dedication is remarkable, and these challenges deserve our attention. Let's examine our department's performance metrics, budget parameters, and staffing ratios to develop a sustainable solution that addresses this situation's emotional and operational aspects". This response maintains an empathetic connection while ensuring decisions remain grounded in objective criteria rather than emotional appeals.

Tactic Two: Anchoring

One of the most prevalent tactics you'll encounter is Anchoring, a cognitive bias in which negotiators rely too heavily on an initial piece of information – the "anchor" – when making decisions. This tactic is frequently employed against healthcare professionals, particularly in high-stakes purchasing scenarios. Consider a medical device company that opens negotiations by stating that its new surgical robot costs $2.3 million. This deliberately high price point serves as an anchor, attempting to frame all subsequent discussions around this inflated figure.

To effectively counter Anchoring, healthcare professionals must be prepared to reset the anchor entirely. The most effective approach is to disregard the initial anchor and establish a new one based on objective market criteria. Rather than engaging with the vendor's $2.3 million anchor, redirect the conversation by stating, "Let's start by looking at the average cost of comparable systems in the market, which is closer to $1.9 million. From there, we can discuss how your system's unique features – like the enhanced visualization software or smaller footprint – might justify a modest premium. We should also examine how the maintenance and service contract could be bundled to provide better long-term value rather than focusing solely on the initial purchase price". This response effectively reframes the negotiation around market reality and total value rather than the vendor's artificial starting point.

Tactic Three: Tactical Flinching

When healthcare professionals encounter Tactical Flinching, they often witness a carefully orchestrated display of shock or concern designed to provoke justification or concession. Though appearing spontaneous, these reactions – sharp intakes of breath, widened eyes, concerned expressions – are typically calculated moves in contract discussions and budget planning. An administrator might gasp audibly at proposed staffing ratios or appear visibly distressed by budget requests, hoping to create immediate psychological pressure for modification.

Healthcare professionals can transform these theatrical moments into opportunities for substantive exploration. Rather than becoming defensive or retreating from their position, they might respond: "I appreciate your reaction, and it highlights the need for deeper understanding. Could you walk me through your specific concerns about these ratios, and let's examine how they compare to evidence-based staffing models?" This analytical redirection maintains professional credibility while addressing legitimate concerns hidden behind the performance.

Tactic Four: Tactical Silence

The artful use of Tactical Silence creates some of the most challenging moments in healthcare negotiations. During critical discussions about resource allocation or organizational change, a skilled negotiator might meet proposals with extended silence, maintaining unwavering eye contact while allowing tension to build. What makes this tactic particularly effective is its simplicity – the natural human impulse to fill uncomfortable voids often leads to hasty concessions or unnecessary modifications. Success in countering such silence requires transforming these weighted pauses into structured reflection time. Consider responding with: "Let's take a moment to consider the full implications of this proposal. While we reflect, I'd like us to specifically consider how these changes might impact patient care outcomes and staff workload". This approach acknowledges the pause while redirecting its purpose toward constructive analysis.

Tactic Five: Pivots and Turns

Pivot and Turn maneuvers often surface at crucial decision points in healthcare negotiations, reflecting a tactical attempt to redirect discussions away from immediate challenges. Watch for the hospital executive who smoothly shifts conversations about current staffing shortages toward futuristic technological solutions or the department head who deflects budget discussions into theoretical long-term efficiency gains. These artful redirections, while appearing strategic, often mask an unwillingness to address pressing current needs.

Breaking through this tactical fog requires firm but diplomatic redirection to immediate priorities. A skilled negotiator might respond: "I see how technology might offer long-term solutions. However, let's first address our immediate staffing challenges with specific metrics and timelines; then, we can explore how technological innovations might enhance those solutions". By acknowledging future possibilities while maintaining focus on current needs, this approach prevents productive discussions from dissolving into vague future promises.

Tactic Six: "Yes, And…"

In the complex landscape of healthcare negotiations, few tactics require more nuanced handling than the "Yes, And…" technique. Initially developed as an improvisational tool, this approach has evolved into a subtle method for expanding agreements beyond their original scope. Watch for the clinical director who transforms a simple request for shared resources into an increasingly complex web of interconnected commitments, each "and" adding another layer of obligation or complexity to the original proposal.

The key to managing this expansive technique lies in resistance and careful boundary setting. When faced with cascading additions, consider this measured response: "Yes, the shared staffing model could work, and to ensure its success, let's establish specific criteria for staff allocation, clear cost-sharing frameworks, and measurable outcome metrics before expanding the scope". This approach honors the collaborative spirit while maintaining practical constraints.

Tactic Seven: The Double Magnet Approach

The Double Magnet Approach dilemma emerges most insidiously in healthcare technology and service negotiations, where vendors craft seemingly distinct choices that ultimately serve their interests equally well. Like a skilled magician's forced card trick, this tactic presents what appears to be a meaningful choice between options – perhaps a "premium" immediate implementation versus a "basic" phased rollout – while obscuring the fact that both paths lead to similar vendor-favorable outcomes.

Experienced negotiators recognize that escaping this false dichotomy requires creating new options rather than choosing between existing ones. A tactical response might be: "While both options have merit, let's explore a hybrid approach that combines immediate implementation of core features with a customized expansion timeline based on our utilization data and Return on Investment (ROI) metrics". This reframing breaks free from the artificial constraints while building toward a solution better aligned with organizational needs.

These counter-tactics provide healthcare professionals with actionable responses to maintain leverage and balance in complex negotiations, ensuring adaptability and alignment with patient-centered outcomes across all healthcare pillars. By mastering the ability to recognize and counter advanced negotiation tactics, healthcare professionals can provide more balanced, productive, and patient-centered negotiations.

Conclusion: The Value of a Tactical Approach

Mastering advanced negotiation tactics is crucial for healthcare professionals in today's complex, high-stakes environment. While strategies provide the foundation for achieving long-term goals, tactics offer real-time adaptability that can turn obstacles into opportunities and build momentum toward successful agreements. As explored in this chapter, tactical tools like Anchoring, Pivots and Turns, Flinching, Tactical Silence, "Yes, And…" thinking, and the Double Magnet Approach offer nuanced approaches to enhance flexibility, maintain rapport, and foster innovation.

When applied thoughtfully, these tactics enable negotiators to manage dynamics across healthcare's three pillars: The Practice of Medicine (Operating Room), Delivery of Care (Exam Room), and Business of Health (Boardroom). By integrating these tactics with ethical considerations and patient-centered goals, healthcare professionals can achieve better outcomes and build stronger, more sustainable partnerships. Ultimately, the true value of these tactics lies in their ability to adapt to ever-changing circumstances while maintaining a clear focus on delivering high-quality patient care.

REFLECTION EXERCISE: MASTERING ADVANCED HEALTHCARE NEGOTIATION TACTICS

Consider a challenging negotiation situation you're currently facing or anticipate in your healthcare role. Take 30 minutes to work through this structured reflection:

1. **Tactical Analysis**:
   - Map the emotional dynamics and power relationships in your negotiation setting.
   - For each key stakeholder, identify:
     - Their likely emotional triggers and concerns.
     - Areas where Tactical Empathy might be most effective.
     - Potential resistance points requiring strategic pivots.
   - Consider which advanced tactics (Tactical Empathy, Anchoring, Tactical Silence, etc.) might be most effective with each stakeholder.
2. **Tactical Planning**: For each identified tactic, develop a specific implementation plan:
   - Plan three moments to employ tactical empathy, writing out specific Acknowledgment statements.
   - Identify two potential anchors you could set and how you'll frame them.
   - Draft three tactical pivots you could use if facing resistance.
   - Prepare two "Yes, And..." responses to likely objections.
   - Map out situations where Tactical Silence might be most effective.
3. **Integration and Implementation**: Consider:
   - How will you combine multiple tactics effectively?
   - What signals will indicate when to switch tactics?
   - How will you maintain authentic engagement while employing these tactics?
   - What safeguards will ensure tactics don't compromise patient care priorities?

Document your insights and create an action plan for implementing these tactics. After the negotiation, reflect on which tactics proved most effective and what adjustments you would make in future negotiations.

Key Takeaways

1. The foundation of healthcare negotiations lies in calibrating tactics across each pillar, demanding skilled navigation of emotional dynamics and power relationships. Success requires thoughtful consideration of psychological safety and stakeholder needs while maintaining adaptability to each context's unique demands. By carefully balancing these elements, healthcare professionals can deploy advanced tactics that strengthen rather than strain relationships throughout clinical, operational, and administrative discussions.
2. Mastery of tactical preparation transforms healthcare negotiations by establishing comprehensive situational awareness before discussions begin. This methodical groundwork spans stakeholder analysis, power mapping, and scenario planning while maintaining a focus on authentic engagement. Through disciplined preparation, healthcare professionals develop the tactical precision needed to advance negotiations effectively without compromising trust or patient care standards.
3. Advanced negotiation tactics offer healthcare professionals vital tools for managing dynamic discussions, with each technique addressing distinct challenges, from building psychological safety to creating meaningful choice. Skilled practitioners use these instruments to transform obstacles into opportunities while preserving momentum and trust across all healthcare pillars. The resulting tactical adaptability allows negotiators to pivot seamlessly between approaches based on real-time dynamics while keeping patient care at the center.
4. Recognizing and countering complex negotiation tactics require healthcare professionals to develop precise defensive capabilities that protect core interests without damaging relationships. By combining Emotional Intelligence with tactical redirection and data-driven reframing, negotiators can effectively respond to manipulative approaches across all healthcare settings. This balanced defensive approach ensures patient care priorities remain paramount even when facing challenging tactical maneuvers from counterparts.

Notes

1. Daniel Goleman, Richard Boyatzis, and Annie McKee, *Primal Leadership: Unleashing the Power of Emotional Intelligence* (Cambridge, MA: Harvard Business Review Press, 2013); Chris Voss and Tahl Raz, *Never Split the Difference: Negotiating as If Your Life Depended on It* (New York: HarperBusiness, 2016).

2. Alison Wood Brooks and Maurice E. Schweitzer, "The Negotiation Dance: Time, Culture, and Behavioral Sequences in Negotiation," *Organization Science* 22, no. 1 (2011): 60–76.
3. Amos Tversky and Daniel Kahneman, "Judgment under Uncertainty: Heuristics and Biases," *Science* 185, no. 4157 (1974): 1124–1131.
4. Adam D. Galinsky and Thomas Mussweiler, "First Offers as Anchors: The Role of Perspective-Taking and Negotiator Focus," *Journal of Personality and Social Psychology* 81, no. 4 (2001): 657–669.
5. Dan Phuong Ly, Paul Gregory Shekelle, and Zirui Song, "Evidence for Anchoring Bias During Physician Decision-Making," *JAMA Internal Medicine* 183, no. 8 (2023): 818–823, 10.1001/jamainternmed.2023.2366.
6. Albert Mehrabian, *Silent Messages: Implicit Communication of Emotions and Attitudes* (Belmont, CA: Wadsworth Publishing Company, 1981).
7. Erving Goffman, *Frame Analysis: An Essay on the Organization of Experience* (Cambridge, MA: Harvard University Press, 1974).
8. William Ury, *Getting Past No: Negotiating in Difficult Situations*, rev. ed. (New York: Bantam, 1993).
9. Roger Fisher and William Ury, *Getting to Yes: Negotiating Agreement without Giving In* (New York: Penguin Books, 1981).
10. Amos Tversky and Daniel Kahneman, "The Framing of Decisions and the Psychology of Choice," *Science* 211, no. 4481 (1981): 453–458; Deepak Malhotra and Max H. Bazerman, *Negotiation Genius: How to Overcome Obstacles and Achieve Brilliant Results at the Bargaining Table and Beyond* (New York: Bantam, 2007).
11. Kazuhisa Takemura, *Behavioral Decision Theory: Psychological and Mathematical Descriptions of Human Choice Behavior* (Tokyo: Springer, 2014); "Behavioral Decision Theory," VAIA, accessed November 17, 2023, https://www.vaia.com/en-us/explanations/business-studies/operational-management/behavioral-decision-theory/; Jack S. Levy, "An Introduction to Prospect Theory," *Political Psychology* 13, no. 2 (1992): 171–186.

Chapter 9

The Negotiation Planner

A Guide to Complex Healthcare Negotiations

The most successful negotiator is the one who has found the order which is inherent in the situation.

– Mary Parker Follett

DOI: 10.4324/9781003336013-11

HEAR Negotiation Planner

Introduction

The HEAR Negotiation Planner is a tool designed to guide providers through complex healthcare negotiations. This planner helps healthcare professionals navigate the three pillars of healthcare – the Operating Room (Practice of Medicine), the Exam Room (Delivery of Care), and the Boardroom (Business of Health) – by integrating the principles of Empowerment, Acknowledgment, and Recasting with traditional negotiation strategies and tactics. Note that not all elements of the chapters or all parts of individual elements are represented in the planner; users are encouraged to review the chapters for details as needed.

Individual Use

1. Set aside dedicated time to work through each step of the planner.
2. Be honest and thorough in your responses to gain the most benefit.
3. Revisit and refine your responses as you gather more information or insights.

Team Use

1. Have each team member complete the steps of the planner independently.
2. Schedule a team meeting to discuss individual responses and insights.
3. Use the collective input to develop a cohesive negotiation approach.
4. Consider creating a shared document for asynchronous contributions and collaboration.

This planner is a living document. Revisit and update it throughout your negotiation process to maintain alignment with your goals and the evolving situation.

Step One: Negotiation Context

This step helps you establish the foundation for your negotiation by considering the broader healthcare context and identifying key factors that may influence the negotiation process.

- Briefly describe the situation, including the background and parties involved.
- Identify the specific healthcare pillar involved.
- List potential obstacles or challenges.

HEAR Negotiation Planner Reflection Prompts

- How might the specific healthcare pillar(s) involved influence your approach to this negotiation?
- In what ways could the potential obstacles you've identified become opportunities for creative problem-solving?

Reference: Chapter 3: Mastering Multifaceted Negotiations in and Across Healthcare's Three Pillars

Step Two: Stating Your Purpose

This step guides you in articulating your negotiation goals while maintaining a focus on building positive relationships and considering broader healthcare objectives.

- Define your specific goal or objective for this negotiation, considering tangible outcomes and relationship-building goals.
- Identify how your purpose considers the perspectives and potential benefits for other stakeholders.
- Explain how your purpose aligns with broader healthcare goals and supports positive relationships across pillars.

HEAR Negotiation Planner Reflection Prompts

- How does your stated purpose balance concrete objectives with relationship-building goals?
- In what ways does your purpose consider the perspectives and potential benefits for other stakeholders?
- How might you articulate your purpose differently when addressing stakeholders from different healthcare pillars?

Reference: Chapter 2, "Setting the Stage for Effective Healthcare Negotiations: Defining Your Purpose."

Step Three: Adopting the Right Mindset

This step focuses on shifting from siloed thinking to a more holistic, integrated approach that balances clinical excellence, operational efficiency, and financial sustainability while prioritizing patient-centered care.

- Define your specific goal or objective for this negotiation, considering tangible outcomes and relationship-building goals.
- Explain how your purpose aligns with broader healthcare goals.
- Outline both objective and relational success measures.

Theory of Mind Assessment

- Reflect on your ability to understand others' perspectives.
- How might other stakeholders view this negotiation differently from you?
- What unique experiences or motivations might influence their stance?
- How can you demonstrate your understanding of their viewpoint during the negotiation?

Relational Mindset Check

- Consider how your approach can foster long-term relationships and mutual understanding.
- Identify opportunities to create value for all parties involved.
- Reflect on how you can maintain an "us" rather than "me" perspective throughout the negotiation.

HEAR Negotiation Planner Reflection Prompts

- How can you apply the Relational Mindset to create a more collaborative negotiation environment?
- How can you use the Theory of Mind assessment to proactively anticipate and address others' concerns?
- What measures can you use to determine success when it comes to negotiations?

Reference: Chapter 2, "Theory of Mind" and "The Relational Mindset: The Foundation of the HEAR Approach™."

Step Four: Empowerment as Aligning Interests

This step helps you prepare mentally and emotionally for the negotiation, recognizing Empowerment as an ongoing process of self-reflection and adaptation that fosters more collaborative and effective healthcare outcomes.

Internal Scan

- List your core interests, motivations, and priorities for this negotiation.
- Evaluate how these align with your organization's mission and values.
- Identify potential emotional triggers or biases that might impact your approach.

Emotional Intelligence Self-Assessment

- Recognize and manage your own emotions during high-stakes discussions.
- Understand and consider others' emotions and perspectives.
- Adapt your communication style to build rapport and foster collaboration.

Empathy Mapping

- Create a self-empathy map to gain deeper insight into your own perspective.
- Create a brief profile including demographics, background, and context.
- Populate the Empathy Map.
- Use the Empathy Map to inform your negotiation strategies, tactics, and communication approaches.

RESET Framework Application

- Recognize your emotional triggers.
- Evaluate the intensity of your reactions.
- Step back to gain perspective.
- Empathize with others' viewpoints.
- Transform your response to a constructive approach.

HEAR Negotiation Planner Reflection Prompts

- How has this self-assessment changed your perspective on the upcoming negotiation?
- What specific steps can you take to leverage your strengths and address your limitations?
- How might empathy mapping enhance your ability to build rapport and foster collaboration?

References: Chapter 2, "Relational Mindset Tools and Practices: Empathy Mapping," and Chapter 4, "Enhancing Negotiation Effectiveness: A Guide for Internal Scans," "Emotional Intelligence Assessment," and "RESET: Regulating Emotional Responses"

Step Five: Acknowledgment as Understanding Diverse Perspectives

This step guides you in understanding diverse viewpoints to create an environment of mutual understanding, leading to innovative problem-solving and patient-centered healthcare.

Stakeholder Mapping

- Identify key stakeholders for each pillar.
- Use the Healthcare Negotiation Mapping Tool to understand priorities and connections.

Empathy Mapping

- For each stakeholder, create a brief profile including background and context.
- Create Empathy Maps to identify potential emotional triggers for each stakeholder.
- Prepare empathetic responses for these scenarios.
- Use the Empathy Maps to inform your negotiation tactics and communication approaches.

Multiple Selves Framework

- Identify each stakeholder's External, Internal, and Vulnerable Selves to gain deeper insight into their perspective.
- Consider how these "selves" might influence their perspective and approach to the negotiation.

Active Listening and Appreciative Inquiry Preparation

- Prepare open-ended questions that encourage the sharing of perspectives.
- List key phrases for demonstrating active listening.
- Develop appreciative, forward-looking questions to foster collaboration.

HEAR Negotiation Planner Reflection Prompts

- How has the combination of stakeholder and empathy mapping deepened your understanding of the negotiation landscape?
- In what ways can you use your insights about stakeholders' Multiple Selves to foster a more collaborative environment?
- How might combining active listening with Appreciative Inquiry help navigate conflicts?

References: Chapter 2, "Relational Mindset Tools and Practices: Empathy Mapping," Chapter 3, "Healthcare Negotiation Mapping Tool," Chapter 5, "Understanding Multiple Selves in Negotiations," "Putting Acknowledgment into Practice: Active Listening as a Catalyst for Mutual Understanding," and "Connecting the Puzzle Pieces of Acknowledgment Through Appreciative Inquiry."

Step Six: Recasting for Collaborative Solutions

This step helps you prepare to recast the negotiation, focusing on shared interests and collaborative problem-solving, while building upon the understanding of diverse perspectives developed in previous steps.

Reframing the Negotiation

- Redefine the negotiation's purpose to focus on shared goals and values.
- Identify areas of common ground or mutual benefit across stakeholders.

- Draft a new collaborative purpose statement that addresses all parties' core interests.

Joint Problem Definition

- List the key issues or challenges from each stakeholder's perspective.
- Craft a shared problem statement that incorporates all viewpoints.
- Identify how this joint definition differs from initial individual perspectives.

Transforming External Selves to Internal and Vulnerable Selves

- For each stakeholder (including yourself), consider how their External Self can be reframed as an Internal or Vulnerable Self?
- What shared values or vulnerabilities might emerge from this reframing?
- Prepare strategies to address these Internal and Vulnerable Selves during the negotiation.

Creative Problem-Solving and Contingency Planning

- Use the 360-degree Stakeholder Analysis to identify potential resources and solutions.
- Apply the Problem Reframing Matrix to explore alternative perspectives on key issues.
- Conduct a Future-Back Thinking exercise to work backward to achieve ideal outcomes.
- Develop "If-Then" scenarios for potential roadblocks or unexpected developments.
- Use the RESET technique and prepare strategies for navigating emotional hotspots.

HEAR Negotiation Planner Reflection Prompts

- How has reframing the purpose open up new possibilities for mutual gain?
- In what ways does joint problem definition create opportunities for collaborative solutions?
- Which creative problem-solving technique feels most promising for your situation?

Reference: Chapter 6, "Recasting: Navigating New Realities Together."

Step Seven: Advanced Negotiation Strategy Toolbox

This step helps you select and prepare appropriate strategies from your negotiation toolbox while maintaining alignment with HEAR principles and healthcare objectives.

Understanding and Setting Your Value

- Evaluate your unique value proposition across multiple dimensions and translate value metrics into terms that resonate with specific stakeholder groups.
- Present a comprehensive value framework that demonstrates both immediate and long-term impacts while aligning with stakeholder priorities.

Logrolling for Mutual Benefit

- Start by mapping out potential trade packages by carefully identifying high-value/low-cost items for each party.
- Identify multiple package combinations that could create mutual value.
- Develop clear fallback positions for each proposed trade, and carefully plan the timing of your offers to maintain negotiating momentum.

Multiple Equivalent Simultaneous Offers

- Create a set of three proposals that emphasize different benefits and appeal to different stakeholder priorities but maintain equivalent value and allow clear comparison.
- Prepare concise explanations of key differences that highlight the unique advantages of each approach and anticipate questions about specific elements of each offer.

Contingency and Post-Settlement Agreements

- Begin by identifying key uncertainties that could impact agreement success.
- Structure your implementation process around well-defined trigger points that automatically initiate specific responses.

- Set regular review periods that allow for timely adjustments based on performance data.

HEAR Negotiation Planner Reflection Prompts

- How do your selected strategies align with HEAR principles?
- Which combination of strategies might work best for your specific situation?
- What potential challenges might arise, and how will you address them?

Reference: Chapter 7, "Advanced Negotiation Strategies for Complex Challenges"

Step Eight: Advanced Negotiation Tactics Toolbox

This step helps you select and prepare appropriate tactics from your negotiation toolbox while maintaining alignment with HEAR principles and healthcare objectives.

Tactical Empathy

- Learn to identify emotional triggers that might arise during negotiations and prepare thoughtful acknowledgment statements for each.
- Create a framework of follow-up questions that deepen mutual understanding while maintaining professional boundaries.

Anchoring and Framing

- Select strategic anchor points and craft framing statements that establish favorable reference points while maintaining ethical standards.
- Gather supporting evidence that validates your chosen anchors and prepares alternative framing approaches for different stakeholder perspectives.

Tactical Flinches

- Master the art of demonstrating appropriate concern by identifying moments when measured reactions could be most effective.

- Practice delivering responses that convey legitimate apprehension while maintaining professionalism.
- Prepare follow-up questions that transform moments of concern into opportunities for deeper discussion.

Pivots and Turns

- Map out potential points in your negotiation for tactical redirection and develop a repertoire of redirection phrases that maintain dialogue momentum while shifting focus.
- Create multiple pathways for discussion that allow flexible navigation of complex topics.

HEAR Negotiation Planner Reflection Prompts

- How do your selected tactics align with HEAR principles?
- Which combinations might work best for your specific situation?
- How can you maintain flexibility while executing your tactical plan?

Reference: Chapter 8, "Mastering Real-Time Negotiation Tactics"

Step Nine: Reflection and Learning

This step encourages ongoing learning and adaptation, reinforcing the iterative nature of the HEAR Approach™ introduced in Chapter 1.

Post-Negotiation Reflection

- Reflect on what worked well and areas for improvement.
- Challenge assumptions you've made about stakeholders or the negotiation context.
- Identify key lessons learned and insights gained.
- Plan how to refine your approach for future negotiations.

HEAR Negotiation Planner Reflection Prompts

- What has been the most surprising or insightful realization as you've worked through this planner?
- How has your understanding of the HEAR Approach™ evolved through this planning process?

- How can you apply the insights gained from this planning process to other aspects of your professional life in healthcare?
- How might you continue to develop your skills in each component of the HEAR Approach™?

Reference: Chapter 1, "The HEAR Approach™: An Overview of Transformative Healthcare Negotiations."

This pediatric cancer drug negotiation offers a compelling illustration of how the HEAR Negotiation Planner can guide real-world strategy. The scenario checks all the boxes outlined in the decision framework: a clearly defined healthcare domain (pharmaceuticals), identifiable stakeholder groups, and measurable success metrics. These factors made it an ideal case for applying the Planner.

What follows is a step-by-step analysis of how Julie Grant and her team systematically used the HEAR framework to navigate a high-stakes negotiation that spanned science, business, and mission-driven advocacy.

In the early 2020s, the landscape of pediatric cancer treatment was marked by a stark disparity. While adult oncology had seen significant advances, children with cancer continued to face a severe shortage of new treatment options. This gap caught the attention of Julie Grant, a venture capitalist with a rare blend of scientific training and business insight. "It was a market that was behind", she observed, "and so you could see the roadmap of what was possible".[1]

As co-founder of Day One Biopharmaceuticals, Grant was operating at the intersection of medical innovation, business strategy, and regulatory complexity. Her academic and professional background – degrees in biophysics and biochemistry from the University of Pennsylvania, an MBA from Stanford, and experience at Genentech in both clinical development and commercial strategy – uniquely positioned her to take on this challenge. "I felt very confident about my ability to understand what the parameters were of what could build a market that could get investor dollars".

"Working at Genentech really opened my eyes to the complexities of bringing new drugs to market", she added. "Over twenty years, the FDA approved over 200 new oncology drugs to treat adults", she explained, her voice tinged with frustration. "Yet fewer than ten new drugs have been FDA approved for children with cancer".

This realization led to the founding of Day One Biopharmaceuticals in 2020. The company emerged from Grant's vision to address the critical gap in pediatric cancer treatments while simultaneously creating a sustainable business model that could attract necessary investments. Moreover, Grant recognized the need to navigate the complex regulatory landscape for pediatric drug development, a challenge that required a delicate balance of scientific innovation, strategic planning, and regulatory expertise. "We couldn't just focus on the science," Grant emphasized. "We needed to convince pharmaceutical companies to partner with us, attract investors who understood the long-term value proposition, and work closely with regulatory bodies to streamline the approval process for pediatric drugs."

As Grant described the stakeholders involved in these negotiations, the complexity of the challenge became evident. "We were dealing with pharmaceutical companies wary of the limited market size, investors seeking a balance between social impact and financial returns, and regulatory bodies tasked with ensuring drug safety while expediting access to critical treatments," she explained. "And of course, we always had to keep in mind the pediatric oncologists, researchers, and most importantly, the families desperate for new treatment options."

A pivotal moment in Day One's journey illustrated the intricate negotiations required. "We identified this promising drug candidate for pediatric brain tumors," she said. "But it was owned by a large pharmaceutical company initially developing it for adult cancers. They considered divesting it because it didn't fit their primary oncology focus. That's when we knew we had to act."

This scenario required Grant to navigate the interests of multiple stakeholders simultaneously. She faced the challenge of convincing the pharmaceutical company of the drug's potential in pediatric oncology while demonstrating to investors the long-term value of pursuing this opportunity. Concurrently, Grant needed to work with regulatory bodies to expedite the development process for this critical need, collaborate with pediatric oncologists to design effective clinical trials, and always keep in mind the urgent needs of affected patients and their families. Each of these stakeholders had distinct priorities and concerns, creating a complex web of interests that Grant had to carefully balance and address.

In recounting this complex landscape, Grant emphasized the importance of a structured negotiation approach. "We couldn't rely on traditional, single-focus negotiation strategies," she explained. "We needed a comprehensive framework to address the interconnected nature of all these stakeholders' interests."

By recognizing the interplay between clinical innovation, operational feasibility, and financial sustainability, Grant and her team at Day One Biopharmaceuticals were ultimately able to forge a path forward in the challenging landscape of pediatric cancer drug development. Their story underscores the critical importance of holistic, multi-stakeholder negotiation strategies in driving meaningful progress in healthcare.

The Negotiation Planner: A Comprehensive Framework

The Negotiation Planner is a comprehensive tool that guides healthcare professionals through complex, multi-stakeholder negotiations. It provides a structured approach to preparing for, executing, and reflecting on negotiations across various healthcare settings. Using Grant's experience, healthcare professionals will see how it can guide them through the negotiation process.

Step One: Negotiation Context

As Grant began to apply the Negotiation Planner to her work at Day One Biopharmaceuticals, she faced a pivotal moment: negotiating to license a promising drug candidate for pediatric brain tumors from a large pharmaceutical company. "When we identified this drug," Grant recalled, "I knew we were at a crossroads. This wasn't just another business deal – it was a potential lifeline for children with few options." Grant's approach involved her team "understanding the full landscape – the science, the business, the regulations, and, most importantly, the human impact. We couldn't rely on just knowing our own position."

In assessing negotiation context, a healthcare negotiator should:

1. describe the situation,
2. identify the relevant healthcare pillars involved, and
3. note potential obstacles or challenges.

Here's how Grant approached each of these elements:

1. **Describe the Situation**: Grant meticulously analyzed critical elements, including:
   - The drug's potential to improve outcomes for children.
   - The pharmaceutical company's priorities and divestment reasons.
   - Day One's limited resources versus the large company's portfolio.
   - Regulatory considerations for pediatric drug repurposing.
   - The urgency of bringing new treatments to market for children with cancer.
2. **Identify the Healthcare Pillars**: Grant identified multiple relevant stakeholders spanning the Business of Health, Practice of Medicine and Delivery of Care:
   - Pharmaceutical companies wary of limited market size.
   - Investors balancing social impact and financial returns.
   - Regulatory bodies ensuring safety while expediting access.
   - Pediatric oncologists and researchers.
   - Patient advocacy groups and families.
3. **Note Potential Obstacles or Challenges**: Grant recognized several key challenges, including funding and a business plan that led to successful treatments. She added, "They don't give medicines away for free. They don't give their assets away for free, not when they've spent hundreds of millions of dollars on them," underscoring the difficulty in acquiring rights to promising drug candidates. Grant also faced the challenge of convincing investors of the viability of focusing on a niche market like pediatric oncology: "We pitched to over 50 VCs to join the syndicate."

By following Grant's example of thoroughly analyzing their negotiation context, healthcare professionals can lay the groundwork for more effective, empathetic, and successful negotiations. This approach extends beyond the Business of Health; healthcare professionals involved in the Delivery of Care and Practice of Medicine would equally benefit from such thorough contextual analysis:

Clinical Parallel: A neurologist advocating for a new stroke treatment protocol would need to consider factors such as potential improvements in patient outcomes, interdepartmental workflows, costs of new equipment and training, and possible resistance to change. Their stakeholders might include emergency physicians, radiologists, hospital administrators, and nursing staff.

Operational Parallel: A hospital operations manager proposing a new patient scheduling system would need to analyze factors such as potential improvements in patient wait times, impact on staff workload, integration with existing IT infrastructure, implementation costs, and possible resistance from different departments. Their stakeholders might include IT staff, department heads, front-desk personnel, finance officers, and patient representatives.

Step Two – Stated Purpose

Grant emphasized the importance of having a clear, multifaceted purpose to guide her negotiations: "Our purpose wasn't just about developing drugs. It was about changing the entire landscape of pediatric cancer treatment".

In Step Two of the Negotiation Planner, healthcare negotiators are encouraged to:

1. Identify their core objectives.
2. Consider the perspectives and benefits for other stakeholders.
3. Align their goals with broader healthcare missions.

For the licensing negotiation, Grant crafted a purpose statement that balanced business needs with Day One's broader mission:

> To negotiate a licensing agreement with [Pharmaceutical Company] for [Drug Candidate] that allows Day One Biopharmaceuticals to develop and commercialize the drug for pediatric brain tumors while ensuring sufficient rights, resources, and flexibility to effectively bring this potentially life-saving treatment to children in need.

Core Objectives:

- Secure licensing rights for the drug candidate.
- Ensure sufficient resources for development and commercialization.
- Maintain flexibility in development and distribution.
- Build a sustainable business model focused on pediatric oncology.

Stakeholder Perspectives and Benefits:

- For pharmaceutical companies: an opportunity to extend impact to a new patient population.

- For investors: a rare blend of social impact and financial return.
- For pediatric oncologists: access to targeted, evidence-based treatments.
- For families: renewed hope for therapies that serve children directly.

Broader Mission Alignment:

- Address the unmet need in pediatric oncology.
- Demonstrate the viability of mission-driven pharmaceutical innovation.
- Build a model that bridges the gap between adult and pediatric drug development.

"Every word in that statement was carefully chosen", Grant later explained. "We needed to be clear about our business goals, but also emphasize our commitment to patients. It wasn't just about getting the rights to the drug – it was about securing the means actually to get it to the kids who needed it".

By following this approach, healthcare professionals can create purpose statements that serve as both strategic anchors and moral compasses – guiding negotiations across the Business of Health, Delivery of Care, and Practice of Medicine.

Clinical Parallel: A CMO at a community hospital crafted a stated purpose for implementing a new telemedicine program: "To establish a comprehensive telemedicine program that expands access to specialist care for our rural patients, improves health outcomes, and creates a sustainable model for remote healthcare delivery while addressing the concerns of our in-person care providers and maintaining the financial health of our hospital."

Operational Parallel: A hospital's COO might craft a stated purpose for redesigning the inpatient discharge process: "To streamline the discharge process, ensuring timely and safe patient transitions, reducing readmission rates, improving communication across care teams, and enhancing patient satisfaction, while addressing staff workload concerns, minimizing bottlenecks, and maintaining cost-effectiveness for the organization."

Step Three – Adopting the Right Mindset

A Relational Mindset serves as the foundation of effective healthcare negotiation. It enables professionals to build trust, foster collaboration, and achieve mutually beneficial outcomes that enhance patient care and drive change across all facets of healthcare delivery.

Julie Grant emphasized the importance of adopting this mindset in her negotiations:

> "We needed capital – but also a business plan that showed we wouldn't just generate data and stall. The pharmaceutical company wanted a partner they could trust: a small biotech fully committed to completing trials and getting treatments approved for kids with cancer".

The payoff, she added, was deeply personal: "It allows you to be human. It's just this incredible moment to be able to try and help people".

In Step Three of the Negotiation Planner, healthcare negotiators are encouraged to:

1. Define specific relationship-building goals or tangible outcomes.
2. Align their purpose with broader healthcare goals.
3. Outline both objective and relational success measures.

The Relational Mindset is built on these three core components, and Grant exemplified each in her approach.

1. Define Specific Relationship-Building Goals or Tangible Outcomes:

Grant prioritized building trust and long-term collaboration with key stakeholders:

- With pharmaceutical companies, to secure drug licensing rights.
- With pediatric oncologists and researchers to support trial development and credibility.
- With investors, to attract mission-aligned capital partners.

2. Align Purpose with Broader Healthcare Goals:

Grant's negotiation strategy was anchored in a larger healthcare mission:

- Addressing the treatment gap in pediatric oncology: "We looked at more than 50 assets. It's incredibly rare to find a medicine that's truly ready to be advanced into human trials".

- Demonstrating scientific and business viability: "We cared very much about applying the most advanced knowledge on the genetics and underlying causes of pediatric cancers to find great medicines that would work".

3. Outline Both Objective and Relational Success Measures:

Grant tracked both concrete outcomes and relationship milestones:

- Objective measures: Securing the licensing deal and raising capital: "We will create a company dedicated to this. And here are the people who we're gonna recruit, and we will raise money".
- Relational measures: Building Day One's credibility with stakeholders: "They were essentially pre-qualifying us – asking, 'Who are you? Who's your head of quality? Your head of regulatory? Your chief medical officer?' They needed to know we were credible".
- Long-term measures: Establishing a replicable model: "The idea is to do what we did with our first asset. Again and again and again".

By following Grant's example, healthcare professionals can apply a Relational Mindset to acknowledge diverse interests, foster cross-sector trust, and co-create solutions that serve the Business of Health, the Delivery of Care, and the Practice of Medicine.

Clinical Parallel: A pediatric surgeon adopting a Relational Mindset when introducing a new minimally invasive surgical technique might focus on building trust with the surgical team, fostering collaboration with anesthesiology and nursing staff, and developing partnerships with the hospital administration to secure necessary resources.

Operational Parallel: A hospital facilities manager adopting a Relational Mindset when proposing a major renovation project might emphasize building relationships with department heads to understand their needs, collaborating with finance to develop a cost-effective plan, and partnering with staff representatives to address concerns about disruptions during construction.

Step Four – Empowerment as Aligning Interests

Empowerment in negotiation begins with self-awareness. It requires individuals to understand their motivations, strengths, and emotional triggers, then align those insights with their organization's mission and negotiation strategy.

Julie Grant was deeply attuned to how her passion intersected with Day One's broader goals:

"I had to be honest with myself about how emotionally invested I was in this mission. It was crucial to stay clear-eyed about the challenges ahead".

"We were not going to start a company unless we found something truly meaningful", she added. "We had a very specific focus for what we were looking for".

In Step Four of the Negotiation Planner, healthcare negotiators are encouraged to:

1. Conduct an Internal Scan of their interests, values, and potential blind spots, assess their emotional intelligence.
2. Apply the RESET framework to regulate emotional responses and maintain relational alignment. Grant's approach exemplified each of these elements.

1. **Internal Scan**

Grant's self-assessment revealed how personal values and professional discipline converged:

- **Core interests and motivations**: "We cared deeply about applying the most advanced understanding of pediatric cancer genetics to find medicines that would work".
- **Link to mission and identity:** "We basically tattooed it on the company: we are P-DOC – a pediatric oncology – driven organization".
- **Awareness of emotional bias:** Grant was acutely aware of how powerful emotion could be when working with families affected by cancer.

"It's the sentinel moment of a parent's life", she said, referring to the devastating experience of learning that your child has cancer. "That affects you".

To prevent emotion from clouding judgment, Day One implemented a rigorous drug screening protocol and conducted extensive due diligence with each potential pharmaceutical partner. The goal was to remain mission-driven while avoiding reactive or overly optimistic decisions.

2. **Emotional Intelligence Self-Assessment**

Grant demonstrated high Emotional Intelligence across multiple domains:

- **Self-awareness:** "I always branded myself as the acting CEO. I held the seat so I could eventually recruit someone better".
- **Self-regulation:** "We had a rule: no rookies. I was the only rookie allowed".
- **Empathy:** "I get emotional. I've heard from so many parents about what this experience has been like for them".
- **Social skills:** "I went out with my co-founder to raise money from other VCs. It was about making the case in person".

3. **RESET Framework Application**

Grant drew on the RESET approach – Recognize, Evaluate, Step back, Empathize, Transform – to stay grounded and productive amid emotional intensity:

- **Recognize emotional triggers:** "I get chills – it was actually unbelievable".
- **Evaluate the intensity of reactions:** "I thought, 'Oh my God, what is that?'"
- **Step back for perspective:** "We needed to move past that. That's why I really think we have a problem right now with how medicines are developed".
- **Empathize with others' views:** "I've been so inspired by these people. They're not jaded or cynical. They're just so pure in their mission of service".
- **Transform response into constructive action:** "That was the big aha moment for me – realizing this community wasn't just a stop along the way. It was the destination".

Grant summarized this mindset clearly:

"Understanding my own triggers was critical. I knew frustration could make me combative, which wouldn't serve our goals. I had to channel that emotion into constructive energy".

By following Grant's example of self-awareness and emotional regulation, healthcare professionals can enter negotiations across all three healthcare pillars with greater confidence, clarity, and the ability to navigate the emotions these conversations inevitably stir up.

Clinical Parallel: A department head at a teaching hospital applied similar empowerment techniques when preparing to negotiate changes to resident work hours. His Internal Scan revealed several driving interests: improving resident well-being while preserving educational quality, drawing on his dual experience as both a former resident and current attending. He also identified potential biases stemming from his past training and emotional triggers around perceived dismissals of resident concerns. By naming those factors in advance, he was able to enter the negotiation with greater clarity, empathy, and composure, balancing institutional needs with frontline realities.

Operational Parallel: A hospital's CFO used similar empowerment strategies while negotiating a new budget allocation system. Her Internal Scan surfaced key priorities: ensuring long-term financial sustainability while protecting care quality. Drawing on her background in both clinical operations and healthcare finance, she recognized how her corporate training could unintentionally lead to rigidity. In particular, her frustration with departments that routinely overspent risked hardening her stance. Acknowledging this trigger, she developed flexible, data-informed budgeting models that could accommodate unexpected demands while maintaining fiscal discipline – creating a more collaborative negotiation environment across departments.

Step Five – Acknowledgment: Understanding Diverse Perspectives

Effective negotiation requires more than asserting your own interests – it demands genuine understanding of others. Acknowledging diverse perspectives builds trust, prevents blind spots, and opens space for collaboration, especially in high-stakes, multi-stakeholder negotiations.

Julie Grant emphasized that understanding each stakeholder group's emotional and cultural dimensions was just as critical as analyzing the data.

"Understanding the cultural aspects of how people operate in this community is crucial", she said. "It's about training yourself to navigate complex emotional landscapes".

"Being able to have hard conversations grounded in data, with the right stakeholders at the right time, is really important", she added.

"There's always a mix of capital strategy, scientific risk, and the willingness to step into new markets or patient populations", she explained. "That's exactly what venture dollars should fund – and what entrepreneurs are built to do".

In Step Five of the Negotiation Planner, healthcare negotiators are encouraged to:

1. Conduct stakeholder mapping.
2. Develop Empathy Maps to explore key perspectives.
3. Apply the Multiple Selves framework to anticipate emotional and strategic positioning.

Grant's negotiation process reflected all three elements.

1. **Stakeholder Mapping**

For the drug licensing negotiation, Grant identified a broad and interdependent network of stakeholders:

- Pharmaceutical company executives.
- Day One's board and investors.
- Regulatory bodies such as the FDA.
- Clinical researchers and frontline physicians.
- Patient advocacy groups and families.
- Potential competitors.

2. **Empathy Mapping:**

Grant built Empathy Maps to understand how different stakeholders might think, feel, say, and act in response to the negotiation. For example, her conversations with pediatric oncologists revealed how deeply committed they were to their patients:

"I've never seen anything like it in my life", she said. "It's so inspiring to be around them because they'll do absolutely anything to help one kid. It's just... super cool".

Her ability to listen deeply and appreciate stakeholders' motivations helped shape a negotiation approach that felt both strategic and humane.

3. **Multiple Selves Framework**

Grant used the Multiple Selves approach to think through each stakeholder's different identities and pressures:

- **External Self**: The professional role they hold publicly (e.g., investor, regulator, clinician).
- **Internal Self**: Their underlying goals, beliefs, and concerns.
- **Vulnerable Self**: The emotional or reputational risks they may carry in the negotiation.

"We had to understand every angle", Grant explained. "It wasn't enough to know our own position. We needed to grasp the full landscape".

She used this approach to identify where stakeholder hesitation might stem from personal risk or unspoken constraints, not just the official talking points.

By following Grant's example of acknowledging and understanding diverse perspectives, healthcare professionals can develop negotiation strategies that are more inclusive, anticipatory, and adaptive.

"Each stakeholder had their own priorities and concerns", she noted. "We had to understand and address each one to build a successful strategy".

Whether working in the Business of Health, the Delivery of Care, or the Practice of Medicine, healthcare professionals must learn to balance stakeholder needs with organizational goals and acknowledgment is the critical bridge between the two.

Clinical Parallel: A hospital chief of staff used similar Acknowledgment techniques when negotiating to implement a new EHR system. Her stakeholder map included hospital IT staff, physicians from various departments, nursing leadership, hospital administration, and EHR vendor representatives. She created Empathy Maps for each group, considering their potential thoughts, feelings, and concerns about the EHR implementation.

Operational Parallel: A hospital's Director of Supply Chain Management used similar Acknowledgment techniques when negotiating a new group purchasing agreement for medical supplies. His stakeholder map included procurement staff, clinical department heads, finance team members, hospital administration, and vendor representatives. He created Empathy Maps for each group, considering their potential thoughts, feelings, and concerns about the new purchasing agreement. For instance, he recognized that clinical staff might prioritize product quality and familiarity, while finance would focus on cost-savings. The director used this understanding to develop a negotiation strategy that balanced clinical preferences with financial constraints, ultimately leading to a more inclusive and effective purchasing agreement that satisfied diverse stakeholder needs.

Step Six – Recasting: Exploring Shared Interests and Collaborative Solutions

Recasting is the art of transforming a negotiation from a fixed-position standoff into a shared problem-solving process. It involves shifting the conversation from "What do I want?" to "What are we trying to solve together?" For Julie Grant, this shift was pivotal in negotiating drug development partnerships across the healthcare ecosystem.

"When you get past the perceptions and the branding disaster that is the pharmaceutical industry, and you get to the core of what you're trying to accomplish for people, they get it", Grant said. "It just took so much effort to try and get past that".

By reframing the negotiation around outcomes for children, she was able to move the conversation away from costs and toward shared value.

"That's when everything changed. I really wish the rest of our healthcare system was like that", she reflected. "It's kind of a magic place. It's how it should be".

In Step Six of the Negotiation Planner, healthcare negotiators are encouraged to:

1. Reframe the negotiation to focus on shared goals.
2. Collaboratively define the problem with stakeholders.
3. Help stakeholders surface internal and vulnerable selves.
4. Engage in creative problem-solving.

Grant's strategy reflected each of these practices.

1. **Reframing the Negotiation**

Grant redefined the purpose of the licensing conversation to center on shared values, not just business metrics.

- She focused the mission on leveraging cutting-edge genomic research and disease pathway insights to bring new therapies to children with cancer.
- She identified common ground across stakeholders: pharmaceutical partners who wanted to see unused assets put to good use, investors interested in long-term impact, and regulators aiming to increase access to pediatric treatments.

To succeed, Grant needed more than capital – she needed partners who understood the complexity of building a sustainable operational model for pediatric drug development.

2. **Joint Problem Definition**

Grant worked actively to surface the challenges each stakeholder faced and reframe them as part of a collective problem to solve:

- **Pharmaceutical companies** were wary of small market sizes.
- **Investors** were balancing humanitarian goals with ROI expectations.
- **Regulators** had to weigh safety rigor against the urgency of unmet medical need.

Ultimately, Grant's team reframed the entire challenge as one of systems integration:

> "We realized that drug development wouldn't succeed unless we figured out reimbursement pathways, secured regulatory buy-in, and brought in industry partners who believed in the long-term value of pediatric innovation".

3. **Transforming External Selves to Internal and Vulnerable Selves**

Grant's negotiations encouraged stakeholders to move beyond scripted roles and show what truly motivated them:

- By pitching to more than 50 venture capital firms, she demonstrated not just perseverance, but a willingness to expose her internal mission: to build something sustainable and meaningful.
- She also allowed space for her own vulnerability:

"Hearing from parents – what they've gone through – it hits you. That emotion fuels you but can also overwhelm you if you don't acknowledge it".

- Through that process, Grant helped coalesce a shared mission around pediatric innovation, grounded in science, empathy, and action.

4. **Creative Problem-Solving**

Grant's approach was deeply strategic but also highly inventive. She conducted a 360-degree stakeholder analysis to uncover tensions: pharmaceutical hesitation, investor skepticism, and regulatory complexity.

- She applied future-back thinking, asking what success should look like in the long term and then working backward:

"We looked at the genetics, what was already developed, and said – how do we match this with what kids actually need? These mutations, these fusions, these drivers – we believed we could go after them".

By following Grant's example of Recasting negotiations, healthcare professionals can shift from positional bargaining to collaborative design. This approach opens space for innovation, inclusion, and long-term alignment across the Business of Health, the Delivery of Care, and the Practice of Medicine.

Clinical Parallel: A CMO used Recasting techniques when negotiating for a new patient safety initiative. He reframed the discussion from a cost-centered debate to a collaborative effort to improve patient outcomes and reduce long-term expenses and encouraged creative problem-solving by involving front-line staff in generating solutions and developing contingency plans for potential implementation challenges.

Operational Parallel: A director of facilities management used Recasting techniques when negotiating for a hospital-wide energy efficiency upgrade. She developed a phased implementation plan that addressed immediate concerns about disruption to hospital operations while showcasing the long-term benefits of reduced energy consumption and improved building performance. By Recasting the negotiation in terms of shared goals like environmental responsibility and financial stewardship, she was able to gain support from diverse stakeholders across the organization.

Step Seven – Negotiation Toolbox of Advanced Strategies

Successful negotiators don't rely on isolated tactics – they build a cohesive strategy where each move reinforces the next. Julie Grant took this systems-level approach seriously, ensuring her negotiation strategy aligned with Day One's mission and stakeholder priorities.

"The strategies I choose need to support both our mission and market potential", she explained. "But more importantly, they need to work together to create a cohesive approach".

Her negotiation plan didn't emerge in a vacuum. Grant drew directly from insights developed during earlier planning stages:

- From her stakeholder analysis:

"Investors will focus on market size and return potential, but some may also value social impact. Finding ways to speak to both priorities will be crucial".

- From her empathy mapping:

"Risk tolerance varies significantly among potential investors. I'll need flexibility in how we structure any agreements".

- From her purpose statement:

"Maintaining our mission focus while securing adequate funding is non-negotiable".

With these principles in place, Grant built an advanced negotiation strategy that demonstrated both vision and flexibility. Her approach reflects two core components of Step Seven in the Negotiation Planner: (1) understanding and articulating your value, and (2) designing flexible but principled offers that meet diverse stakeholder needs.

1. **Understanding and Setting Your Value**

Grant began by establishing a clear and compelling value proposition tailored to each stakeholder group: "First, we need to be very clear about our value", she said. "It has to resonate with the people we're talking to".

- She framed Day One's work not just as a business opportunity but as a moral and medical imperative:

"The pediatric oncology space represents more than just a market. It's a chance to transform children's lives while building sustainable value. With fewer than ten FDA-approved drugs for children with cancer in the past two decades, we're positioned to be first-movers in addressing this critical need".

Her value statement did more than justify investment – it reframed the conversation around shared purpose and societal impact.

2. **Multiple Equivalent Simultaneous Offers (MESOs)**

Grant also used advanced deal-structuring techniques like MESOs to keep negotiations flexible while protecting core priorities. When an investor raised concerns about market size, she offered a tailored response:

> "You raise an important point. That's exactly why we've developed multiple investment approaches that balance impact with sustainable returns".

She then laid out three distinct paths:

- One offered structured traditional equity with milestone-based returns.
- A second link returns to specific FDA approval phases.
- A third proposed a hybrid model that balanced short-term incentives with long-term value creation.

This approach allowed her to address varying appetites for risk and return, without compromising on mission.

By integrating these advanced strategies, Grant remained aligned with her purpose while adapting to the needs of complex, multi-stakeholder negotiations. Her example demonstrates that even in high-pressure environments, it is possible to stay anchored in values while building dynamic, collaborative deals.

This level of strategic fluency is essential not just in the Business of Health but across the Practice of Medicine and the Delivery of Care – where stakes are high, relationships are layered, and alignment often requires innovation.

Clinical Parallel: A Surgical Division Chief successfully restructured operating room (OR) block time by identifying complementary priorities across departments. Recognizing that while all surgical teams preferred morning slots, orthopedics had a critical need for increased total weekly block time. The Chief created a contingent agreement where orthopedics received additional weekly blocks by agreeing to take some afternoon slots, with the option to temporarily adjust schedules based on seasonal volume fluctuations. This nuanced approach not only optimized OR utilization but also fostered interdepartmental collaboration and mutual trust, as each group felt their core needs were understood and accommodated. The resulting framework became a model for other resource-sharing agreements across the hospital system.

Operational Parallel: A Chief Nursing Officer leveraged strategic negotiation methods when revamping hospital staffing models. She created unit-based working groups where staff nurses collaborated with management to design custom scheduling solutions. Her approach balanced administrative priorities (coverage ratios, overtime costs) with front-line concerns (work-life balance, patient assignments). By emphasizing shared outcomes, including a 25% reduction in agency costs and improved nurse satisfaction scores, she secured buy-in across departments and created a model for managing complex operational changes through collaborative negotiation.

Step Eight – Negotiation Toolbox of Advanced Tactics

Tactical success in negotiation often appears effortless, but in reality, it's the result of rigorous preparation. Julie Grant's ability to respond calmly and strategically during high-stakes discussions was grounded in the work she had done in advance: researching stakeholder concerns, anticipating emotional responses, and crafting targeted, empathetic counterpoints.

"If you know what people care about, you don't have to scramble. You can plan how to respond to what they're most likely to say", she explained.

Grant's tactical approach reflects key elements from Step Eight of the Negotiation Planner: using Tactical Empathy, employing Tactical Silence, and layering advanced cues to deepen trust and forward movement.

1. **Tactical Empathy**

Rather than reacting defensively to objections, Grant prepared acknowledgment statements in advance, validating concerns while reinforcing confidence through evidence.

During one negotiation, she anticipated that an investor might challenge Day One's projected returns.

"These projections seem optimistic given the market size", the investor said.

Because she had anticipated that very response, Grant was ready:

> "I appreciate your scrutiny of the numbers. Let me share the data behind our projections..."

She then used that opening to walk the investor through the analysis, demonstrating both transparency and respect for their due diligence.

2. **Follow-Up Questioning and Strategic Silence**

Grant understood that acknowledgment alone was not enough, especially when trust or skepticism was on the line. She paired her responses with follow-up questions designed to elicit deeper concerns or open new areas of exploration. But she also knew when to pause.

"We've structured contingencies around key development milestones to manage risk", she added.

Then she stopped. Rather than rushing into technical detail, she paused for five full seconds, letting the weight of her comment land.

Her nonverbal cues were intentional: steady eye contact, open posture, and silence that signaled confidence, not defensiveness.

"It's uncomfortable", she admitted. "But sometimes, silence says more than another slide".

By combining empathy, data fluency, and controlled pacing, Grant cultivated credibility in even the most skeptical rooms. Her tactics allowed her to build trust, stay aligned with Day One's mission, and maintain forward motion, without overexplaining or defensively pivoting.

In the fast-moving world of healthcare negotiation, these micro-moves matter. Whether leading boardroom discussions, clinical collaborations, or operational reviews, professionals who master tactical empathy and silence can shift the energy of a conversation in subtle but powerful ways.

Clinical Parallel: A Chief of Surgery used advanced negotiation tactics to implement a new intraoperative checklist to reduce post-surgical complications. Recognizing that surgeons might resist perceived intrusions on autonomy, she led with data showing a 25% drop in preventable complications in hospitals using similar protocols. Anticipating emotional pushback around workflow disruption, she hosted department-specific briefings that invited feedback and allowed teams to co-design checklist modifications. When pushback surfaced during a department meeting, she responded with a pause, then used empathetic framing:

> "I know this feels like another box to check. But if we can cut our complication rate even by half of what other hospitals are seeing, that's dozens of patients whose recoveries get easier".
>
> By acknowledging concerns while holding space for silence and collaborative input, she secured buy-in for a change that ultimately elevated both safety and team communication.

Operational Parallel: A hospital's Chief Operating Officer used tactical negotiation techniques while redesigning inpatient bed allocation procedures. Facing growing tension between medical and surgical units over priority access, she avoided a top-down directive. Instead, she collected real-time data on bed turnaround times and case urgency, then presented it to both groups in a neutral, transparent format.

Rather than mandating a single policy, she introduced three tactical options: a tiered access model based on patient acuity, a rotating prioritization schedule, and a dynamic algorithm updated daily. When surgical leaders expressed concern about how delay penalties might affect their workflow, she paused before responding, acknowledging the concern and reframing the issue:

> "We're not choosing who gets priority – we're building a system that ensures patients get to the right bed at the right time".
>
> By combining data, silence, and empathy, she shifted the energy of the discussion and secured buy-in for a flexible system that reduced conflict and improved patient flow across departments.

Step Nine – Reflection and Learning

The final step of the Negotiation Planner emphasizes the value of ongoing reflection and adaptation. Effective negotiators don't just prepare for the moment – they learn from it. Julie Grant's ability to navigate complex, multi-stakeholder healthcare negotiations wasn't solely based on her strategy or preparation. It was also rooted in her willingness to analyze each negotiation, surface new insights, and adjust accordingly.

"There's always going to be some combination of market dynamics, scientific risk, and the challenge of entering new populations or commercial markets", Grant explained. "That's exactly what venture dollars should support – and what entrepreneurs need to get comfortable doing".

This mindset of continuous learning guided both her process and her progress.

In Step Nine of the Negotiation Planner, healthcare professionals are encouraged to:

- Conduct post-negotiation reflection.
- Challenge assumptions and close knowledge gaps.
- Distill key insights.
- Adjust planning for future negotiations.
- Grant's process aligned closely with each of these practices.

1. **Post-Negotiation Reflection**

After major discussions, Grant would debrief with her team to assess what worked, what needed adjustment, and what the negotiation revealed that they hadn't fully understood before.

"We'd unpeel the layers – asking, 'What do you really want?'" she recalled.

"What I came to understand is that people want high-quality medicine that works. But they also need it to be covered by insurance, because that's how the U.S. system functions. That piece is just as important".

2. **Challenging Assumptions and Closing Information Gaps**

Grant continually examined gaps in both public understanding and internal planning. One recurring realization was how misunderstood the drug development process remains, even among sophisticated stakeholders.

"Most people in the U.S. don't realize where medicines actually come from", she said. "And it's not because they don't care – it's because no one's ever told that story. The truth is, medicines often come from small biotech companies like ours".

This awareness shaped how she communicated Day One's mission in future negotiations.

3. **Lessons Learned and Insights Gained**

Grant came to appreciate the sheer complexity of getting a pediatric drug to market – and how many hands are involved in the process.

"Everyone plays a role. Most medicines pass through dozens of decision points before they're approved", she reflected.

She also noted how difficult it was to shift public perception around pharmaceutical work:

> "It took so much effort to move past the assumptions. That's why I think we're stuck – we haven't done a good job explaining how innovation actually happens".

4. **Planning for Future Negotiations**

Grant didn't just reflect – she codified lessons into actionable updates. She made margin notes in her Negotiation Planner after each deal:

- "Strengthen value proposition with immediate supporting market data".
- "Move FDA statistics earlier in pitch deck".
- "Keep empathetic response, but make a cleaner transition into investment structure".
- "Add concrete examples of risk management contingencies".

She also emphasized that future efforts would focus on education:

> "We need to help people understand what's really holding innovation back. If we don't, I worry we'll miss the next wave of breakthroughs".

By embracing reflection as a core part of the negotiation process, healthcare professionals can evolve beyond tactical wins and into more meaningful, mission-aligned leadership. Whether in the Business of Health, the Delivery of Care, or the Practice of Medicine, continuous learning transforms good negotiators into great ones – and great negotiators into trusted, long-term collaborators.

Clinical Parallel: A hospital's CMO applied similar reflection and learning techniques after implementing a new patient safety protocol. She conducted a thorough post-implementation review, gathering feedback from various departments and analyzing outcome data. This process helped her identify unexpected challenges, refine the protocol, and develop strategies for future implementations.

Operational Parallel: A hospital's Director of Human Resources applied reflective learning techniques after rolling out a new staff wellness initiative. Rather than moving on after launch, he initiated a post-implementation review – collecting data on participation rates, surveying frontline staff about usability and relevance, and analyzing trends in absenteeism and morale.

The reflection process revealed both strengths and blind spots. While uptake was high among clinical departments, administrative teams felt underrepresented in the program design. He also uncovered a disconnect between leadership messaging and on-the-ground awareness.

Using these insights, he convened a cross-functional debrief, made targeted adjustments to communication strategies, and added department-specific wellness modules tailored to distinct roles. The revised plan launched with clearer alignment, broader buy-in, and stronger outcomes.

By embedding reflection into the rollout process, he turned a static program into an adaptive, stakeholder-informed initiative, mirroring the Negotiation Planner's emphasis on learning as a core component of strategic success.

CHALLENGES AND STRATEGIES IN IMPLEMENTING THE NEGOTIATION PLANNER

While the Negotiation Planner offers a comprehensive framework for healthcare negotiations, several significant challenges require careful consideration and proactive management:

The pressure of *time constraints* presents a significant hurdle in healthcare negotiations. Medical professionals regularly encounter situations demanding immediate decisions, leaving minimal opportunity for detailed preparation. Success in these scenarios requires developing and internalizing efficient negotiation processes. By creating streamlined versions of planning tools and practicing their implementation regularly, healthcare professionals can build the muscle memory needed to navigate time-sensitive negotiations effectively.

Emotional intensity poses a unique challenge in healthcare negotiations, where high-stakes decisions and personal investment can cloud objective judgment. The key to managing these emotionally charged situations lies in systematic emotional regulation and self-awareness. Incorporating structured approaches to acknowledge and process emotions, combined with practical techniques like mindfulness, enables negotiators to maintain their composure while engaging meaningfully with sensitive topics.

The reality of *power imbalances* significantly impacts healthcare negotiations, where authority and influence often vary considerably among participants. Successful navigation of these dynamics requires a methodical approach focused on understanding and acknowledging diverse perspectives. By emphasizing evidence-based discussions and ensuring all viewpoints receive proper consideration, negotiators can work toward more balanced and equitable outcomes despite inherent power differentials.

Managing the *complexity of stakeholders* represents a critical challenge in healthcare negotiations. The involvement of multiple parties, each with distinct priorities and interests, necessitates careful coordination and strategic planning. Success in these multi-stakeholder scenarios depends on comprehensive stakeholder analysis and the ability to identify areas of mutual benefit. By investing time in understanding various perspectives and actively seeking common ground, negotiators can build more cohesive and sustainable agreements.

Resistance to change within healthcare organizations can significantly impede the adoption of new negotiation approaches. Overcoming this resistance requires a gradual, demonstrative approach to implementing new methods. By beginning with personal implementation and documenting successful outcomes, negotiators can build credibility for new approaches. This allows for organic adoption across teams as colleagues witness the tangible benefits of structured negotiation processes in achieving favorable outcomes.

Conclusion: Successfully Navigating Healthcare Negotiations

Julie Grant's journey from venture capitalist to biotech pioneer illuminates the high-stakes world of healthcare negotiations. Her story offers invaluable lessons for all healthcare professionals across various settings. By systematically applying the Negotiation Planner and integrating advanced strategies and tactics, Grant successfully navigated complex negotiations to bring hope to children battling rare cancers.

As demonstrated throughout this chapter, the Negotiation Planner is a versatile tool adaptable to diverse healthcare contexts. Whether you're in the Operating Room advocating for new equipment, in the Exam Room discussing treatment options, or in the Boardroom negotiating partnerships, the structured approach strategies and tactics here can help you achieve better outcomes.

Mastering the Negotiation Planner is an ongoing process, with each negotiation offering healthcare professionals an opportunity to refine their skills and adapt the planner to their specific context. But regular use leads to effective healthcare negotiations that transcend simply winning deals to focus on creating value, fostering collaboration, and improving patient care. By embracing the HEAR Approach™, consistently using the Negotiation Planner, and applying advanced strategies, you can advocate more effectively for your patients, team, and healthcare mission.

REFLECTION EXERCISE: TAKING A 360-DEGREE VIEW OF THE NEGOTIATION PLANNER

Choose a complex negotiation you are currently facing – or one you anticipate – in your healthcare role. Use this exercise to reflect on how you might apply the HEAR Negotiation Planner holistically. Take 30 minutes to assess the negotiation from multiple vantage points.

1. Context Analysis
   - Define the negotiation and its significance to your role or organization.
   - Map out key stakeholders and consider their priorities, emotional drivers, and potential sources of resistance.
   - Identify possible power imbalances, cultural dynamics, or time pressures that could shape the negotiation.
2. Strategic Planning
   - Draft a clear Purpose Statement that aligns organizational goals with stakeholder needs.
   - Identify where you might recast the negotiation to highlight shared values or systemic benefits.
   - Pinpoint opportunities to demonstrate empathy while advancing strategic objectives.
   - Consider what emotional responses this negotiation might trigger – for you or others – and how you'll stay grounded in patient-centered outcomes.

3. Implementation Planning
   - Think through how you'll adapt the Planner's steps in time-sensitive or high-pressure environments.
   - Establish metrics or reflection checkpoints to evaluate success.
   - Plan for how you'll balance institutional priorities with the broader mission of improving patient care.

Document your insights and draft an action plan for your next negotiation. Afterward, revisit your plan: What worked well? What surprised you? What would you do differently next time?

Reflection isn't just how we close – it's how we grow.

Key Takeaways

1. The Negotiation Planner provides a structured yet adaptable framework that guides healthcare professionals through complex, multi-stakeholder negotiations. Systematic application of the planner's nine steps enables negotiators to comprehensively analyze contexts, align stakeholder interests, and maintain focus on core healthcare missions. This methodical approach proves valuable across healthcare's three pillars, allowing organizations to pursue innovation while maintaining commitment to patient care.
2. Successful healthcare negotiations require a sophisticated balance of Emotional Intelligence and strategic thinking. Healthcare professionals must recognize and manage their own emotional triggers while demonstrating empathy toward stakeholders' concerns. The integration of personal awareness with structured planning enables negotiators to transform potentially adversarial situations into collaborative problem-solving opportunities, particularly when addressing high-stakes healthcare challenges that affect patient outcomes.
3. Effective Recasting and Acknowledgment represent critical capabilities in healthcare negotiations. Success often hinges on reframing discussions from purely financial considerations to shared missions of improving patient care, thereby aligning diverse stakeholder interests. This approach, combined with comprehensive stakeholder and empathy mapping, enables healthcare professionals to identify common ground and develop solutions that address both immediate concerns and long-term healthcare objectives while maintaining focus on patient welfare.

4. Healthcare negotiators must proactively address common challenges like time constraints, emotional intensity, power imbalances, and stakeholder complexity. Success requires building organizational credibility through demonstrated outcomes while gradually implementing new negotiation approaches that can overcome institutional resistance to change. Thorough preparation, the use of planning tools, and regular practice enable professionals to navigate complex decisions while maintaining strategic focus.

Note

1. This case study draws from a June 25, 2024, interview with Julie Grant, co-founder of Day One Biopharmaceuticals, as well as publicly available information about the company's development and achievements. While key facts, outcomes, and direct quotes are preserved from these sources, additional context and dialogue have been reconstructed to illustrate negotiation principles. These interpretative elements, while grounded in documented events, serve pedagogical purposes. The case combines actual events with illustrative examples to demonstrate cross-pillar healthcare negotiation strategies. All financial data and business outcomes described reflect publicly documented information as of the interview date.

Chapter 10

The Trilingual Planner

A Guide to Multi-Pillar Healthcare Negotiations

Better is possible. It does not take genius. It takes diligence. It takes moral clarity. It takes ingenuity. And above all, it takes a willingness to try.

– Dr. Atul Gawande

DOI: 10.4324/9781003336013-12

HEAR Trilingual Planner

Introduction

The HEAR Trilingual Planner builds directly on two foundational tools introduced earlier in this book: the Healthcare Negotiation Mapping Tool (Chapter 3) and the HEAR Negotiation Planner (Chapter 9). While the Negotiation Planner supports negotiations within a single healthcare pillar, the Trilingual Planner extends the Healthcare Negotiation Mapping Tool framework to manage negotiations that span all three pillars: Practice of Medicine (Operating Room), Delivery of Care (Exam Room), and Business of Health (Boardroom).

Drawing on the Healthcare Negotiation Mapping Tool four core components – Key Stakeholders, Negotiation Focus, Trilingual Skills, and Interconnectedness Insights – this planner follows the same nine-step HEAR Framework as the Negotiation Planner while adapting each step for cross-pillar application.

Like the Negotiation Planner, this tool can be used individually or with teams:

Individual Use

1. Set aside dedicated time to work through each step.
2. Be honest and thorough in your responses across all pillars.
3. Revisit and refine your responses as you gather more information.
4. Consider implications for each healthcare domain.

Team Use

1. Have team members from different pillars complete steps independently.
2. Schedule team meetings to discuss varying perspectives.
3. Use collective input to develop integrated solutions.
4. Create shared documentation for ongoing reference.

This planner is a living document that should be regularly updated throughout the negotiation process.

Step One: Negotiation Context Analysis

This step helps establish the foundation for your negotiation by mapping the landscape across all three healthcare pillars using the Healthcare Negotiation Mapping Tool framework.

Multi-Pillar Context Analysis

- Briefly describe the situation and background.
- Identify how each healthcare pillar is involved.
- Map key stakeholders across domains.
- List potential obstacles or challenges for each pillar.

Cross-Pillar Impact Framework

- Document direct effects between pillars
  - How decisions in one pillar affect others.
  - Resource dependencies across domains.
  - Communication flow between pillars.
- Map indirect consequences
  - Secondary stakeholder impacts.
  - Long-term system effects.
  - Cultural implications.

HEAR Trilingual Planner Reflection Prompts

- How do the three pillars intersect, and what ripple effects might decisions in one domain create in others?
- How do different professional cultures and stakeholder priorities influence communication and decision-making across domains?
- What formal and informal influence patterns exist across professional boundaries, and how do they shape outcomes?
- Where might hierarchies and cross-pillar dynamics create tension points, and how can these be addressed?

Reference: Chapter 3, "Healthcare Negotiation Mapping Tool" and "Understanding the Interplay of Medicine, Care Delivery, and Business"

Step Two: Stating Your Purpose

This step guides you in articulating negotiation goals that resonate across all three pillars while maintaining focus on building positive relationships.

Value Translation Matrix

- Produce Operating Room value propositions spanning:
  - Clinical outcomes.
  - Quality measures.
  - Professional standards.
- Create Exam Room value statements that include:
  - Patient experience.
  - Care coordination.
  - Service delivery.
- Identify Boardroom value metrics that reflect:
  - Financial sustainability.
  - Resource optimization.
  - Strategic alignment.

Cross-Pillar Purpose Development

- Create pillar-specific objectives and messages that resonate with each domain's unique context.
- Identify shared goals and develop communication bridges that connect stakeholders across domains.
- Design multi-level engagement strategies that facilitate cross-pillar collaboration and understanding.
- Craft unified purpose statements with clear success measures that speak to all stakeholders.

HEAR Trilingual Planner Reflection Prompts

- How can you frame your purpose to resonate across different professional cultures and identities?
- What common ground and shared value propositions exist that could bridge professional boundaries?
- How do pillar-specific goals and definitions of success align or conflict with system-wide objectives?

- Where might differences in professional language and culture create misunderstandings between stakeholders?

Reference: Chapter 2, "Setting the Stage for Effective Healthcare Negotiations: Defining Your Purpose"

Step Three: Adopting the Right Mindset

This step focuses on developing a mindset that can bridge professional cultures and create alignment across healthcare domains.

Theory of Mind Assessment Across Domains

- Map stakeholder perspectives by pillar.
- Identify potential cultural misalignments.
- Plan perspective-taking approaches.
- Design empathy-building activities.

Cross-Pillar Mindset Framework

Cross-Reference: See Negotiation Planner Step Three for foundational mindset development.

- Assess cultural competency and professional identity dynamics across pillars to develop adaptive communication approaches.
- Map relationship-building requirements while considering power dynamics and hierarchical structures.
- Design trust development approaches that respect and bridge diverse professional cultures.
- Cultivate a system-wide perspective that integrates cross-pillar relationships and cultural understanding.

HEAR Trilingual Planner Reflection Prompts

- How comfortable are you operating in each pillar's culture, and how do professional identities affect cross-domain relationships?
- What adaptation skills and cultural bridges need to be developed to work effectively across pillars?

- Where do you see opportunities for building trust across professional boundaries?
- How might power dynamics and cultural differences create challenges in cross-pillar relationships?

Reference: Chapter 2, "Theory of Mind" and "The Relational Mindset: The Foundation of the HEAR Approach™"

Step Four: Trilingual Empowerment

This step builds on the Negotiation Planner's empowerment framework while addressing the unique challenges of maintaining confidence and capability across multiple professional domains.

Cross-Pillar Internal Scan

- Assess primary pillar expertise and comfort while mapping domain-specific triggers and confidence patterns.
- Evaluate secondary pillar knowledge and professional culture sensitivities that affect cross-domain work.
- Analyze cross-domain communication skills and power dynamic responses in multi-stakeholder contexts.
- Map relationship strengths across pillars while considering emotional responses to different professional cultures.

Cross-Pillar Emotional Intelligence

- Navigate authority structures and influence patterns while recognizing interconnected impacts across pillars.
- Adapt to diverse decision-making norms while developing an understanding of resource dependencies.
- Build flexible communication styles that strengthen relationships across professional boundaries.
- Develop cultural bridges that enhance system-wide awareness and cross-pillar collaboration.

HEAR Trilingual Planner Reflection Prompts

- How does your confidence vary across pillars, and how do power dynamics shift across professional boundaries?

- What support and cultural adaptations might you need when operating in less familiar domains?
- Where are your strongest professional relationships, and how can they bridge cross-pillar divides?
- How might professional identities and cultural differences create tension or opportunities for growth?

Reference: Chapter 4, "Enhancing Negotiation Effectiveness: A Guide for Internal Scans" and "Emotional Intelligence Assessment"

Step Five: Trilingual Acknowledgment

This step expands the Negotiation Planner's acknowledgment practices to address diverse professional perspectives and creates psychological safety across domains.

Stakeholder Validation

- Recognize domain-specific expertise and professional language while respecting diverse authority structures.
- Understand pillar-based priorities and decision-making preferences that shape stakeholders' perspectives.
- Navigate operational constraints and communication norms unique to each professional culture.
- Acknowledge quality standards while demonstrating cultural sensitivity across professional boundaries.

Cross-Pillar Bridge Building

- Identify shared values and validate professional identities across domains while developing common ground.
- Build trust through role-based perspective-taking and cultural adaptation skills.
- Develop collaboration frameworks that respect diverse professional cultures and identities.
- Enhance boundary-spanning capabilities while integrating multiple professional perspectives and approaches.

HEAR Trilingual Planner Reflection Prompts

- How can you validate expertise and acknowledge value across different professional cultures and domains?
- What common values and cultural bridges could strengthen cross-pillar relationships?
- Where might acknowledgment and recognition build trust across professional boundaries?
- How do hierarchies and professional cultures affect trust development and collaboration?

References: Chapter 2, "Relational Mindset Tools and Practices: Empathy Mapping," Chapter 5, "Putting Acknowledgment into Practice: Active Listening as a Catalyst for Mutual Understanding," and "Connecting the Puzzle Pieces of Acknowledgment Through Appreciative Inquiry"

Step Six: Trilingual Recasting

This step adapts the Negotiation Planner's Recasting approaches for complex, multi-domain challenges while creating sustainable, cross-pillar solutions.

Opportunity Identification

- Identify cross-pillar synergies and resource optimization possibilities while developing coordinated implementation timelines.
- Map process improvement opportunities and establish clear success metrics across domains.
- Enhance quality through strategic resource allocation and progress monitoring.
- Create integrated value propositions that maximize cross-pillar benefits and measurable outcomes.

Integration Development

- Design cross-boundary solutions that enhance workflows and transform collaborative processes.
- Build cultural bridges while advancing communication and professional practices.

- Develop sustainable partnerships that strengthen relationships across professional domains.
- Create system-wide innovations that evolve professional practices and integration approaches.

HEAR Trilingual Planner Reflection Prompts

- How might professional cultures affect innovation and create opportunities for mutual gain?
- Where can resources and expertise be integrated across pillars to create new value?
- How might current challenges become catalysts for system-wide transformation?
- What cross-pillar opportunities exist to optimize resources and foster collaborative innovation?

Reference: Chapter 6, "Recasting: Navigating New Realities Together"

Step Seven: Cross-Pillar Advanced Strategies

This step adapts advanced negotiation strategies for complex multi-domain scenarios while maintaining alignment across healthcare pillars.

Understanding and Setting Your Value Across Pillars

- Create value propositions that resonate in each pillar's language.
- Develop metrics that demonstrate benefits across domains.
- Build comprehensive business cases showing system-wide impact.

Cross-Pillar Logrolling

- Design trade packages that leverage different pillar priorities.
- Map interdependencies between proposed exchanges.
- Create implementation timelines respecting all domains.
- Structure trades that build sustainable cross-pillar partnerships.

Multi-Domain Multiple Equivalent Simultaneous Offers

- Develop equivalent offers appealing to different pillar priorities.
- Create hybrid options combining benefits across domains.
- Ensure proposals maintain value balance across pillars.
- Design clear comparison frameworks for cross-pillar evaluation.

Cross-Pillar Contingency Agreements

- Structure triggers considering impacts across domains
- Design review mechanisms involving all affected pillars.
- Create adaptive implementation pathways
- Build flexibility for different professional cultures

Post-Settlement-Agreement Integration

- Establish cross-pillar review processes
- Create ongoing value-enhancement mechanisms.
- Design sustainable partnership frameworks.
- Maintain alignment across professional boundaries.

HEAR Trilingual Planner Reflection Prompts

- How do your strategies translate across professional cultures?
- What interdependencies need to be managed between pillars?

Reference: Chapter 7, "Advanced Negotiation Strategies for Complex Challenges"

Step Eight: Cross-Pillar Advanced Tactics

This step adapts negotiation tactics for complex scenarios spanning multiple healthcare domains.

Cross-Pillar Tactical Empathy

- Validate concerns using pillar-specific language.
- Demonstrate understanding of different professional perspectives.
- Build psychological safety across domains.
- Navigate cultural differences effectively.

Multi-Level Anchoring and Framing

- Set reference points meaningful to each pillar.
- Frame proposals using domain-appropriate metrics.
- Create bridges between professional value systems.
- Maintain credibility across boundaries.

Cross-Pillar Pivots and Turns

- Redirect while maintaining multi-stakeholder engagement.
- Navigate between professional perspectives smoothly.
- Build momentum across boundaries.
- Create new pathways for collaboration.

The "Yes, And..." Technique Across Pillars

- Build on ideas from different professional perspectives.
- Create connections between pillar-specific proposals.
- Foster cross-domain innovation.
- Maintain forward momentum across boundaries.

The Double Magnet Approach Across Domains

- Create choices appealing to different professional cultures.
- Design options with cross-pillar benefits.
- Enable meaningful choices while maintaining progress.
- Build sustainable cross-domain solutions.

HEAR Trilingual Planner Reflection Prompts

- How must tactics be adapted for different professional cultures?
- What signals indicate the need for tactical shifts across domains?
- How will you maintain alignment while being tactically flexible?

References: Chapter 8, "Mastering Real-Time Negotiation Tactics"

Step Nine: Cross-Pillar Learning and Integration

This step creates structured opportunities for continuous improvement in multi-domain negotiations.

Multi-Pillar Assessment Framework

- Process Evaluation
  - Analyze stakeholder engagement across pillars.
  - Assess communication effectiveness between domains.
  - Review implementation coordination.
  - Evaluate feedback loop effectiveness.
- Outcome Measurement
  - Track goal achievement by pillar.
  - Document system-wide benefits.
  - Identify unintended consequences.
  - Measure cross-pillar impact.
  - Assess cultural integration progress.
- Relationship Development
  - Map trust-building across domains.
  - Evaluate collaboration enhancement.
  - Assess partnership sustainability.

HEAR Trilingual Planner Reflection Prompts

- What insights have you gained about cross-pillar dynamics?
- What cultural bridges have proven most effective?
- How has your approach to multi-domain negotiations evolved?
- Where are opportunities for enhancing future integration?

Reference: Chapter 1, "The HEAR Approach™: An Overview of Transformative Healthcare Negotiations"

The Health and Education Alliance case illustrates how and when a comprehensive planning approach becomes essential. According to the decision framework, negotiations that span multiple healthcare domains and involve diverse, interdependent stakeholders require the expanded scope of the Trilingual Planner.

This negotiation checked every box: it crossed departmental boundaries, engaged interconnected networks of influence, and had system-wide implications. The following case analysis shows how the team used the Trilingual Planner to navigate that complexity – and build a solution that aligned strategy, care delivery, and business viability.

Despite being just blocks from Mount Sinai's world-class medical facilities, East Harlem schools struggled to support their most vulnerable students, lacking both adequate resources and consistent access to healthcare. As a medical student at Mount Sinai and Finance Chair of the East Harlem Health Outreach Partnership, Krishna Patel saw the disconnect firsthand. But he also recognized it wasn't simply a matter of funding. It was a systems failure: education and healthcare were operating in silos, not in partnership.

Drawing on a unique combination of skills, a Wharton economics degree, biology training, and hands-on experience through the Vagelos LSM Program, Patel developed a new model. He founded the Health and Education Alliance (HEA) to create sustainable, school-based health partnerships supported by a blended-billing approach that could unify clinical, educational, and financial systems under one strategy.

While the idea was born from Patel's work in East Harlem, its first real test came in Pittsburgh's Woodland Hills School District. There, administrators were grappling with rising special education costs, limited access to care, and educators stretched far beyond their formal roles. Patel would need to persuade a broad network of stakeholders – school board members, union leaders, healthcare providers, and community advocates – that HEA's model was not only viable, but transformational.

"We weren't just proposing a partnership", Patel reflected. "We were asking them to reimagine how education and healthcare intersect – and that meant speaking the languages of clinical excellence, service delivery, and financial sustainability all at once".

HEA's model required Patel to negotiate across all three core healthcare domains:

Clinical Excellence (Operating Room): Ensuring high-quality care delivery in non-traditional, school-based settings.

Service Delivery (Exam Room): Coordinating complex care across educational environments.

Financial Sustainability (Boardroom): Designing a reimbursement model that made long-term fiscal sense for all stakeholders.

This was not just a new program launch – it was a case study in cross-pillar negotiation. Success would require Patel to map stakeholder interconnections, tailor communication to each group's needs, align incentives across sectors, build trust through acknowledgment and empathy, and create a sustainable strategy that worked at scale.

The Trilingual Planner: Elevating Cross-Pillar Healthcare Negotiations

Building on the Healthcare Negotiation Mapping Tool introduced in Chapter 3, the Trilingual Planner provides a comprehensive framework for managing the complexities of advanced, multi-stakeholder healthcare negotiations. While Chapter 3 equipped professionals to recognize cross-pillar tensions, the Trilingual Planner offers a step-by-step guide to navigating and resolving them, especially when decisions must simultaneously align with the Practice of Medicine (Operating Room), Delivery of Care (Exam Room), and Business of Health (Boardroom).

These negotiations often involve competing priorities, system-wide interdependencies, and unpredictable ripple effects. The Trilingual Planner challenges healthcare professionals to become fluent in all three domains and to lead with strategies that account for their interplay, not just their boundaries.

Step One – Cross-Pillar Context Analysis

The statistics in front of Krishna Patel were staggering: $140 billion in unclaimed federal safety net aid each year – $80 billion of it tied to CHIP and Medicaid. But to him, this wasn't just an administrative inefficiency. It was an opening to rethink healthcare delivery for underserved students.

The next morning, he would present to leaders from Woodland Hills School District, where 80% of students qualified for federal assistance. The district faced mounting special education costs, overburdened teachers functioning as de facto mental health providers, and few nearby healthcare options. Patel knew that the success of the HEA model hinged on understanding the full context, not just what services were missing, but how the existing system was stretched across three distinct but interconnected domains.

Opening the Trilingual Planner, Patel began mapping the multi-pillar terrain:

Practice of Medicine: The district's medical director raised concerns about liability and clinical standards for school-based care.

Delivery of Care: School nurses managed complex cases without enough support, and teachers were overwhelmed by emotional and behavioral crises in the classroom.

Business of Health: Administrators needed to improve services while cutting costs, and healthcare providers doubted the financial viability of bringing care into schools.

"Our biggest challenge wasn't just delivery", Patel reflected. "It was helping each group see past their own constraints, and recognize a shared opportunity".

Using the Cross-Pillar Impact Framework, Patel identified how decisions in one domain could trigger ripple effects in the others. For example:

A new clinical protocol for managing student mental health would directly affect classroom environments and require funding for implementation.

Adding staff to improve care coordination would shift responsibilities for both school personnel and healthcare partners.

Resource allocation decisions wouldn't just influence program viability – they'd shape educational outcomes and long-term community trust.

"Every adjustment created friction – but also revealed connection points", Patel said. "Each decision had to work within its domain and ripple productively across all three".

That insight became central to his strategy. When the superintendent added HEA's proposal to the upcoming board meeting agenda, Patel knew success would require more than individual stakeholder buy-in. It would take a framework capable of holding shared priorities, mutual pressures, and cross-domain alignment all at once.

Step Two – Cross-Pillar Purpose Definition

The $300,000 grant HEA received from a Pittsburgh-based foundation opened doors – but also posed risks. Patel had learned from experience that leading with funding could backfire. Just months earlier, healthcare partners had jumped at the opportunity, only to insist on using the money their way – a path that consistently proved unsustainable.

Reviewing his notes, Patel spotted the pattern: whenever he led with philanthropic support, stakeholders saw HEA as another well-meaning initiative without staying power. He knew he had to reframe the conversation around value, not charity.

"We can't position this as a feel-good grant", Patel explained. "We need to show each stakeholder how this creates lasting value – in their language".

Using the Value Translation Matrix he'd developed, Patel outlined tailored outcomes across the three pillars:

Practice of Medicine (Operating Room):

- Physicians gain earlier intervention opportunities.
- Nurses receive standardized care protocols.
- Specialists expand access while improving continuity.

Delivery of Care (Exam Room):

- Teachers return to teaching, not counseling.
- School nurses receive clinical backup.
- Administrators reduce behavioral incidents and improve attendance.

Business of Health (Boardroom):

- Healthcare providers earn revenue and staff bonuses.
- District finance offices realize annual savings.
- Taxpayers benefit from better services without higher rates.

Still, Patel knew the real breakthrough would come from a unified message. While analyzing federal funding data, he reframed the purpose of HEA's proposal:

> "We're not asking anyone to do more with less", he realized. "We're showing them how to unlock resources they already have".

That insight shaped his pitch to the Woodland Hills school board:

> "The district leaves about $2 million in federal safety net aid unclaimed each year. That's not a criticism – it's an opportunity. By improving coordination with healthcare providers, we can access those funds and improve services".

When board members asked whether it would require new staff or costly expansion, Patel responded:

> "Actually, no. This is about optimizing what you already have. Counseling delivered on-site is Medicaid-reimbursable at higher rates. Preventive

care reduces ER visits, which reduces costs. It's not a new program – it's a smarter system".

In a later meeting with 25 concerned teachers, Patel resisted the urge to defend HEA's model. Instead, he framed it through shared interest:

> "I'm not here to outsource anyone's job", he said. "I'm here to increase the size of the resource pie. When we tap unused federal funds, we can add support staff so you can focus on teaching, not crisis management".

The tone shifted immediately. One teacher asked, "So we'd actually get more resources, not less?"

"Exactly", Patel replied. "Every dollar saved through better healthcare coordination goes back into the classroom".

Patel even reframed the opening of a new community center:

"It's not a cost – it's a retention tool. For every student who stays in the district, the state provides $18,000–50,000 in annual funding. Everything connects".

"Most importantly", he later reflected, "we proved this isn't charity. It's good business that transforms communities. If you can tell a superintendent that eight hours of planning can generate millions in sustainable savings while improving services – that's a purpose everyone can get behind".

The result was a cross-pillar purpose statement that didn't just align with HEA's values – it became a scalable blueprint for future negotiations.

Step Three – Cross-Pillar Mindset Adaptation

The call from the teachers' union president caught Patel off guard.

"Do you know who I am?" the voice on the other end asked. "You got the school board to approve this plan without consulting us".

Standing in a hospital corridor, lunch delivery forgotten in his hands, Patel felt the weight of his oversight. He'd been so focused on aligning his proposal with funding opportunities and board priorities that he had failed to engage the union early.

His clinical instincts kicked in: assess, listen, adapt.

"You're absolutely right to call", he replied, softening his tone. "I made an assumption I shouldn't have. Can you help me understand your concerns?"

That conversation became the inflection point for Patel's shift from message control to mindset adaptation. It wasn't enough to frame HEA's model differently for each audience – he needed to internalize how each group viewed change, risk, and value.

Using the Cross-Pillar Mindset Framework, Patel began mapping not just what stakeholders needed, but how they *thought*:

- **The school board** needed data, pilot outcomes, and implementation timelines.
- **The union** needed early inclusion and assurance that HEA would reduce, not increase, teacher burdens.
- **Healthcare providers** needed clinical integrity, evidence-based protocols, and assurances that their autonomy wouldn't be threatened.

"What I initially saw as a communication oversight", he reflected, "was actually a much deeper disconnect. Each group had its own rhythm, its own rules".

Rather than defending his model, Patel immersed himself in their worlds:

- For the school board, he developed a phased rollout tied to performance metrics.
- For teachers, he reframed the initiative as a way to reduce emotional overload and classroom disruptions.
- For clinicians, he emphasized sustainable funding streams and quality-of-care benchmarks.

In a pivotal union meeting, Patel didn't open with slides – he opened with a question:

> "What's your biggest challenge in supporting students' well-being?"

The responses shifted the tone immediately:

- "We're trying to be teachers, counselors, and social workers at the same time".
- "When a kid's in crisis, we have nowhere to send them".

Patel reframed:

"What if, instead of asking you to do more, we brought in the resources you've always needed?"

The impact was real. Teachers became advocates. Healthcare partners who had once been skeptical began volunteering to join the pilot. Administrators who'd questioned the feasibility of the model became vocal champions.

"Success wasn't just about respecting each group's identity", Patel later reflected. "It was about proving that integration makes everyone better at their core mission – whether that's teaching, healing, or managing resources".

The Trilingual Mindset became foundational to HEA's expansion strategy. Word of the model spread: unions across the state requested similar programs, administrators shared improved outcomes, and clinicians recognized a scalable approach to school-based care.

By aligning his mindset – not just his message – Patel helped transform a fragmented system into a shared solution.

Step Four – Cross-Pillar Empowerment

Krishna Patel walked into that early stakeholder meeting with two things: a $300,000 grant in his back pocket and the growing realization that it might hurt him as much as help.

"Having the grant opened doors", he later said, "but if I wasn't careful, it would define the conversation before I even opened my mouth".

Some stakeholders saw funding as validation. Others saw it as a red flag: another outsider-backed project that would leave them with the cleanup.

Patel quickly realized that success would depend on more than the model or the money – it required a Cross-Pillar Internal Scan, a structured assessment of how his own strengths, triggers, and perceived authority would be interpreted across domains.

As a medical student, he risked being dismissed as inexperienced.

With grant funding, he could be seen as short-term or naïve.

With deep systemic knowledge, he risked alienating people who didn't want their systems "diagnosed" from the outside.

He also had to map formal and informal power structures:

School boards controlled budgets.
Unions influenced implementation.
Healthcare providers policed standards.
Community leaders guarded trust.
This awareness sharpened his Cross-Pillar Emotional Intelligence. He didn't just adapt what he said – he adapted how he showed up in the room.
With administrators, he emphasized data.
With clinicians, he spoke about sustainability and clinical rigor.
With teachers, he focused on reducing burdens, not increasing expectations.

During the most high-stakes moments, Patel relied on the RESET technique – a structured tool for managing emotional intensity across systems:

1. Recognize your emotional triggers

Patel acknowledged the frustration that surfaced when his intentions were questioned.

2. Evaluate the intensity of your response

"This isn't just a miscommunication – it's a potential derailment", he noted privately.

3. Step back to gain perspective

He paused, reflected on what he hadn't yet heard, and shifted his tone accordingly.

4. Empathize with others' viewpoints

"I can see why this caught you off guard", he told one union leader.

5. Transform your response into constructive engagement

"What if we designed this together, based on what support would look like for you?"

That final step often unlocked collaboration. One school nurse who had been skeptical told him:

"It's the first time someone's asked what I actually need, rather than just what I can do".

By using empowerment not as self-assertion, but as a relational skill, Patel reframed HEA's role. It wasn't about leading from the front, it was about co-creating from within.

"We weren't telling people what to do", he said. "We were building from the ground they were already standing on".

The Cross-Pillar Empowerment strategy gave Patel more than confidence. It gave him a way to validate others – teachers, clinicians, administrators, without minimizing their roles. And that's what turned resistance into partnership.

Step Five – Cross-Pillar Acknowledgment

Step Five of the Trilingual Planner marks a critical shift: from understanding others' contexts to explicitly validating their expertise. For Patel and the HEA team, this wasn't a rhetorical exercise – it was the foundation for building cross-sector trust.

"Real acknowledgment goes beyond politeness", Patel later reflected. "It's about showing each stakeholder how collaboration strengthens their core purpose".

To educators, acknowledgment began by naming the unspoken emotional load they carried:

"You're being asked to teach, counsel, and stabilize all at once – and we see that", Patel told a group of union leaders. "We're not here to add to your plate. We're here to rebuild the support you've been missing".

This reframing transformed hostility into dialogue. As Patel explained elsewhere:

"When teachers said, 'We're doing three jobs already,' we didn't counter. We listened. And we showed them how the model could restore their actual role – teaching".

To healthcare providers, acknowledgment meant elevating their clinical standards, not bypassing them:

"We're not asking you to lower the bar", Patel emphasized. "We're asking you to help us build a model that meets your bar – in a setting where your patients already are".

This message resonated, especially with providers concerned about risk dilution. Patel reinforced their value by integrating bonus structures and staffing supports, ensuring school-based care wouldn't mean cutting corners.

To administrators, acknowledgment required navigating their dual mandate – improve outcomes, cut costs – and doing so without condescension:

"You're not running a clinic", Patel told one skeptical CFO. "But when we reduce ED visits and absenteeism, that translates to measurable fiscal gains. Our job is to make that math work in your language".

That kind of respect opened space for honest conversations – not just about cost savings but also implementation timelines, data ownership, and political optics.

Across all three pillars, acknowledgment became the bridge from transactional approval to transformational alignment.

Rather than pushing a one-size-fits-all pitch, Patel developed micro-strategies rooted in each group's identity:

For teachers: refocus on instructional autonomy and classroom stability.

For providers: maintain excellence and clinical credibility.

For finance leaders: deliver outcomes without creating fiscal cliffs.

This strategy was codified through internal planning templates and external materials, which Patel called "value language playbooks" tailored for each pillar.

And it worked.

Senior administrators who had initially questioned the scope became champions. Healthcare partners who feared dilution began advocating for the model. And the same union leaders who once sent angry emails were soon calling school boards to request pilot expansions.

"Acknowledgment isn't just about hearing concerns", Patel said. "It's about showing people that their expertise is essential – and proving that shared success is possible without professional sacrifice".

As HEA expanded, this approach continued to shape every conversation. It didn't just defuse tension. It created a coalition.

Step Six – Cross-Pillar Recasting

For Patel, federal funding data wasn't just policy background – it was a lever.

"We're not asking anyone to do more with less", he said. "We're showing how to unlock $140 billion in resources that already exist".

That mindset became the heart of HEA's Recasting strategy: shifting the frame from cost burden to shared opportunity.

School administrators were among the most cautious. When they voiced concern that healthcare services might drain already stretched budgets, Patel flipped the frame:

"Imagine turning every health intervention into a revenue opportunity", he offered.

"When a student gets counseling here instead of being referred out – that's billable to Medicaid at a higher rate. When we prevent emergency room visits, we're not just improving care – we're generating savings that fund more support".

This cross-pillar alignment transformed friction into traction. Teachers worried about job loss – Patel showed them how the model created more classroom support, not less. Healthcare providers feared diluted standards – he highlighted the rigor and reach of school-based delivery. Finance leaders feared complexity – he showed how integration streamlined systems, making each role more efficient.

"Everyone wins when incentives align", Patel explained. "But someone has to do the work of showing how they align".

The real power of recasting came from connecting goals that had previously seemed siloed:

- Better student mental health meant fewer classroom disruptions.
- Lower absenteeism translated to higher district funding.
- Increased access to care stabilized family engagement and built community trust.

As the initiative evolved, these aligned interests gave rise to something bigger than the original scope: integrated community health centers. These weren't just service hubs – they were physical embodiments of recasting in action. Teachers gained direct support. Providers secured stable revenue. Administrators saw measurable academic gains. And families accessed care without leaving their neighborhoods.

"Recasting isn't about changing what people do", Patel said.

"It's about showing how collaboration makes everyone better at what they already do".

That's when the model stopped being a pitch and started becoming a movement.

Step Seven: Cross-Pillar Advanced Strategies

As implementation moved forward, resistance emerged – not around the model's intent, but its execution. School board members raised concerns about the funding flow. Healthcare providers asked for guarantees that billing would be feasible. Teachers wanted firm assurances that classroom support would show up in practice, not just on a slide.

Patel responded by applying Cross-Pillar Logrolling, the strategic art of trading what different groups value most.

"We proposed that healthcare providers could receive staffing bonuses funded by reductions in emergency care costs", Patel said.

"That gave teachers immediate classroom relief, while administrators saw measurable savings. Each group got what mattered most – without sacrificing the others".

These trades weren't improvised. Patel had spent months mapping interdependencies across systems:

- Improved mental health support reduced behavioral incidents.
- Fewer disruptions improved academic performance.
- Better attendance unlocked increased per-pupil state funding.

These chains formed the logic of his trades. And timing mattered.

"We aligned the rollout with both academic and healthcare calendars", Patel explained. "That reduced disruption and helped ensure visible early wins".

But timelines alone weren't enough to sustain momentum. To protect against uncertainty, Patel introduced Contingency Agreements: flexible structures that triggered benefits only when success was measurable.

One such agreement tied classroom support expansion to verified reductions in ER utilization. Another unlocked additional resources only if student attendance improved across a full grading period. These trigger-based structures helped skeptical leaders see HEA not as a promise – but as a model that scaled with outcomes.

"The superintendent needed assurance this wasn't just another unfunded mandate", Patel said.

"By linking expansion to verified success, we made the program self-sustaining".

To maintain trust and calibrate expectations, Patel built a formal assessment framework: quarterly stakeholder reviews, data-driven implementation planning, and adaptive cross-pillar workshops. These weren't just check-ins – they were collaborative design sessions.

"Each review brought administrators, educators, and clinicians to the table", he noted. "Every decision – on staffing, workflows, even classroom design – became co-owned".

That co-ownership became a strategic advantage. Teachers shaped how new staff were embedded. Healthcare providers helped revise care protocols for school settings. Administrators tied budget reallocations to metrics that all parties endorsed.

"Each trade had to work across all three pillars", Patel said.

"Better healthcare led to fewer classroom disruptions, which boosted performance, which increased funding. That's not a pitch, it's a strategy map".

The strength of these Advanced Cross-Pillar Strategies wasn't just in creativity. It was in alignment. Patel built a system where structure met flexibility and where each win became a shared success.

Step Eight – Cross-Pillar Advanced Tactics

After months of stalled conversations with healthcare providers, Patel realized he needed to rethink his entry point.

"Initially, I avoided school districts because of the bureaucracy", he said. "But the providers were locked into their models. We had to shift the center of gravity".

That decision became a defining tactical move. By approaching state legislators and school board leaders instead, Patel gained not only access but influence. Once districts began asking for provider partnerships, momentum flipped. The very stakeholders who had been resistant were now responding to demand from their own community partners.

That redirection illustrates one of Patel's core tactical strengths: knowing when to adjust the narrative based on where leverage lives.

He also learned to shift language based on stakeholder pressure points in real time. When teachers expressed concern about added responsibilities, he didn't defend logistics. He reframed the conversation around restored focus and reduced disruption. With administrators, he linked resource questions directly to revenue triggers. With providers, he emphasized staffing bonuses and risk-managed integration.

These micro-Pivots and Turns weren't about charm – they were about continuity. Patel used cross-pillar tactics to maintain forward motion, even as objections arose.

One of the most powerful tools in his toolkit was the "Yes, And…" technique – an improvisational method repurposed for negotiation:

To administrators:

> "Yes, we understand budget constraints, and by accessing unused federal funds, we can generate savings while improving services".
>
> This turned fiscal skepticism into strategic planning.

To teachers:

> "Yes, your focus should be on teaching, and integrated health services mean fewer classroom disruptions and more support for behavioral challenges".
>
> This reframed the program as a teaching aid, not a competing mandate.

To healthcare providers:

> "Yes, school-based care must meet clinical standards – and our model includes staffing bonuses and rigorous protocols to ensure exactly that".
>
> Here, Patel bridged clinical caution with operational reassurance.
>
> "The goal wasn't to argue", Patel said. "It was to build on what people were already telling us – and show how that insight made the model stronger".
>
> These moments added up. The tactics worked not because they shut down resistance, but because they converted objections into design

improvements. Teachers shaped rollout plans. Providers adjusted scheduling frameworks. Administrators codified performance metrics.

What began as separate conversations across pillars became a single, integrated dialogue – driven by a tactical approach that elevated stakeholder concerns into co-ownership.

The "Yes, And..." approach didn't just keep the conversation moving. It made the solution stronger.

Step Nine – Cross-Pillar Learning and Integration

"It's easy to get caught up in the success metrics", Krishna Patel said, "but the real learning came from understanding how each pillar's perspective shaped what we became".

HEA's impact at Woodland Hills was significant, but its staying power came from something deeper: its ability to reflect, adapt, and evolve across systems.

The post-implementation assessment surfaced a crucial lesson: healthcare-led models struggled to gain traction. Communities needed to lead.

"This should start with the school district", Patel noted. "When the community initiates and we support – everything shifts".

That shift reshaped HEA's entire expansion strategy. Instead of launching top-down with providers, future rollouts would begin with district leadership, community anchors, and localized planning teams. It wasn't just better politics – it was better design.

HEA also refined how it communicated its purpose.

"We stopped leading with systemic change", Patel recalled. "Instead, we showed how this reduced the taxpayer burden while improving services. That message resonated across all three pillars".

And the results followed:

Financially, the district saved $3.1 million annually, reinvesting nearly $1 million into provider bonuses. Even the district's credit rating improved.

Clinically, students accessed mental health support more consistently, ER usage declined, and preventive care became standard.

Relationally, trust deepened. Stakeholders reported higher satisfaction, smoother coordination, and stronger cross-role respect.

Most striking: a 29% drop in behavioral incidents, improved student retention, and long-term provider sustainability.

But numbers weren't the full story. HEA also learned that relationships are infrastructure. Sustainable success came not from performance dashboards alone, but from:

- Consistent delivery on commitments
- Quarterly cross-pillar reviews
- Stakeholder-designed modifications
- Cultural fluency across professions

"Assessment isn't just about metrics", Patel emphasized. "It's about understanding how each pillar experiences change – and maintaining the trust that makes integration possible".

As HEA expanded to new districts, that mindset became foundational**: listen first, learn continuously, build across.** Every new setting brought different politics, policies, and partners – but the same insight applied:

"When you show each stakeholder how collaboration strengthens their core mission", Patel said, "transformation becomes possible".

That's the heart of cross-pillar learning: progress that doesn't just scale – it sustains.

POTENTIAL CHALLENGES AND LIMITATIONS OF THE TRILINGUAL PLANNER

While the Trilingual Planner offers a powerful framework for cross-sector integration, its implementation presents real-world challenges that require thoughtful navigation and strategic adaptation.

The **complexity of simultaneous translation** across the three pillars remains one of the most significant hurdles. Healthcare professionals often struggle to explain how a single decision impacts clinical practice, operational workflows, and financial outcomes all at once. These cognitive demands can overwhelm even experienced practitioners. Success depends on developing structured approaches to cross-domain communication. Standardized translation frameworks and well-designed visual tools can clarify interdependencies and help teams communicate more effectively across professional languages.

Conflicts rooted in professional identity and culture also pose barriers. Deeply held norms and role definitions within each pillar can foster resistance to integration. Clinicians may push back against changes perceived as business-driven, while administrators might undervalue clinical context or classroom dynamics. Overcoming these cultural divides requires more than messaging – it demands deliberate efforts to demonstrate respect for each domain's core values. Engaging trusted voices within each group as bridges can help build mutual understanding and foster collaboration.

Time and resource constraints are practical limitations. In fast-paced environments, comprehensive cross-pillar planning may seem unrealistic. The demands of integrated decision-making often compete with urgent operational needs. Addressing this tension calls for the development of efficient planning models that adapt to real-world conditions. Streamlined templates and "lite" versions of the Trilingual Planner can help organizations benefit from integrated thinking without overwhelming limited bandwidth.

Power dynamics and authority structures frequently complicate multi-domain initiatives. Competing hierarchies and misaligned decision-making processes can create friction or stall progress. These issues require early identification and active management. Mapping both formal reporting lines and informal influence networks can surface potential bottlenecks. Building cross-level coalitions and working with trusted connectors across domains can create more stable pathways to shared decision-making.

The **challenge of aligning data and metrics** across pillars is another recurring obstacle. Each domain defaults to its own success measures – cost savings, patient outcomes, academic performance – making unified assessment difficult. Integrated measurement frameworks can bridge this gap. Comprehensive "value dashboards" that translate impact across domains, supported by illustrative case studies, can create shared language around results.

Managing multiple stakeholder relationships is also a central challenge. Cross-pillar initiatives often bring together a large and diverse cast of participants, which can lead to communication breakdowns or decision-making paralysis. Clear stakeholder mapping, consistent communication protocols, and defined input channels are critical. Establishing structured forums for engagement ensures that input is collected efficiently and progress is not derailed by ambiguity.

Implementation complexity can turn even the most promising cross-pillar plan into a logistical challenge. Coordinating changes across clinical, operational, and administrative systems requires disciplined execution. Detailed rollout plans, milestone-based roadmaps, and cross-functional oversight teams can help manage complexity. Regular assessment checkpoints and the flexibility to recalibrate as needed are essential to long-term sustainability.

Finally, **resistance to change** is inevitable. Siloed systems often feel familiar and safe, and integrated approaches can provoke uncertainty or pushback. Overcoming this resistance requires a phased approach: demonstrate success early, document results, and recruit champions across all three pillars. When stakeholders see that integrated planning enhances their ability to fulfill their primary mission, the case for change becomes stronger.

Mastering Multi-Pillar Healthcare Negotiations

Krishna Patel's work with the Health and Education Alliance offers more than a case study – it's a blueprint. Through his use of the Trilingual Planner, Patel showed how even deeply siloed systems can be transformed into integrated, sustainable care and support networks. By translating fluently across the Boardroom, Exam Room, and Operating Room, he turned misalignment into momentum – and built solutions that worked for educators, clinicians, families, and finance leaders alike.

The Trilingual Planner is more than a tool – it's a mindset. It challenges healthcare professionals to think across systems, speak across roles, and design across disciplines. Whether you're launching a new clinical initiative, renegotiating interdepartmental workflows, or leading a district-wide change effort, this framework helps make complex negotiations more coherent, collaborative, and actionable.

Mastery doesn't come from reading – it comes from repetition, reflection, and adaptation. The more you use the Planner, the more attuned you'll become to where systems break down – and how they can be rebuilt to align mission, metrics, and meaning.

In a world where healthcare challenges rarely live inside a single department or domain, trilingual thinking isn't a luxury – it's a leadership imperative. By embracing the tools and strategies outlined in this chapter, you can become the kind of cross-pillar leader healthcare needs now: clear-eyed, adaptable, and relentlessly focused on integrated solutions that work.

REFLECTION EXERCISE: MASTERING CROSS-PILLAR INTEGRATION

Choose a complex healthcare initiative you're currently navigating – or expect to face – that requires coordination across the three pillars: the Operating Room (clinical care), Exam Room (day-to-day service delivery), and Boardroom (financial and strategic oversight). Using the Trilingual Planner, take 30 minutes to reflect on the following:

1. **Cross-Pillar Mapping**
   - Identify key stakeholders from each pillar affected by the initiative.
   - For each, outline their priorities, professional culture, and likely points of resistance.
   - Consider how power dynamics or resource constraints might complicate coordination.
   - Map where interdependencies or bottlenecks are most likely to appear.
2. **Communication Strategy**
   - Craft key messages that align with each pillar's goals.
   - Translate complex concepts into language that resonates with each group.
   - Identify tactics that show value in terms meaningful to each audience.
   - Develop a plan for bridging communication gaps between pillars.
   - Pinpoint trusted "cultural mediators" who can help build alignment.
3. **Integration Plan**
   - Sequence stakeholder engagement in a way that builds momentum.
   - Establish coordination mechanisms across pillars (e.g., standing committees, shared dashboards).
   - Define what success looks like in each pillar – and how you'll measure it.
   - Anticipate areas of friction and develop conflict-resolution processes.
   - Stay grounded in the overall healthcare mission as a unifying guide.

4. **Implementation Roadmap**
   - List the critical resources you'll need from each pillar.
   - Outline how you'll maintain collaboration throughout the project.
   - Establish clear feedback loops and progress review points.
   - Identify metrics that will show traction early, and over time.
   - Prepare contingency strategies for unexpected challenges.

After completing your plan, identify 1–2 immediate actions you can take to move forward. Revisit this reflection after major milestones to refine your approach. Track what worked, what changed, and how each pillar contributed to (or complicated) system-wide progress.

Great cross-pillar negotiators aren't just translators. They're integrators – able to turn misaligned systems into shared momentum.

Key Takeaways

1. The Trilingual Planner provides a comprehensive framework for navigating healthcare's complex intersections across the Operating Room, Exam Room, and Boardroom. Through systematic application of intersectionality mapping and cross-pillar analysis, healthcare leaders can better understand stakeholder connections, identify interdependencies, and maintain focus on shared healthcare missions. This structured yet adaptable approach enables organizations to pursue integrated solutions while ensuring alignment across all three pillars of healthcare delivery.
2. Effective healthcare integration requires mastery of trilingual communication and strategic relationship building. Healthcare leaders must develop fluency in translating key concepts between domains while cultivating cross-pillar partnerships through regular collaboration and shared accountability. The integration of pillar-specific communication strategies enables leaders to transform siloed operations into cohesive, collaborative initiatives that strengthen organizational performance across all domains.
3. Value creation and continuous learning represent critical capabilities in cross-pillar healthcare leadership. Success depends on establishing balanced scorecards that track benefits across domains while maintaining robust monitoring systems for implementation. This approach enables healthcare professionals to demonstrate tangible value to diverse stakeholders while systematically improving their integration capabilities over time.

4. Healthcare leaders must proactively address common challenges like stakeholder resistance, resource constraints, and cultural conflicts across pillars. Success requires the strategic application of advanced negotiation tactics while maintaining flexibility through phased implementation approaches. By activating cross-pillar resources and establishing clear mechanisms for resource sharing, organizations can overcome institutional barriers while building sustainable integrated solutions that serve all stakeholders.

Chapter 11

Final Thoughts

Better Healthcare Through Better Negotiations

When we think about healthcare delivery, we often picture massive hospital systems, complex insurance networks, and sweeping government policies. But the reality is both simpler and more profound: healthcare happens through negotiations. It happens when a nurse negotiates medication compliance with a patient, when a physician negotiates treatment approaches with colleagues, or when an administrator negotiates with community partners to expand services. These daily negotiations – these pivotal moments of engagement – are where healthcare truly lives.

What we've explored together in this book isn't just another set of negotiation strategies and tactics. The HEAR Approach™ represents something more fundamental: a recognition that every healthcare interaction carries the potential for positive change. Whether you're in the exam room discussing treatment options with a hesitant patient, in the operating room coordinating complex care protocols, or in the boardroom advocating for resources, you're engaging in negotiations that ripple far beyond that moment.

When Dr. Sarah Shapiro first met Alex, a 16-year-old with poorly controlled Type 1 diabetes, the situation epitomized the complexity of modern healthcare delivery. Despite having access to the latest insulin pumps and continuous glucose monitors, Alex's A1C remained dangerously high. His parents were frustrated, his school nurses felt overwhelmed, and his previous endocrinologist had labeled him "non-compliant." But Dr. Shapiro saw

 DOI: 10.4324/9781003336013-13

something different: not a difficult patient but a web of negotiations waiting to be transformed.

In the exam room, Dr. Shapiro didn't just review glucose numbers – she negotiated a new understanding with Alex and his family. Instead of lecturing about compliance, she acknowledged Alex's expertise in his own daily routines. "You live with this disease 24/7," she told him. "Help me understand what works for you and what doesn't." This simple shift – from telling to collaborative problem-solving – changed everything. Alex began sharing the real challenges: how the recommended meal schedule clashed with his basketball practice, how the pump alerts disrupted his sleep, and how he felt embarrassed managing his diabetes at school.

But Dr. Shapiro's negotiations didn't stop at patient care. In the operating room pillar, she brought Alex's insights to her practice's weekly case conference. Instead of presenting another case of "poor compliance," she negotiated a fundamental shift in their adolescent diabetes protocols. "We're not failing these patients," she argued. "Our protocols are failing to account for their real lives." Her negotiations led to a complete overhaul of their teenage diabetes management approach, one that prioritized flexibility and patient autonomy over rigid compliance.

The ripple effects reached the boardroom, where Dr. Shapiro leveraged Alex's story and their practice's improved outcomes to negotiate system-wide changes. She helped create a youth diabetes advisory council that now shapes hospital policies. The resulting program – combining peer support, flexible protocols, and technology that adapts to patient lifestyles – has reduced emergency department visits for diabetic ketoacidosis by 40% across their healthcare system.

One doctor, through a series of thoughtful negotiations, didn't just help one patient – she catalyzed changes that transformed hundreds of lives. And while Dr. Shapiro's story illustrates the extraordinary potential of skilled healthcare negotiation, it's not an isolated example. Every healthcare professional has similar opportunities to create meaningful change through their daily interactions. Whether you're a nurse navigating complex care coordination, a physician implementing new treatment protocols, or an administrator building community partnerships, you're driven by a desire to improve people's lives. What we've explored together isn't just about becoming a better negotiator – it's about becoming a more effective catalyst for the changes you already want to make.

Tomorrow, you'll engage in dozens of negotiations that impact healthcare delivery. Some will feel significant – like presenting a proposal for a new service line or implementing a major protocol change. Others might seem routine – discussing treatment adherence with a patient, coordinating care across departments, or allocating daily resources. But here's what I've learned from years of working with healthcare professionals: it's often those seemingly routine negotiations, handled skillfully and thoughtfully, that create the most profound and lasting improvements in healthcare delivery.

Dr. Shapiro's story illustrates what's possible when healthcare professionals apply thoughtful negotiation practices across all three pillars. Whether you're managing complex chronic conditions, implementing new care protocols, or advocating for system-wide changes, you have the same potential to create transformative change. And now you have tools specifically designed for healthcare's unique challenges.

Understanding these principles is just the beginning. To help you translate this knowledge into consistent practice, you'll want to develop habits that reinforce effective negotiation strategies. When Dr. Shapiro was faced with updating chronic disease management protocols, the sections on tactical empathy and the double magnet approach, combined with the trilingual planner, helped structure her negotiations across departments.

So keep this book within reach. Use the advanced tactics section when you need to manage a particularly complex negotiation. Reference the HEAR Framework when you find yourself stuck in an unproductive discussion. Return to the case studies when you encounter similar scenarios in your practice. The more you integrate these tools into your daily work, the more natural they'll become, and the greater impact you'll have on healthcare delivery.

The next negotiation you engage in is an opportunity to create positive change. Start with one interaction tomorrow. Make it count by using what you've learned and put this knowledge into practice. Notice the difference and then do it again, building on what works. Because while policies and systems matter, it's these daily negotiations that truly transform healthcare.

Index